Praise for Evelyn's books...

"Wisdom like this can change lives and Brooks' book serves up plenty. A self-improvement recipe with plenty of ingredients worth nibbling on their own." --*Kirkus Reviews (You Were Born to Triumph: Create a Five-Star Life in Your Quantum Kitchen)*

"A metaphysical masterpiece of easy to digest steps for manifesting the life of your dreams." *(You Were Born to Triumph: Create a Five-Star Life in Your Quantum Kitchen)*

"The best gift you can give yourself is to understand who you really are and what you are capable of achieving when you take action and work in consonance with the universal laws. The laws are always working, whether you're aware of them or not. Evelyn Brooks shows you how to work on purpose and in harmony with the laws! "– Bob Proctor *(You Were Born to Triumph: Create a Five-Star Life in Your Quantum Kitchen)*

"The way we make progress in the world is by people stepping into the light with their gifts, talents, and passion. Restoring Tibet is a beautiful example of that. What if the Dalai Lama was able to go home? This book will inspire you, and it will trigger you to think creatively and ask what's possible in anything in life. I love the book for its simple message, with potentially profound results. It's short, yet it's packed with value for the mind and heart." – Pattie Craumer, The Mosaic Effect *(Restoring Tibet: Global Action Plan to Send the Dalai Lama Home)*

"Some great advice from a real 'results expert.' Self-sabotage is surprisingly common. Many of us engage in it without knowing it. This book taught me some useful tools to use to stop shooting myself in the foot and start going forward with my dreams. I learned how to identify some of my own problem areas, about just how vitally important gratitude is, writing down my goals. The author did a good job of showing me the track to get on and how to stay on it. Empowering!" *(5 Proven Methods to Stop Self-Sabotage)*

"Although we're repeatedly told that it's futile, many of us are people pleasers and don't know how to fix it. Beginning with an eye-opening quiz to see if you are indeed a people-pleaser, the author proceeds to plainly teach us how to adjust our reactions to others and situations. Some of it might be hard to hear for those of us trying to control our environment. But as with all the Born to Triumph books, there are some real tools contained here to help readers. If you're tired of being a doormat, this book is for you." *(Do's and Don'ts for Recovering People-Pleasers)*

"I was deeply encouraged by this book. It gave me a better perspective on things and hope for the future. All Lightworkers should read this book." *(Calling All Lightworkers: Claim Your Role in the World-Wide Awakening)*

"I was afraid it was going to be just a lot of fluffy cheer-up type of reminders to look on the bright side and keep smiling, but she gets down to the practical techniques of stress management, and includes a 5-step program of lessons to give you something solid to hang onto and start doing things differently. I was pleasantly surprised to find a lot of fresh new ideas I'd never seen any place else. This is a great book and I highly recommend it." *(Forget Your Troubles: Enjoy Your Life Today)*

"Using well-written characters and LOTS of dialogue (I love that), *Dream Spinners* doesn't shy away from the deep questions. A beautiful story with an interesting perspective." *(The Dream Spinners,* novel)

America's New Breed
of
Freedom Fighters

AMERICA'S NEW BREED
OF
FREEDOM FIGHTERS

2nd edition

by

Evelyn Roberts Brooks

America's New Breed of Freedom Fighters / Evelyn Roberts Brooks –2nd Ed.

Photo credits: The cover and chapter images are from bigstockphotos.com, used with permission. Cover design by Pixel Studios, Bosnia.

ISBN 978-0-9998408-0-1 ebook
ISBN 978-0-9998408-1-8 paperback

Categories:

1. Nonfiction > Politics & Social Sciences > Politics & Government > Ideologies & Doctrines > Democracy;

2. Nonfiction > Politics & Social Sciences > Politics & Government > Elections & Political Process > Practical Politics;

3. Nonfiction > Religion & Spirituality > New Age > Self-Help

Evelyn explains the laws of the mind in her big fat juicy book *YOU WERE BORN TO TRIUMPH: Create a Five-Star Life in Your Quantum Kitchen*

To learn more about Evelyn and read her hundreds of informational articles and blog posts about spiritual healing, stress relief, and using the laws of the mind, do a Google search for: "Evelyn Roberts Brooks" … or simply go to her central website evelynbrooks.com

Would you like to learn how to dissolve guilt, reduce your stress, and stop letting regrets for the past and worry about the future tie your stomach in knots? Stop by today to claim free Instant Download Access to a powerful **Serenity Gift Collection** at evelynbrooks.com

Follow Evelyn at:

twitter.com/evelynbrooks
facebook.com/evelynbrooksauthor
youtube.com/evelynbrooks
pinterest.com/evelynRbrooks

View and share the Freedom Fighters videos:
FreedomFightersVideos.com

Born to Triumph

Books by Evelyn Roberts Brooks

When you finish the book, please take a moment to review it (and give me a 4- or 5-star rating if you'd like) so other readers can find me, too. I really appreciate it. I love hearing from readers—contact me at evelynbrooks.com or Facebook.com/EvelynBrooksAuthor

Nonfiction

AMERICA'S NEW BREED OF FREEDOM FIGHTERS: With Liberty and Justice for All (Liberty and Justice Series)

WHAT WERE THEY THINKING? Inside the Minds of Trump's Voters (Liberty and Justice Series) [HUMOR]

WHAT TRUMP'S VOTERS WERE REALLY THINKING: The Complete Report Unedited (Liberty and Justice Series) [HUMOR]

WHEN THEY GO LOW WE GO HIGH: How to Raise Your Vibration to Manifest What You Want (Liberty and Justice Series)

RESTORING TIBET: Global Action Plan to Send the Dalai Lama Home

YOU WERE BORN TO TRIUMPH: Create a Five-Star Life in Your Quantum Kitchen

FORGET YOUR TROUBLES: Enjoy Your Life Today

GET HAPPY TODAY: No More Excuses!

CALLING ALL LIGHTWORKERS (Born to Triumph Series)

HEAL YOUR TOXIC FRIENDSHIPS (Born to Triumph Series)

DO'S AND DON'TS FOR RECOVERING PEOPLE-PLEASERS (Born to Triumph Series)

CHOOSE HAPPINESS NOW (Born to Triumph Series)

5 PROVEN METHODS TO STOP SELF-SABOTAGE (Born to Triumph Series)

6 SECRETS FOR A HARMONIC MARRIAGE (Born to Triumph Series)

YOUR HAPPINESS COMPASS (Born to Triumph Series)

YOUR GRIEF RELIEF (Born to Triumph Series)

BE HEALTHY, BE RICH: Secrets of Wellness and Wealth (classics by Wallace D. Wattles, annotated)

Fiction: Adult and Young Adult

THE DREAM SPINNERS (a novel about love, loss, and second chances with a little help from the Other Side)

THE GYPSY TALISMAN

THE CALICO TAPESTRY

VAMPIRE MISCHIEF

Juvenile

PROFESSOR BUBBLES AND THE MISSING FORMULA

MY DAYS OF THE WEEK UNDERWEAR

Contents

DEDICATION

To everyone who loves freedom, growth and happiness,
and is willing to protect and defend these inalienable rights.
Let no one defile our democracy.

*"The thing you dislike or hate will surely come upon you,
for when man hates, he makes a vivid picture
in the subconscious mind and it objectifies."*

Florence Scovel Shinn

***

*"Everybody's been there, everybody's been stared down
By the enemy
Fallen for the fear and done some disappearing
Bow down to the mighty
Don't run, stop holding your tongue
Maybe there's a way out of the cage where you live
Maybe one of these days you can let the light in
Show me how big your brave is…*

from the song *Brave* by Sara Bareilles

AUTHOR'S NOTE FOR THE 2ND EDITION

Dear Reader,

This is the advanced training manual for Freedom Fighters who refuse to be overrun by The Trump Circus, and its right-wing extremist agenda of hate, greed, white supremacy, misogynism, and voter repression.

You've already got progressive petitions to sign, social media posts to write and share, marches and Town Hall events to attend, but this book will take you deeper—into the realm of the creative mind, where we can access our unlimited power to manifest the results we want to experience.

Does that sound like mere wishful thinking? It's not. We are fully capable of using mental abilities we've given little attention to before. Even if you've watched films, read books and attended seminars about using the law of attraction more skillfully, we're going to explore things you might not have considered, as it relates to working together and collectively changing the direction this country is going in, and thus create lasting progress.

At this time, we are being eagerly watched by the many who have gone before us and are no longer in physical form, by those who know first-hand the hard fight to gain justice and liberty and the fruits of democracy. They are on our side, cheering our goals and actions. Listen for that whisper of encouragement and love when you focus on the desired outcome of expansion in civil rights and freedom.

However, showing Trump and his pals, the exit door is only a beginning, not a culmination. Let's vote them out of office, but we'll

1

have to keep up the good work and prevent their clones from springing up in this battle for human evolution and a healthy environment to live in.

The work will continue beyond our own lifetimes, but this will be our legacy to future generations. I invite you to make a simple commitment to progress.

In fact, I believe each member of the resistance deliberately chose this lifetime to be on hand for the big changes ahead, and to be part of making them happen.

This is a new type of revolution the world has never seen. Gandhi would recognize elements of it, as would Nelson Mandela and other proponents of peaceful change. So, of course, would our nation's founding fathers and mothers, who established a new way of living that has the seeds of worthy achievement firmly planted in its soil.

In times of great trouble, when a nation's citizens are under attack from within or from without, people begin to gather from all backgrounds and communities to form a resistance. These people have one important thing in common—whether they are fighting the Nazis or resisting Donald Trump and his elitists—they are willing to stand up and speak out for freedom.

As Tom Brokaw put it, in regards to hostile acts by the Trump administration and the Republicans in Congress: "Make no mistake about it—we are at war."

Books and films offer us a window into history's traditional wars, such as World War Two, during which brave resistance fighters risked their lives and the safety of their family and friends to combat Hitler's takeover of their own countries or the countries of allies.

They had to meet in secret, create code names, and establish enigmatic cyphers and elaborate lines of communication with the underground. They stockpiled weapons and supplies. They went hungry, they rationed, they mended their clothes, and did without the comforts we take for granted.

They furtively disseminated news bulletins and information, at the risk of being discovered, arrested, tortured, shot. At all times, their personal safety was at risk. They led a double life, and especially for agents infiltrating enemy territory, they had to leave the relative safety of home with perhaps only a clandestine radio for company.

Today, we've got it far easier than any band of Freedom Fighters in history.

With the incredible power of the internet at our fingertips, we can battle the Republican leaders from home, on the go, or at the neighborhood coffee shop. We click "Sign" and submit a petition to our representatives in government, adding our single voice to the voices of millions. We share our messages in social media. We write letters to our Congressional, state and local leaders, demanding accountability, insisting that they stand up to Trump and his cohorts. We meet openly in our communities. And we march in the streets in nonviolent protests against the Trump administration's extremist agenda.

You may have felt all your life that there was some elusive purpose you were meant to be fulfilling. If you feel in alignment with the statements in this book, then I believe you've found your purpose: you're a Freedom Fighter!

I am pleased to present this second edition of *America's New Breed of Freedom Fighters* for all the Democrats, Progressives, and Liberals who are watching the news and wondering frantically: What on earth can we do about this powder-keg situation?

As I write this, we've already survived long months of mind-boggling behavior and legal restrictions imposed by the Republicans in Congress and their figurehead, Mr. Trump.

Trump's role? He's not really the "leader" of the Free World. Despite his claim that he is a "stable genius," and that he is "the least-racist" person in the country, he's merely the clown on a jerry-rigged stage who keeps the media distracted and the crowd roaring in either glee or outrage, while his henchmen systematically loot the country.

If you feel strangled by fear, nervous to pick up a newspaper or turn on the television, I hope you will find relief in this book. My life mission is to help people heal and be happier, and be more effective in creating results that improve life and are for the greater good of the many, not the few.

Together we can uplift the collective consciousness to create a Blue Wave bigger than a tsunami to wash away the filth of greed and self-aggrandizement.

As we join together, open your mind to replacing worry with a deeper understanding of how today's new breed of Freedom Fighters need to think and behave in order to defeat tyranny.

To truly make progress in long strides, we must shift our collective focus away from Trump and toward what we want to achieve, using the best practices of the law of creation, a.k.a. law of attraction.

We create what we picture in our minds and then steep with emotion (whether fear or happy anticipation). We create in our environment a reflection of our most heartfelt thoughts.

When we allow anger and anxiety to muddy our mental pictures, we inadvertently align our creative energy with the "Dark Force."

Are you ready for your hero's journey? Perhaps you've already embarked on it and would like to sharpen your tools and hone your skills at creating what you desire.

In this volume, along with a new section titled "The Heart of Progress," you will find the first edition of the book (issued on Inauguration Day 2017) in its entirety. I also reviewed the original material for the purpose of creating a spiritually uplifting experience as you read.

We communicate with words, which set up a vibrational reaction as we read, but also with the invisible energy called "body language" which is present even when we are not physically near one another.

Just as your computer is connected to the same internet the rest of us access, there is an inescapable energy of connection between all of us within the One Mind. The higher we go in the stream of consciousness, up where love, peace, compassion, and joy thrive, the more alive and calm we feel, and the more powerful we become as Freedom Fighters for democracy.

Reading this book will energize and enliven you, as you come into harmony with ideals that uplift and inspire you to bring your most glorious self into play.

You will feel a wonderful sense of confidence, peace and wellbeing inside, and at the same time realize more fully just how powerful a being you are, fully capable of creating the results you want in life.

In the conclusion of *Walden*, Henry David Thoreau wrote, "I have learned this, at least, by my experiment: that if one advances confidently in the direction of his dreams, and endeavors to live the life which he has imagined, he will meet with a success unexpected in common hours; he will put some things behind, will pass an invisible boundary; new, universal, and more liberal laws will begin to establish themselves around and within him or the old laws be expanded, and interpreted in his favor in a more liberal sense, and he will live with the license of a higher order of beings."

As we join together and move forward with determination and fervor in the name of justice, you may feel that you have been catapulted into that higher order of beings to which Thoreau refers.

That exhilarating feeling will expand as we actively engage with our government at all levels to create a stronger and more robust democracy.

In the new section called **The Heart of Progress**, in addition to describing the urgency of our **Code Blue** crisis, I address our need to, as Barack Obama phrases it, tend to **The Garden of Democracy**. The valuable work of **Marchers & Protestors** is summarized, and I share some of the **Voices of Progress** and a review of the **Voices of Destruction** we've heard since Trump's taking office.

We'll also be investigating how our words and deeds can act as **Boomerangs for the Greater Good** in this inside-out universe of ours, and how to harness your own words to create the most effective results possible.

Let's look at a more vibrant approach to understanding the **Paradigm of Progress** and why it's critical to elevate our collective belief system and thus advance human evolution.

I invite Democrats to **Take Back Our Flag**, and I offer a new series of affirmations in **Fortune Cookies for Freedom Fighters**.

In listing my personal **Five Freedoms**, I hope you will feel inspired to enumerate your own goals and dreams for progress that help you stay motivated to march and be involved in our government...of the people, by the people, and for the people.

I urge you to begin doing these three things, starting today:

ONE In social media, especially in Twitter, <u>unfollow</u> Donald Trump in all his guises, and unfollow all Republican members of Congress and your local and state Republicans.

If enough of us do this, they will see a significant drop in their popularity rating. Yes, of course, they can have their social media managers use bot techniques to add a few million fake followers, but by removing your energetic interest in what they share, you begin detaching from that Dark Force.

Do not retweet or pass along Republican social media and email marketing material.

In your own inbox, stop opening email with alarming subject lines, no matter who the email is from. When you read a scary prediction such as "Oh no!--We're LOSING!" it sets up an unhealthy vibration in your mind and body. You immediately picture a result you <u>don't</u> want: the Republicans winning!

That statement and similar ones were, unfortunately, repeated again and again by Democrats in the presidential campaign of 2016. I realize the email marketing managers probably thought it was a great idea to get people to open the email and hopefully make a donation. However, the unfortunate tactic of embedding the collective picture of losing in the minds of Democrats resulted in the surprise election of a man who claims he never thought he'd win.

We cannot continue to align with thoughts and images of what we don't want to happen. We must keep our sight on being in harmony with the good we desire to create, and that means disciplining our emotions to <u>respond</u> rather than react to stimulus.

TWO Stop being a news junkie. You don't need to have the news on all day long in order to keep up with what's going on. Get the news in brief, and then turn it off. We used to call it brainwashing or propaganda when short, emotionally charged statements are reiterated to such a degree they become embedded in the minds of the listeners. Now we call it The News. Or, even more devastatingly: Fox News.

You do not need to fill your mind with a nonstop stream of negativity and fear-inducing messages. When we do this, we diminish our own ability to vibrate at the high level of energy needed to create the awe-inspiring changes we have in mind for our country and, indeed, the entire world.

THREE Discard unwanted images in your mind of what Trump and his team are doing to destroy the environment and devastate the lives of millions. Keep a strong vision of what you do want to help create. Happy, healthy children who have access to education. Compassionate caring and support for the elderly, the impoverished, those who are unable to care for themselves. Sensible gun control, tax reform, medical care. Ease of voting for all eligible citizens. Keep the pictures strong of America as the beautiful melting pot which welcomes immigrants onto its bright shores of opportunity.

As the ripples of our efforts bring forth a harmonious song of the universe, we will prevail over the destructive agenda of the Republican leaders.

Let's continue what we've begun.

Our Allies are watching to see how we will handle this crisis in America: let's not disappoint them by hiding under the covers.

Expanding liberty and justice for all is not an impossible dream. All we need to do is collectively live and serve at a higher level than the opposition, and keep marching.

Welcome to the Resistance,

Evelyn

Evelyn Roberts Brooks

PS I love hearing from my readers (well, other than those who accuse me of lying about Donald Trump). Please connect with me on Twitter @evelynbrooks or Facebook.com/EvelynBrooksAuthor

THE HEART OF PROGRESS

"We are in the preliminary stage
of one of the greatest battles in history."

Winston Churchill, May 1940

1

CODE BLUE

The informal term for a situation in which a hospital patient is going into cardiac arrest and needs immediate help is "CODE BLUE!"

On November 9, 2016, the United States of America was jolted into a CODE BLUE condition.

And, oddly enough, the <u>BLUE</u> WAVE is the solution for bringing this patient back to a thriving state and on the road to recovery and greater health.

This may sound strange, but it's actually a good thing that the "urgent care" team needed to rush to the scene—because it's not just this patient's "heart" that needs help. The entire body is filled with issues that have grown cancerous.

Many social, financial, medical, and environmental issues have come to the forefront because of Trump's election. Millions of people who never felt the urge to become involved in petitions or marches are fired up and ready to do their part to resuscitate our beautiful country.

Following are just some of the national ailments and wounds that are now out in the open and being discussed. These can be seen as part of the bigger problem of a dying patient, who requires life support and healing in many areas in order to recover and thrive:

   – The ancient culture of patriarchy that allows men to fondle, grope, sexually assault women in the name of male entitlement, and then claim that either his victim is lying or she invited the activity. #MeToo stories are busting this old culture wide open. We won't go back again.

– Health care, Social Security, Medicaid and Medicare. As a wealthy, technologically advanced nation, we have the responsibility to help all our citizens obtain the five basic necessities of life: food, clothing, shelter, transportation and health care. And yet, Trump's Administrations and the Republicans in Congress are eager to rescind established support. Why? Because big business profits and kickbacks are more important to them than the citizens of the United States.

– Freedom of speech. Did you know that, when Donald Trump found out about the book *Fire and Fury: Inside the Trump White House* by Michael Wolff, he demanded that the publisher cease and desist publishing it? Macmillan refused. Score one for Freedom of Speech, but gag rules are the order of the day with Republicans, who scramble like crazy to undo what they were heard saying, and try to refute words that are in writing.

– Immigration and the Mexican Border Wall. I don't think anyone denies that we need sensible regulations related to immigration, work permits, student visas, etc. But Trump's "solution" is to build a $33 billion wall (estimated cost), and to deport thousands of people who have lived and worked in our country, and the DREAMERS, too. Indeed, the Republican Party's approach to immigration is a malignant growth that must be excised.

I'm sure you can add to this list. Just take a look at today's headlines and your Twitter feed to see the rampant destruction Trump and his team are enacting each day. Their actions are well documented by recordings in their own words, in newspaper, television and radio interviews, by Congressional records, and social media shares from their own thumbs.

2

THE GARDEN OF DEMOCRACY

Democracy is government by the common people. Voters elect their representatives, and those reps are supposed to pay attention to what their constituents want.

In a recent speech at the Economic Club of Chicago, Barack Obama cited Hitler's rise to power in Germany as a cautionary, chilling example of the direction the United States is heading under the Trump Administration.

The former president said, "I do think because we've been so wealthy and so successful that we get complacent and assume that things continue the way they have been, just automatically. And they don't. You have to tend to this garden of democracy, otherwise things can fall apart fairly quickly. And we've seen societies where that happens."

Moving away from the example of the Nazis and their Fascist regime which slaughtered millions of people, let's look to a more commonplace scene that is closer to home.

Imagine the worst bullies of the school yard have been given a hall pass and the keys to the office safe as well as the keys to the gate for the students' vegetable garden. What do you suppose they'll do? Will they stay true to their inner paradigm of contempt for everyone else, or magically become model students just because they've been given a responsibility they never trained for? Will they lovingly protect the rights of the students, or trample all over them?

Trump's staff members have admitted in the media that since they never expected him to win, no plan for administration of the nation was even drafted. While Trump was gleefully tweeting nuclear threats to North Korea, his underlings were vainly trying to find what the Trump Administration had set in place as a strategy for handling a nuclear threat if it came our way instead of being outgoing. They didn't find a plan. Because nothing had been done, other than moving into the White House and setting up their offices.

Incompetent is hardly a strong enough word to describe Trump and his team.

When we look at the words "common people" we shouldn't instantly think of red vs. blue states, or Republicans vs. Democrats. Party divisions have shifted and changed dramatically over the years, particularly since 1964. If you take a moment to search the history of the two main political parties of this country, you may be surprised to see Republican Party agendas in Abraham Lincoln's time that champion immigrant rights and abolition of slavery, and Democratic party agendas in the early 20th century that promote giving power to corporate entities.

Today, with the extremist right wing's having taken over the Republican Party, the line between Democrats and Republicans has become a sharp difference in two ideologies, and it seems that never the twain shall meet.

However, if sanity can prevail in the grassroots of the Republican Party, and they institute reform of their platform, and vote out the extremists who have given their party a vile reputation, then they will have a chance to restore a party of decent values.

Republicans, if you are disgusted by the actions of the Trump administration and the Republicans in Congress, consider taking a page from Theodore Roosevelt's book. He left the Republican Party in 1912, and founded the short-lived "Progressive Party" also known as the "Bull Moose Party."

John Avion, CNN Contributor, summarizes that reform party's agenda by saying, "[Theodore] Roosevelt's Progressive Party definitely did not shy away from taking fearless stands on the vital issues of the day. The party's platform backed giving women the right to vote, the abolition of child labor, minimum wages, social security, public health standards, wildlife conservation, workman's compensation, insurance against sickness and unemployment, lobbying reform, campaign finance reform and election reform."

Doesn't that sound much more like the Democratic Party of today than the Republicans? That's why I feel it's dangerous to make sweeping statements that label "all" Republicans as being against social change and the rights of the individual. Many millions of Republican voters are simply hypnotized by Fox News and think they are learning the facts about Trump and his Administration.

While we tend to our Garden of Democracy, let's look to the words of the Dalai Lama in his new book, *An Appeal to the World: The Way to Peace in a Time of Division.*

The book is the compilation of interviews between the Dalai Lama and his long-time co-author Franz Alt, primarily on the topics of world politics and the growing urgency to understand that no nation should put itself first. He suggests that America should follow the example of the European Union, whose members have been at peace with each other for the past 60 years—unheard of in the long history of Western European nations warring against each other.

The Dalai Lama specifically addresses the issue of Donald Trump's presidency. In what Franz Alt describes as an anti-Trump program, His Holiness outlines several ideas for what Trump should be doing differently, and chastises Trump for withdrawing the United States from the Paris Climate Agreement, as well as Trump's anti-ecology, isolationist platform in a time of growing global unions among nations.

3

MARCHERS & PROTESTORS

The first political march I attended was in 1969 in Washington, D.C., protesting the Viet Nam War. Richard Nixon was President of the United States at that time. I still have the button I bought that day.

Fast forward a few decades…okay, stop at January 21, 2017 for my second political march: the Womens March in NYC.

I have never thought of myself as a political activist, but when the need arises, I'm like so many other millions of Democrats: willing to stand up and be counted on the side of progress and human rights.

But why do we do this? Why do we set aside other tasks in our busy lives, and join together to march through the streets of our country?

Some of the reasons that come to mind are:

We individually march to speak up for a specific cause that is near and dear to us.

We collectively march to add our message to the voices of progress.

We march to inform the public and our government that we will not be passive observers of the destruction of civil liberties and our environment.

We march because we believe in the chant we call out while marching in public for all to see and hear: Show me what democracy looks like! THIS IS WHAT DEMOCRACY LOOKS LIKE!

And when we march, these wonderful things begin to happen:

We reinforce our commitment to democratic principles of liberty and justice, and freedom of speech.

We feel energized by taking physical action, and this action also reinforces our determination to succeed against all odds.

We make new friendships and renew old ones, as we join together in a growing coalition for progress.

In this era of instant communication, each time someone shares about the march in social media, our actions and protest signs are multiplied again and again on behalf of those who had to stay home.

When we have a big goal in mind, it is all too easy to feel discouraged and isolated, to falter in the action steps, and to feel confused about what we should do next. One of the great benefits of the resistance is that by joining together we bolster our individual strength. We create a synergy that is stronger than all of us separately.

Unlike a mindless group that is simply obeying a dictator's injunctions and marching as if hypnotized, we retain our individuality and our own preferences for what is important to us as we join the larger resistance and take action.

Let's time travel for a moment back to the morning of Wednesday, November 9, 2016 when we woke up to the stunned, heart-wrenching, unfathomable realization that Donald Trump was the President-elect of these United States.

All Democrats and Progressives can recall that awful feeling in the pit of your stomach. That sense of being in the Twilight Zone. *Somebody please wake me from this terrible nightmare—it can't possibly be true!*

But on that Wednesday, each one of us had the innate ability, however unskilled it might be from our lack of using it, to hold firm our innermost conviction that right will always win over might, and that liberty will prevail in the long run.

This planet is on an evolutionary path, and we humans are evolving to a higher level of being with a much broader awareness of who we are and what we are capable.

The push-back from Trump and his buddies is our CALL TO ACTION.

Many millions of Americans have been slumbering in a placid state of complacency, with little caring for what goes on in Washington, D.C. because it seems to so many that their vote doesn't make a difference.

But with Trump's election, millions of people got jolted into awareness that it does indeed matter who is President.

Trump is the figurehead of the Republican Party. Out of all the presidential candidate hopefuls in the Republican Party, the party leaders chose Trump. A man with no political experience. No diplomatic experience. A man with an appalling record of racism, sexual assault, and assorted financial and ethical crimes.

Without needing a peek into back room meetings or secret documents, I can easily imagine they envisioned exactly what would happen in the coming months and years: The Trump Circus!

Trump has delivered the buffoon's performance to their precise expectations, while behind the scenes the Republicans in Congress and their wealthy backers, proceeded with their plan to deconstruct the Constitution by putting unqualified people in each Cabinet position and tear apart the heart of our country's foundation.

Picture this scene: you are on a busy street in a big city, with people coming and going. You notice a crowd up ahead. You're curious to see what they are all looking at.

As you approach, you see a tall man with a suit and red tie, and a big red clown nose and big floppy shoes, and bright orange hair. He's ranting and raving and his thumbs are busy pushing buttons on an oversized smart phone. He strides back and forth, screaming that he's going to bomb North Korea because he's got a nuclear bomb "button" that actually works! He shouts snide remarks to the women in the crowd. You can hardly believe the vile language and snarls coming from this clown's mouth. He spots a woman wearing a hajib headscarf and yells out that she's a terrorist—he convinces a policeman to drag her away.

Meanwhile, the crowd is so stunned by all this, they start taking photos and videos and sharing this clown's antics. News vans and helicopters converge on the scene.

Some people think it is hilarious television show of some kind and they begin chanting white supremacist slogans along with the clown.

Others are worried and upset, but feel helpless to do anything. The number of police protecting the clown increases.

A huge contingent of security people surrounds the clown and prevent anyone from getting closer, while the media give him full coverage – day after day, minute after minute.

Trying to get away from the crushing melee, you manage to skirt some bushes near the building and walk behind the clown. You notice that the doors of a massive old bank have opened to allow teams of hooded R-MoC's (Republican Member of Congress) to slip in and out of the bank, robbing it in open daylight.

How do you want this story to change?

24

Impeach the clown, and we simply have the R-MoC's methodically continue their Party agenda of pillaging and plundering, while they salute the flag and claim to be patriots of the finest caliber.

Until the day that the Republican Party undergoes a gut renovation, like when someone buys an old home and has to get rid of the garbage and stench that built up from neglect, the solution is to vote Republicans out of office.

I hope that you will make or renew a personal commitment that you will vote for Democratic candidates in upcoming elections, and that you will remind your friends to vote, too.

A sensible #swingleft will help this country immensely.

4

VOICES OF PROGRESS

L et us strengthen our ability to speak lovingly to each other, to speak with integrity, truth and compassion.

Abraham Lincoln

"America will never be destroyed from the outside. If we falter and lose our freedoms, it will be because we destroyed ourselves."

"I see in the near future a crisis approaching that unnerves me and causes me to tremble for the safety of my country... corporations have been enthroned and an era of corruption in high places will follow, and the money power of the country will endeavor to prolong its reign by working upon the prejudices of the people until all wealth is aggregated in a few hands and the Republic is destroyed."

Barack Obama

"Change will not come if we wait for some other person or some other time. We are the ones we've been waiting for. We are the change that we seek."

"The best way to not feel hopeless is to get up and do something. Don't wait for good things to happen to you. If you go out and make some good things happen, you will fill the world with hope, you will fill yourself with hope."

"We are reminded that in the fleeting time we have on this Earth, what matters is not wealth or status or power or fame, but rather how well we have loved and what small part we have played in making the lives of other people better."

Bernie Sanders

"Now is the time to alter our government. Now is the time to stop the movement toward oligarchy. Now is the time to create a government which represents all Americans and not just the 1%... No more excuses. We must all become involved in the political process."

"If the environment were a bank, it would have been saved by now."

Earl Nightingale

"Discontent is the greatest motivator of all."

Eleanor Roosevelt

"Basically, we could not have peace, or an atmosphere in which peace could grow, unless we recognized the rights of individual human beings... their importance, their dignity... and agreed that was the basic thing that had to be accepted throughout the world."

"We are given in our newspapers and on TV and radio exactly what we, the public, insist on having, and this very frequently is mediocre information and mediocre entertainment."

Elizabeth Warren

"In a democracy, hostage tactics are the last resort for those who can't otherwise win their fights through elections, can't win their fights in Congress, can't win their fights for the Presidency, and can't win their fights in Courts, for this right-wing minority, hostage-taking is all they have left – a last gasp of those who cannot cope with the realities of our democracy."

"It's a simple idea: We all do better when we work together and invest in our future."

George Washington

"However [political parties] may now and then answer popular ends, they are likely in the course of time and things, to become potent engines, by which cunning, ambitious, and unprincipled men will be enabled to subvert the power of the people and to usurp for themselves the reins of government, destroying afterwards the very engines which have lifted them to unjust dominion."

"Guard against the impostures of pretended patriotism."
"Few men have virtue to withstand the highest bidder."
"The harder the conflict, the greater the triumph."

Hillary Clinton

"It is often when night looks darkest, it is often before the fever breaks that one senses the gathering momentum for change, when one feels that resurrection of hope in the midst of despair and apathy."

"I'm sick and tired of people who say that if you debate and disagree with this [Trump] administration, somehow you're not patriotic. We need to stand up and say we're Americans, and we have the right to debate and disagree with any administration."

His Holiness the Dalai Lama

"The present President [Donald Trump], in the very beginning he mentioned 'America first.' That sounded in my ear not very nice."

"The US is still very powerful. The motto of the forefathers of modern Americans was democracy, freedom, and liberty. Totalitarian regimes don't have a future. As a leading power, the US should affiliate itself more closely with Europe."

"The new reality is that everyone is interdependent on everyone else. The United States is a leading nation of the free world. That's why the US president [Trump] should think more about global-level issues."

Joe Biden

"Don't tell me what you value. Show me your budget, and I'll tell you what you value."

"We must rekindle the fire of idealism in our society, for nothing suffocates the promise of America more than unbounded cynicism and indifference."

"If you do politics the right way, I believe, you can actually make people's lives better. And integrity is the minimum ante to get into the game."

"Our future cannot depend on the government alone. The ultimate solutions lie in the attitudes and the actions of the American people."

John F. Kennedy

"If a free society cannot help the many who are poor, it cannot save the few who are rich."

"Our problems are man-made; therefore, they may be solved by man. No problem of human destiny is beyond human beings."

"The ignorance of one voter in a democracy impairs the security of all."

"Peace is a daily, a weekly, a monthly process, gradually changing opinions, slowly eroding old barriers, quietly building new structures."

"In giving rights to others which belong to them, we give rights to ourselves and to our country."

"We are not here to curse the darkness, but to light the candle that can guide us thru that darkness to a safe and sane future."

Kamala Harris

"There is a lot of work to be done to make sure our leaders reflect the people they are supposed to represent. The more diverse a group of decision makers is, the more informed the decision will be. Until we achieve full representation, we all should understand we are falling short of the ideals of our country."

"Don't give up – our country needs you now more than ever. This is a pivotal moment in the history of our country: Our ideals are at stake, and we all have to fight for who we are."

Kirsten Gillibrand

"When we create hope and opportunity in the lives of others, we allow love, decency and promise to triumph over cowardice and hate."

"When a woman has the opportunity to speak truth to power, it's important that she does, even if it's just trying to get a crosswalk in her neighborhood. That's how social change happens!"

Theodore Roosevelt

"The most practical kind of politics is the politics of decency."

"To announce that there must be no criticism of the president... is morally treasonable to the American public."

"Do what you can, with what you have, where you are."

Thomas Jefferson

"Nothing gives one person so much advantage over another as to remain always cool and unruffled under all circumstances."

"I know no safe depository of the ultimate powers of the society but the people themselves; and if we think them not enlightened enough to exercise their control with a wholesome discretion, the remedy is not to take it from them, but to inform their discretion by education. This is the true corrective of abuses of constitutional power."

"Shall we refuse to the unhappy fugitives from distress that hospitality which the savages of the wilderness extended to our fathers arriving in this land? Shall oppressed humanity find no asylum on this globe?"

5

VOICES OF DESTRUCTION

I refuse to sully the vibrant energy of this book by including quotations from Donald Trump or anyone who claims that he's a great president and is getting things done.

We know what sort of "things" he is doing and what he is getting done, in the name of a white supremacist, greed-first agenda. The list of threats to our civil liberties keeps growing—a list written and endorsed by the Trump Administration and Republicans in Congress.

We all know what he has to say (*ad nauseam*). And not one word of the Racist-in-Chief's rhetoric is worth repeating.

You might point out that thousands slavishly retweet whatever message he eagerly blasts to the world. But I'm talking about something that is "worthy," not just something that the deluded masses of Republican voters take as truth because they walk the party line and never look left even when crossing streets.

Have you ever noticed what happens when a situation is controlled by mob mentality?

We've seen it in real life and we've seen it in films and we've read about it in fiction and non-fiction accounts of people who, once they are anonymously part of a crowd, will abandon moral principles and shout for the sake of shouting, loot for the sake of looting, set fires and smash windows in the adrenaline-charged moment of feeling invincible.

I believe those millions who are still nodding and agreeing with whatever Trump spews are caught up in a not-care mode of refusing to look past the Republican Party rhetoric, because if they looked, they might have to change something in their lives. And it's far easier to just keep going, don't risk an argument with family and friends who are staunch Party members.

Think about the wife who sees all the signs that her husband is cheating, but if she looks away, she can pretend her marriage is okay, and she doesn't have to confront him. In taking the stance of looking honestly, she has a chance of either healing the marriage if it is salvageable, or striking out on her own and creating a far better life for herself. But the very idea of having to break up the marriage, explain to friends and family what is going on, find a place to live, perhaps need to find a job or a higher paying one to allow for a single head of family lifestyle with children in her care—all of those ideas swarming through her mind like a nightmare picture coax her into saying, *Oh it's nothing, maybe a little harmless flirtation at work, he still loves me.*

The "marriage" a voter has with the person(s) they helped elect into a position of power needs that kind of honest look that we usually avoid due to dread at what we might discover. We as a society need to be willing to ask about situations that can be painful to unmask when you realize you've been deluded.

What about believing that guy on the stage who is foaming at the mouth as he rants about making the country great again? In case you don't know your history, Trump's election campaign promise was the same as Hitler's for Germany, a nation still reeling from poverty in the wake of their defeat in the Great War of 1914-1918 after their national resources were drained to pay for a war they expected to win in four months (the goal was to quickly crush their old enemy, France).

Adolf Hitler was elected in 1932 on the promise that he would make Germany great again, and the desperate population listened to his words and began nodding in agreement, wanting to believe someone would step in and fix all that was wrong in their country and in their impoverished lives.

It's been widely quoted that one of Trump's wives revealed Trump keeps Hitler's autobiography *Mein Kampf* (My Struggle) by his bedside. That book sets forth Hitler's anti-Semitic philosophy as well as his plans for the conquest of other nations in the name of a cleansed humanity.

When a populace allows itself to be mesmerized by the glorious image of a country where those pesky people you don't like magically vanish from sight (Deported, gassed, jailed, tortured--who cares! Just get rid of them!), they don't question what "great" actually means.

A similar populace in America didn't bother to look beneath the veneer of the Republican Platform to see how this supposed greatness would be put into effect.

If you were visiting from another planet, you might be fooled that the Republican Party promotes a fair plan for all citizens. They are skilled at double-talk, and soft-soap millions of Americans who keep voting Republican despite what the Republican leaders' true agenda is.

Speaking in a general way, those who look to the short run and what they can get out of a quick grab at raiding America for profits can be defined this way:

They behave as if their actions have no repercussions, and they are entitled to do what they want, when they want, and they won't get caught. And, if they do get caught, it will be a slap on the wrist and they'll still have all the money.

They don't think about who they'll trample and destroy on their so-called righteous path to greatness.

They surrender their morality and their humanity in the name of greed for profits today no matter what devastation that means for others tomorrow.

Republicans are not squeamish about destroying lives as well as the environment. It's strange for a large group to call itself the "Conservative Party" and yet it apparently has little or no interesting in <u>conserving</u> anything good. The policies of greed create environmental destruction, hardship for millions of women, children, infants and disabled people. And the list goes on.

Republicans in Congress, and Trump's Cabinet have a singular purpose: de-construction of the United States Constitution so they can create ever swelling profits for gigantic corporations and the super-wealthy.

Donald Trump has many nicknames in the press and social media around the world, including "Toddler-in-Chief." Of course, that term is referring to his habitual temper tantrums that at first glance are reminiscent of the fury during the stage of development called "the terrible twos."

When a toddler has been thwarted by a rule such as bedtime or no more dessert, the child might erupt in a boiling rage. But let's not belittle children, because the comparison is specious. Donald Trump chose the man he became, whereas a toddler is reacting to life with the only understanding he or she has at that young age, when even a small frustration can lead to shrieks before the child finally falls asleep and gets the much-needed respite from worldly cares over toys and television and treats.

Along the way, growing up, Donald Trump obviously aligned with the bullies, tyrants and abusers of the world. He no doubt felt stronger and bigger when he could make others jump when he said "frog," bow and scrape to earn his favors, and endure his temper. He brags about sexual exploits and harassment of women, whom he objectifies as yet another thing he's entitled to own and discard.

When people of a low level of awareness treat others with cruelty, they assume that if the tables were turned, they would be treated the same way. They can't distinguish their own viewpoint of grabbing at life's goodies from the reality of diversity in the world. They see themselves, and nothing else. And the vacancy in their eyes is all too revealing.

What can we do about people who are firmly convinced that Trump won the popular vote, that he was a "landslide" winner of the presidential election? What can we say to convince them to look at the facts about the tax law, about the Mexican wall, about all the problems Republicans in Congress are creating for our country?

Nothing.

We can't do anything to change their minds. When people are not willing to look beyond the pap fed to them by their favorite news source, Fox News, and the Tweeter-in-Chief himself, they are like the Germans who still supported Hitler on into year thirteen of his "reign," and even killed themselves and their children when they learned about Hitler's suicide in 1945.

The more you try to convince someone that they are "wrong," the more they dig in their heels and defend their position.

We know this. Because we all do the same thing. It takes a certain level of willingness to hear the truth when it doesn't align with what you've been taught all your life to believe.

That is why Trump and his clan had to do such outrageous things that even long-time Republicans are now waking up and saying, in essence, "Whoa, hold on a minute! I never knew he was actually accused of sexual assault! How come we didn't know about this before I voted for him! I didn't know his so-called tax cuts and big breaks for business were all about more relief for super-wealthy and corporations—my mom and pop store is going to be hurt by what he's doing. How come nobody told me! And why didn't anybody make it clear that his special ideas about health care reform mean I won't have coverage and my sick kids are going to be at risk? What about Medicaid...Medicare...Social Security? I was told the Democrats are the ones who were going to make my life miserable—how come so many people lied and I'm just now finding out the truth about all this?"

As more and more Republicans realize what their elected officials are doing in Congress, I hope they will begin a much-needed party reformation at a deep level, and rid themselves of the sexual molesters, misogynists, racists and corrupt officials in their party ranks.

A first step for the Republican with a heart would be to stop watching Fox News and find out what is actually going on. Dig deeper into the real lives of those unqualified men and women whom Republicans keep voting into office in local and state elections, and who perpetuate the climate of sexual abuse and destroying civil liberties.

Let's shun Donald Trump. Narcissists thrive on attention, even when it is negative in nature. They can't tolerate being ignored. Let's turn our backs on him and keep our attention firmly focused on the results that we want to create for the good of our country and its citizens.

6

BOOMERANGS FOR THE GREATER GOOD

"Man receives only that which he gives.
The Game of Life is a game of boomerangs.
Man's thoughts, deeds and words,
return to him sooner or later,
with astounding accuracy."

Florence Scovel Shinn

The law of attraction is a neutral energetic force that automatically draws together those elements that are matching or in harmony with each other.

The common expression "Birds of a feather flock together" was perhaps intended long ago as a lesson about the law of attraction.

The danger of not understanding this law is that we inadvertently misuse its power, and we attract into our lives all sorts of results that we are not happy about. We picture being alone and sad, and boom! –that is what happens.

We don't easily make the connection between thought pictures and what we experience because starting in early childhood we were taught to be practical, to set goals, to look at benchmarks along the way to be sure we are achieving what we want, and also to absorb a whole host of misconceptions about ourselves and why we are here.

In addition, there's often a time lag (thank goodness) between thinking about something and manifesting it. Otherwise, this planet would be a total mess, wouldn't it? You'd angrily notice the garbage a neighbor left on your yard, and wish they'd drop dead—and it would happen.

I feel it's of vital importance that we learn to work more harmoniously with our natural laws such as the law of attraction. Whatever we think about comes back to us—just like a boomerang.

Have you noticed times when you or a friend casually remark, perhaps with a groan of confusion, that the day started off badly and has gotten worse ever since? You can't wait for tomorrow, as if the setting and rising of the sun will create a magical difference in your life experience.

Until we learn that it is our own attitude that sets the emotional tone for our day, and thus our "point of attraction" as Esther Hicks identifies it, we will continue to be the willy-nilly victims of days that seem to run our lives instead of the other way around.

Each time you start to say something, remember that your words are boomerangs, and will come back to you.

7

PARADIGM OF PROGRESS

Let's look at a more vibrant approach to understanding the progressive paradigm, or mindset, and why it's critical to elevate our collective belief system and thus advance human evolution.

Since a paradigm is a collection of a multitude of beliefs, we all walk around with ideas in our mind that have varying degrees of effect on what we do in life. Some paradigms from childhood can be so tightly interwoven with our self-concept that they are difficult to shake loose—and that shaking can only be a voluntary action.

Have you ever been on the other end of an aggressive sales call, or someone you've just met at a party or networking event who is determined to make you change your mind about something? No matter how hard they try to convince you, if something is jarring about their message, you'll be more likely to resist, to dig in your heels and cling to your old belief, than you are to agree with them. The exception is, of course, if what they are telling you resonates with some misgivings you've been secretly having about that very belief.

Let's say you grew up believing that you will never be successful. Teachers and parents reinforced this idea, however unwittingly, with comments that you'd better play it safe and get the kind of job you can handle—don't dream too big or you'll be sorely disappointed.

Yet, over the years, you couldn't give up that tiny idea that maybe they were wrong about you. And along comes a book telling you about people who overcame all odds to live at a higher level, and succeed in sports, or business, or relationships. The experience of learning about others who were in your situation and triumphed over it, opens your mind to wondering where else in life you have shortchanged yourself because of unchallenged beliefs you've been carrying around.

Quantum physics opens the door for us to gain a more enlightened view of our ability and innate power to create our results by our own thought power. Thus we have control over our lives and our destinies, but too often we abdicate that to old paradigms about our own worth.

When we expect hard times and disaster, those thoughts are not idle—they go to work, magnetically drawing together events and circumstances that answer our unwitting request. That is how the natural laws of this universe work, although we are just beginning to get a better understanding of these laws.

When we learn to be careful of what we ask for, we have a much better chance of attracting what we really want to experience for ourselves and others.

There are two ways in which we change our paradigm about a particular topic such as success, or relationships, or life in general and our place in society.

1. By noticing where we are not getting the results we want, and making a deliberate decision to change. This is a progressive changing of the paradigm by repetition of positive statements that affirm the direction we want to go in.

2. By a catastrophe that shocks us into a sudden change of heart or opinion about life. This could be a natural disaster, a horrible accident or fire that destroys your belongings, a

sudden illness… or the election of a man such as Donald Trump as the 45th President of the United States of America.

When we look at the history of the world, we see that the wheels of change grind slowly—and one of the reasons for that is that we collectively <u>believe</u> that change can't be fast!

Looking at our own history, in the United States, freedom for the Colonials was not won overnight; even after the Declaration of Independence, it took nearly another hundred years for slavery to be declared illegal. The women of this nation did not get the right to vote until the country was 150 years old. Labor unions and social change began to benefit the common worker and lower/middle income families in the early part of the 20th century. In the early 1960's, Martin Luther King and other civil rights leaders like James Farmer (founder of the Congress of Racial Equality) followed the example of Mahatma Gandhi and used the methods of nonviolent protest to free the Blacks in the South and in the ghettoes of Northern cities, a freedom they created for themselves by allowing themselves to be beaten, jailed and worse, which was then passed into law in the Civil Rights Act of 1964.

You probably have other stories about the changing of paradigms in your own life and those of your friends and neighbors. The shift away from the stigma of being an unmarried mother; the prevalence of romantic couples living together openly, without benefit of a civil or religious marriage ceremony.

Think about a positive change that you would like to create in your own life, and in your community, and in our country. Then tell yourself: *I can do this…We can do this. And change will be quick!*

It's vital that we remain willing to open our minds to new ideas and new ways of coming together in service of the greater good.

Ask yourself:

- Why do I vote for Democratic candidates?

- What is it about calling myself a "progressive" or "liberal" that aligns with who I really am?

- Where else in my life do I want to see progress, and positive change?

- How can I be of greater service at home, at work, at school, in my community—in my everyday actions and the things I say to others?

- How can I help this world of ours evolve into a higher level of awareness?

For many if not most Republicans, they are stuck in their Paradigm of Entitlement, a mindset that tells them their party is always right, and that they deserve to take what they want no matter who or what it hurts. (Hey, drill the Arctic Refuge because I'm entitled to oil and I'll never go there anyway.) They march in lockstep with their leaders and don't question what is going on behind the scenes. They don't realize the part they are playing in this period of history.

From their viewpoint, I'm guessing, they believe that Trump is being demonized by the Democrats and they think he's actually doing a fine job, keeping his promises to cut taxes, to keep trying to get rid of Obamacare (even though it helps them!), to deport people of a different color or religion than they are.

All you have to do is take a glance in social media and you'll see the men and women who are enthusiastic supporters of Donald Trump. In other words, they drank the Kool-Aid and they're not looking for the antidote.

What we can see from the words and deeds of Republicans is that they have a certain belief set or paradigm deeply embedded in their minds, and it drives what they do.

When people run on automatic pilot in life, simply reacting to everything around them, and doing daily tasks according to established routine, unless something shocking happens, they don't challenge their paradigm and question whether they may have some old or even erroneous beliefs that are not useful to hold onto.

Most people live their entire lives at a level of awareness barely above the animalistic instinct. They react to everything. They don't strive for personal growth, or reach out with a questioning mind to discover a higher way of living.

This is the fault of our centuries-old cultural focus on looking outside of ourselves for happiness, contentment, success and love. Throughout human history only a few students of the mind discovered the truth that we create our reality with our own thoughts.

But we are in an exciting point right now—the shock of Trump's election has catapulted millions of people into a more awake and aware state, and they are looking eagerly for ways to change not only what is going on in our government, but in their own lives.

In a sense, the boom of self-help books in the 1980s has led the way for us to seek new opportunities to assist our country's recovery from the devastation caused by Trump and the R-MoC's. So many of us have already gotten into the habit of meditating, using positive affirmations, opening our minds to new ideas and information about other cultures and religions around the world. We are more expansive in our thoughts and this prepares us to keep going in our fight for liberty and justice for all.

When we live in a state of hypnotic adherence to the multitude of beliefs in our thoughts, and don't question the sanity or truthfulness of them, we are easy prey for the man who rants and raves and makes wild promises about making the nation great and prosperous.

Trump followed Hitler's example with the same kind of rants, and millions of people raised to believe that whatever the Republican Party leaders decided was correct, simply nodded and voted. Their paradigm automatically filtered out conflicting reports about Trump that exposed reality. It wasn't just that they got their "information" from Fox News, they were –and millions remain—cocooned in a false world where the truth of Arctic drilling and tax cuts for corporations who profit from destroying the environment, deportations, and more devastation are simply not believable.

And so the truth is rejected as being merely a sign of Democrats acting out their anger about losing, as those pesky progressives trying to stir up trouble, those bleeding heart liberals chanting to give away the country to every hard luck case.

The Republicans are deeply entrenched in a paradigm of regression, of divisiveness and isolation. As the Dalai Lama commented, Trump's championing "America First" has no place in the world community of today, and neither does Trump's totalitarianism.

Democrats do know. We know we are here at this time to advance progress, to protect human rights, and to protect our beautiful planet.

Surely this must be a nightmare we will awaken from. And yet each day when we get up, there are even more devastating results of his blatantly egoistic presidency as he gleefully allows the far-right Republicans to rape our nation and destroy our liberties.

I'm sure you've seen his daily rants, his tweeted nuclear threats to other countries, his blatant lies and twists of reality, his frankly insane behavior. The list goes on and on. Oddly enough, whatever Trump declares as "fake news" keeps turning out to be a recording of his own words, verified events, and true reportage.

Even as their own rights are abrogated by the tax scam, threats about Medicare, Medicaid, Social Security and other benefits, Republicans tweet their undying loyalty to *der fuhrer* (German for *the leader*). It seems incomprehensible that many millions of United States citizens actually believe Trump is doing a terrific job.

In the following passage from *The Lion, the Witch and the Wardrobe* by C.S. Lewis (the second book in *The Chronicles of Narnia*), we find an analogy to Donald Trump (Witch) and his cabinet members and voters (Edmund) which may help in understanding the Republican Party Paradigm of "me-first":

You mustn't think that even now Edmund was quite so bad that he actually wanted his brother and sisters to be turned into stone. He did want Turkish Delight and to be a Prince (and later a King) and to pay Peter [his older brother] out for calling him a beast. As for what the Witch would do with the others [Peter and their two sisters, Susan and Lucy], he didn't want her to be particularly nice to them—certainly not to put them on the same level as himself; but he managed to believe, or to pretend he believed, that she wouldn't do anything very bad to them, "Because," he said to himself, "all these people who say nasty things about her [the White Witch] are her enemies and probably half of it isn't true. She was jolly nice to me, anyway, much nicer than they are. I expect she is the rightful Queen really. Anyway, she'll be better than that awful Aslan!" At least, that was the excuse he made in his own mind for what he was doing. It wasn't a very good excuse, however, for deep down inside him he really knew that the White Witch was bad and cruel.

Later in the book, when Edmund has been shocked into awareness about the cruelty of the White Witch, he realizes, "All the things he had said to make himself believe that she was good and kind and that her side was really the right side sounded to him silly now." And still later in the story, as Edmund's misery increases, he tries to comfort himself with the idea that it was all just a bad dream and he'd wake up soon.

In the words of a recent Democratic Congressional Campaign Committee (DCCC) survey: "Trump's administration is tearing proud American families apart. Are you prepared to fight back?"

Here's a recent comment about the Trump Administration's assault on the environment from Robert Redford, a Trustee of the Natural Resources Defense Council [NRDC]: "Forty-seven years ago, none other than Richard Nixon established the Environmental Protection Agency. And in the decades since, Republican and Democratic administrations alike have affirmed that environmental issues transcend politics. Now, we're watching the man charged with heading the EPA — Scott Pruitt — break from that tradition and tear down our most basic environmental safeguards left and right. I cannot understand how he will explain himself to his own children."

8

TAKE BACK OUR FLAG

I invite Democrats to start displaying the US Flag at home, and include it in your social media images.

Why?

I'm the kind of person that people call sweet and quiet. But let me tell you something, the Republican Party has gotten my back up.

I'm particularly outraged to see that if you wave the American flag people assume you're a Republican!

It's my flag. It's your flag. It doesn't belong to one party or group. It is OUR FLAG.

We the people of these United States have a beautiful flag that is renowned throughout the world as a symbol of hope and freedom. Or at least it used to have that symbolism.

Donald Trump's election destroyed a lot of that image, but he can't take it away completely, and we will repair the damage and move forward.

But it takes all of us.... #bluewave #humanrights #indivisible #swingleft #womensmarch … and many more… to come together as Freedom Fighters and defeat the Republican agenda of divisiveness and corruption.

So, please start the process of making the Stars and Stripes the flag for all of us, red and blue.

9

FORTUNE COOKIES FOR FREEDOM FIGHTERS

While writing this second edition of *America's New Breed of Freedom Fighters*, I took a break to eat stir fry veggies and rice from a Chinese restaurant around the corner. I cracked open the fortune cookie included in my takeout bag, and read the slip of paper folded inside, which said: "Today, you should spent some time to search in yourself." Grand advice, albeit phrased a bit oddly.

But when I thought about the message, I decided to include in this book Good Fortune affirmations to uplift and inspire all of us during the challenging times ahead.

Each time we repeat a positive concept, we diminish the power of old beliefs that we are not worthy of success, or that life is a hard struggle and then you die.

As you read, imagine you have just opened a fortune cookie and this is the message within, fortuitously meant to give you a personal message that is meaningful to you in this moment. Open your heart and mind to receive blessings each day from every aspect of your life experience.

Look for the good in others, instead of their faults.

Challenge yourself to be more positive each day.

Remember that Fortune favors the brave.

Don't worry, be happy!

Expect miracles.

Believe in your ability to create change.

Let discontent motivate you to expand upward.

Grow, grow, grow.

Each day, align with your higher purpose.

Calm down and speed up—you'll get there faster.

Your life is getting better and better every day.

Discipline is making a promise to yourself and keeping it.

Bloom where you are planted.

Smile until you feel a happy vibe in your toes.

Choose to feel peace in every cell of your body.

Your inner vibration predicts the results you'll see.

Guard the portal of your mind against negative thinking.

How you feel inside is more important than words and actions.

Your seemingly impossible good now comes to pass.

Keep your focus on freedom and hope.

We are all immigrants from a higher realm.

Forgiveness starts in the mirror.

Feel the feeling of your wish fulfilled.

Seize the day—be your best!

54

You become what you think about the most.

Choose self-assurance instead of fear.

Let go of the past—it can't touch you unless you drag it along.

You radiate joy wherever you go.

Know that you are on the side of progress.

Focus only on what you want to manifest.

The Divine Plan for your Life is now speeded up!

10

FIVE FREEDOMS

In listing my personal "Five Freedoms," I hope you will feel inspired to enumerate your own goals and dreams for progress.

When we have a vague sense of wanting "democracy," there is no real picture or vision that goes with that nebulous idea. General wishes don't have any fire under them, they don't have the molecular energy to actually create change.

We have to go deeper. We have to get clearer. We need to be very precise about what we are moving towards.

Knowing exactly what our dreams are is a tool to help us stay motivated to march and be involved in our government...of the people, by the people, and for the people.

When we allow ourselves to indulge in the temporary satisfaction of being outraged, resentful, angry and bitter, we inadvertently slide down into the emotional level where the narcissistic Trump and his ilk reside.

We can do better than that. Much better.

Big change is on the way. If you haven't already joined in, please consider doing so—join the worldwide movement to stand up and fight back against tyranny, corporate greed, and the suppression of human rights.

As we have learned from stories, both true and fictional, of heroes who are imprisoned and yet do not allow themselves to fall into permanent depression over their seeming lack of freedom, all of us are free to <u>think</u> and to <u>feel</u> our own thoughts and emotions.

No one can take away the power of thought from us (with the obvious exceptions of hypnotic drugs, brain surgery, torture, and so on).

Following are five freedoms that came to mind while writing this second edition of "America's New Breed of Freedom Fighters."

I know there are many more but I'd like to invite you to think about the concept of FREEDOM and start making your own list:

FREEDOM to decide our own behavior and outlook.

FREEDOM to speak to others, and to communicate our thoughts and ideas.

FREEDOM to learn from the past and look to the future.

FREEDOM to declare: "I will never give up!"

FREEDOM to define what is meaningful to us.

An intrinsic joy of these freedoms is that each individual has the full freedom to be unique.

Freedom to decide for ourselves means that even though we are loosely organized under a banner of "Democrats," we have our own stories. Each person gets to choose what is important for him or her.

Because of the many liberties that are under attack by Congressional Republicans, we marchers and protestors are coming into political activism for a wide variety of reasons. One person might be personally motivated to focus on health care for all, while her friend or neighbor picks up the banner to fight for automatic voter enrollment and other issues related to helping eligible voters get counted in each election.

QUOTE TO EXPLORE: "He who has a <u>why</u> to live for can bear with almost any <u>how</u>." Friedrich Nietzsche

We are fortunate today that Trump's election did not lead to an outbreak of actual Civil War with weapons of killing.

Our resistance weapons are of a higher order: we march, we protest, we sign petitions, we raise funds to help elect progressive candidates who are more interested in serving the Constitution than in raping the country to fill their own pockets.

When we collectively have a "why" to live for, we can define it as our mission statement. Think about this for a moment: why do you vote for Democrats? What is it about the Democratic Platform, in general, that appeals to you? Is it the idea that we are all citizens together and we should help each other, and also help those who are unable to help themselves (children, elderly, poverty-stricken, those who are sick and suffering)? Are you outraged at the long history of diminished rights for women, minorities, the LGBT community, and you want to do something about it?

We come together from many different streams and creeks into a great ocean of possibilities.

What did Nietzsche mean by saying that with that "why" solidly motivating and inspiring our lives, we can bear with, or put up with, any "how"? What is that "how" all about?

For me, I see it as relating to the steps we have to take in order to create change. Those "how" steps are usually what bogs us down in life. In fact, most of the time, the word "how" is a dream killer.

We get a bright idea to do something, and we're so excited about it—we feel more alive just thinking about it! And then our logical or reasoning mind leaps in with the laundry list of objections we were trained to focus on starting in early childhood (because that's our generational DNA as far as thinking habits go, passed down from one generation to the next): how can I do this? I must be crazy even thinking I can—where will I get the money, the training, the_____?

Fill in the blank with all the practical reasons that come to mind and bring us to a screeching halt, as we reluctantly put aside the big idea and settle for something easier to achieve.

However, with all of us coming together by the millions in a growing community across the land—and with support pouring in from our friends around the world-- that seemingly impossible HOW becomes much more doable.

Starting November 9, 2016 when Trump's election was announced, we Democrats knew that we had tough times ahead that would challenge us every day to bring our best game to the forefront.

We knew that a single womens march on January 21, 2016 was not going to make Donald Trump and his pals vanish from the scene.

We knew we had a road of challenges ahead of us.

We knew that we needed to speak up with the voice of progress and fight back. Our weapons: words of truth, words of #MeToo, words of justice for the oppressed and deported and Dreamers, words of support for what we want our government to stop doing, and what we want our government to start doing.

With our WHY firmly in place—to champion the principles of liberty and justice for all—we can bear the ups and downs of this path we are on.

And we won't give up.

Introduction

(1ST EDITION)

Dear Reader,

Everything we say and do is an affirmation of either fear or love. Although I understand the solidarity behind wearing a T-shirt that reads: "I'm One of 65,844,610 Americans against Trump," if we don't turn around that "against" mindset—we simply empower Trump and his agenda.

In my opinion, this is how Trump got elected:

The Red State voters pictured Donald Trump in the White House (imagining him making good on his promise to roll back progress to their idea of a "Great America" made up only of white bread and pasteurized white milk, with no chocolate milk or squaw bread allowed.)

The Blue State voters pictured Donald Trump in the White House (imagining in horror all the devastation that would follow his election.)

Over 90 million eligible voters (40% of total) did not vote in the 2016 presidential election. Their reasons for abstention added a low-level energy vibration of "whatever" and "it won't matter"—which is down on the frequency scale with Mr. Trump's hate-based campaign.

Combined, all of that fear energy elected Trump.

Unless we progressives begin doing something radically different as a collective whole, Trump's threats will materialize in all the devastating detail we have imagined.

We think in images, and when we get emotionally involved with those movies playing across the screen of our minds, and we picture the scenes in great detail, until they feel so real we can taste the popcorn, then those pictures must materialize.

That is the creative process of our universe, and we can't escape the law of attraction when we push against what we don't want. That doesn't bring us what we do want, it merely makes what we resist even stronger.

We fight terrorism, and the terrorists multiply.

We fight cancer, and it turns into an epidemic.

We fight Donald Trump's agenda, and… Guess what? His agenda grows stronger.

I was born in Texas. My heritage is Anglo-French, and I am qualified for membership in the DAR, "Daughters of the American Revolution." Perhaps the spirit of revolution is in my blood and has helped push me to write this book, although I must admit it is far outside my comfort zone because for much of my life, my outlook was, "Don't rock the boat, whatever you do!"

But I can't sit by and watch, like so many people did with Nazi Germany. I have to speak up and share what I think will help us. We can't allow Trump to get re-elected in 2020. I am writing this book to help Democrats and Progressives gain a better understanding and application of the law of attraction, so that the travesty of a man like Donald Trump in the White House can never be repeated in our country.

Every tyrant, every dictator and despot in history has eventually been defeated, but we cannot wait four years in a hopeless and helpless state of mind and then pray to defeat Trump in the polls. An organization in Alabama called Southern Poverty Law Center reports that in the first ten days post-election, there were 867 hate incidents in our country as white supremacists and avowed neo-Nazis celebrated Trump's election.

Personally, I don't believe the average Trump supporter is an extremist, racist or bigot. I feel that most of the people who voted for him were simply following their belief that a Republican candidate was the best choice no matter what others might be claiming about him. It's sad to realize that the hard-working middle class farmers, laborers, small business owners and factory workers in the Red States will be hit very hard indeed by Trump's widespread economic plans regarding minimum wage, tax benefits for the super-wealthy, and other issues that will adversely impact the lives of so many millions who gave him their blind support.

Wishes and hopes are a start towards creating our manifestation list, but wishing and hoping for change isn't enough.

We have to take inspired action, we have to imagine what we do want for our country, and we have to do all this in great enough numbers to make a difference.

To help mitigate the disaster of Trump's term in office and head off a potential re-election in 2020, in these pages I share how we can use and apply the laws of the mind more effectively and beneficially.

Now is a good time for me to point out that I'm not a political analyst, I'm not someone you would see on the streets shrieking into a news camera, or picketing outside one of the Trump buildings in NYC.

I'm an inspirational writer. I show people how to heal, recover from grief, and be happier. I'm also someone with the gift for making complex issues easier to comprehend and apply. I am a perpetual student of the natural laws of the mind and how we can transition out of humanity's Old Worldview of struggle and war, and into a New Worldview accessible to us from the insight quantum physicists have given us—a new view that explains that as incredible as it may seem at first, we actually create the results we experience, and we create them with our thoughts and the emotional images those thoughts form in our minds.

> *"Mind is the Master power that moulds and makes,*
> *And Man is Mind, and evermore he takes*
> *The tool of Thought, and, shaping what he wills,*
> *Brings forth a thousand joys, a thousand ills: —*
> *He thinks in secret, and it comes to pass:*
> *Environment is but his looking-glass."*

James Allen

When we think "in secret" it means those hidden beliefs that we all hold inside, and which pop up in response to life situations by bringing an image to mind.

I also bring to the table my lifelong experience in relationships with narcissistic men. Donald Trump is an extreme narcissist. People with this "personality disorder" are typically defined as being completely self-absorbed and possessing an unnaturally high level of entitlement: the rules don't apply to narcissists. They demand constant attention to mask their overwhelming insecurities, and erupt in rage when they are inadvertently or purposefully thwarted.

This book offers a new point of view, a new approach to defeating and neutralizing Trumps' radical, hate-based agenda.

We'll use the laws of the mind to attract success in the causes so dear to the hearts of compassionate and progressive people in America. All our friends around the world are welcome to join in visualizing peace. We can prevent the massive havoc and destruction that Trump and his supporters are championing.

When it's a big result like an election, it means many millions of us were involved in the outcome.

Hillary Clinton won the 2016 presidential election as the People's Choice, and now We the People have the amazing opportunity to join together in service to progressive ideals, and then, out of seeming devastation, create tremendous good for our country and global wellbeing.

We the People desire progress that helps the greatest number of people, instead of going back to the insular white bread, pasteurized white milk worldview espoused by Trump and his supporters.

This book includes a crash course in using the laws of the mind such as the law of attraction in a more effective way than most of us ever learned.

For instance, the law of opposites tells us that there is always an equal opposite for everything. If it is 30" from the top of your table to the floor, it must be 30" from the floor to the top of the table. We readily understand similar examples of polarity or opposites such as hot/cold, on/off, dark/light, up/down, back/front.

But a more interesting effect of the law of opposites is that when we are faced with a situation that appears really dreadful, that means there is an equal opposite that would be really wonderful.

I see the potential to create beauty out of the dark night of Trump's election.

The law of grace gives us a shortcut past karma, so that when we invoke grace into our lives, we can accelerate our results to, well, to warp speed.

This book is not a rehash of the campaign. It's not a plea to take action for the many wonderful causes and issues that the Democratic platform supported and continues to support, although I do list the main issues in a separate section for review and inspiration to get involved.

Consider this a call to action of a different variety. It's a pebble tossed into the lake, rippling outwards with the invitation to join me in visualizing progress, and in doing so, think those results into manifestation.

I know from experience in my own life that an undercurrent of panic will pull the rug out from under you and serve up the very results that you dread.

Let's not let that happen to America. Let's not let Trump truly win, by allowing his agenda to proceed into fulfillment.

If we fear and dread his presidency, we become inadvertent collaborators—transmitting our invisible energy straight to him and his cronies and feeding their greed for power.

In **Part One: What Do We Do Now?,** I explore the metaphysical and other reasons behind Trump's win, and what we can do about it. This section includes a special message to the Teens and Tweens who are our up-and-coming voters. I've included a recap of the issues, and messages from various organizations who have mapped out their plans for offsetting Trump's radical agenda.

Then, in **Part Two: Inside the Mind of a Narcissist,** I share my own experiences and perception about what drives an extreme narcissist such as Mr. Trump. I'm not a psychologist—but I survived way too many years of being married to a narcissistic verbal abuser, and I learned a lot about how to handle the situation, and how to change my behavior so I could be happy anyway.

Part Three: Alphabet Soup to Strengthen & Inspire offers words of comfort and, I hope, wisdom, on 26 topics listed in alphabetical order A-Z. The list of topics was gifted to me during meditation, and I am grateful to be of service in this way.

For those readers who weren't aware of or following my Stress Relief Blog Countdown to Trump's Inauguration, I've included all 31 blog posts in **Part Four: 31-Day Countdown to Inauguration 2017** I intended the blog content to be an integral part of the book, so don't skip this section under the assumption it's redundant.

By the way, a warm welcome to any Republicans who did not vote for Trump because of his extremism, or who did vote for him but now realize with horror that the "gossip" about his corruption and right-wing extremism is all too true. I grew up in a family where my dad was a Democrat and my mother was a Republican. But back then the party differences were not as wide apart as they are today, where basic freedoms and inalienable rights for all are truly at risk.

I offer a message of hope for the future in **Part Five: In God We Trust** Whatever your beliefs or lack of them, we all know that we did not create the sun and the moon and this planet we inhabit. Some energy is behind all that we see and experience, and we are all connected in this energy field as part of the whole.

In closing the book, I present my request that you make a commitment for change, described in **Part Six: Call to Action**. Prepare to embark on the greatest adventure of your life as you access a new level of courage you may have thought was meant only for those we call heroes. After all, a hero is someone who saw a need, walked through the fear and said, "Yes, I can do this."

Let's move forward with love in our hearts and get to work on creating a greater country and a better world, with liberty and justice for all.

Namaste—I see the Light in you.

with love,

Evelyn

Evelyn Roberts Brooks

P.S. For free ebooks, access to my studio with webinars, coaching lessons, and other downloadable material related to being a Freedom Fighter, visit your gift page at evelynbrooks.com/readers-freedom-fighters

PART ONE

WHAT DO WE DO NOW?

"It was the best of times,
it was the worst of times."

Charles Dickens (from *A Tale of Two Cities*)

1

THE REAL REASON MR. TRUMP WON

Widespread fear elected Donald Trump.

He won by manipulating terror.

He stirred up enough fear and dread in the hearts of millions to gather in a dark cloud of energy around him and thus gain the electoral votes needed to be declared president.

"All the water in the world cannot drown you
unless it gets inside you."

Eleanor Roosevelt

We the Democrats, Progressives and Moderates let fear get inside us, we allowed terror to overwhelm us with anxiety and worry about the future of our country – we pictured the horror of Donald Trump in the White House…and in our unintentional mis-use of the law of attraction, that picture materialized.

Mr. Trump will succeed with his plan to rape and pillage our democracy if we continue to let fear of his actions control our thoughts.

"Let me assert my firm belief that the only thing
we have to fear is fear itself — nameless,
unreasoning, unjustified terror which
paralyzes needed efforts to convert retreat into advance."

Eleanor's husband

73

This is a democracy. We elect our leaders. Holding up signs and tweeting "Not my president" is no doubt a way of stating your reaction, but it doesn't affect the reality of Trump's being handed the keys to our beloved White House for four years.

Despite the countless protests in social media—Trump is our president for now. Even though he is not the People's Choice, since he was not the winner of the popular vote, the Electoral College declared him the winner, and we must make the best of a bad situation.

In my opinion, there are more than a few factors that contributed to Trump's election.

Failure of the media to hold Mr. Trump accountable.

Failure of the national press to demand and get Mr. Trump's financial records—there is only one reason a businessman hides his tax returns, and that is to conceal the true nature of his business associates and the secrets behind his wealth. The world deserves to know exactly where Mr. Trump's financial interests lie, and the sources of his income.

Anxiety over the issues.

There was too much fear in Hillary's campaign particularly in the final weeks, panicked email subject lines that were probably intended to rally supporters, but instead fed into the fear-energy of Mr. Trump's campaign and made him more successful in his bid for electoral votes.

Inadvertently, Hillary's campaign fed the flames of Trump's fear campaign and made it stronger and more powerful.

Our real problem as Democrats was a serious lack of understanding the laws of the mind. Using the law of attraction more skillfully, we could've won the day because we would've magnetized all the good desired, and attracted in people who wanted the progressive results outlined so clearly in Hillary's campaign.

The fervor of Trump's supporters.

Let's put aside talking about the Trump supporters who are racist, misogynist, bigoted, white supremacists, and determined to gleefully extract all they can in profits while exploiting the workers and giving nothing back to society. I don't believe that they represent all Republicans.

I think "regular" people voted for Donald Trump because he stirred up their emotions with his angry rants, and gained their support with his lies about improving the economy and bringing work back to the U.S. labor force from foreign countries.

Blinded by his razzle-dazzle, they nodded as if hypnotized, and then looked the other way when news of his lack of integrity spread in social media.

The Electoral College system.

Although the system made sense in 1776, when the white male voters (the only ones allowed to vote, in case you fell asleep in history class that day) lived in far-flung villages and towns, and gathering the votes regionally made it easier to come up with a total in the days before calculators and computers, today the Electoral College is dangerously antiquarian, unfair and outmoded, and must be abandoned.

Apathy.

The emotion of "who cares" swept our land from sea to sea. 90 million eligible voters didn't bother to go to the polls or take advantage of absentee voting by mail. The prevailing sentiment seemed to be that people didn't like either candidate.

Trump's soundbites of hate.

Millions of Republicans bought into his demonized portrayal of Hillary Clinton and didn't take a moment to examine the lies and deception, or to question their adherence to the party platform no matter what items were hidden on the glitter and glamor of wild promises for "greatness."

Celebrity-struck Americans.

A celebrity-awed population held and still holds a distorted belief that Trump's ability to get his name on top of tall buildings means he knows how to create economic recovery—and these very people only accessed the type of media and news programs that support that distortion of his lifestyle, his business history and the devastation he has already caused to his employees and others in his path.

Lack of understanding the President's scope of work.

It's as if millions of Republicans were thinking, "Hey, the President goes on television now and then and talks. Trump can do that! He already does more than that, he's got his own show. Reality TV star? Oh, yeah, he's qualified to be president."

> *This election was truly won by the woman.*
> *That which was in the shadows is now in the light.*
> *Keep your voices—let your desire be to be heard.*
> *Change comes from the heart.*
> *Live life through you, by choices that you make*
> *– this is the time to choose. -- **THEO***

Those who thought only about Trump's economic promises found it more convenient to ignore, deliberately or not, the rest of his platform on so many other issues, as if it wasn't an all-inclusive meal, and they could order à la carte when he got in office.

And of course some of his supporters agree with his ideas of an elite white society; they formed alliances with him and stood by him even while decrying and tutting his admissions of groping and assaulting women, and other sordid insights into his view of the world and his place in it.

Did you know that Adolf Hitler was elected? That's right, the people voted him into power in 1932 on the platform of making Germany "great again" after its defeat in the Great War, (later called World War I, but not until we were in the midst of World War II, just in case you were dozing in that history class as well). Hitler's tactics of ranting, bullying, threatening and overriding any opposition landed him in a position of power that he inflated beyond all rationality.

The Third Reich is part of our human history, and we can and should learn from it.

Where do we go from here? Do we simply hope for the best, and wait out the next four years with bated breath, worried what Trump will do next?

Or do we join together and find a way to neutralize Trump's extreme right-wing agenda?

Resistance won't work.

Fighting won't work.

Why? Because pushing against something makes it grow stronger. Fear makes everything worse.

But there is a way we can outwit the bully, and it will be completely nonviolent in nature.

In fact, I believe you'll enjoy the process because every area of your personal life—health, prosperity, self-expression, relationships–will improve as you access the power of your thoughts.

I am here to make a difference. That is why I'm writing this book. And I believe you are here to make a difference, too—a <u>positive</u> difference, not the kind of difference Trump and his supporters are already enacting.

We must make our picture of progressive America—the land of the free and the brave—<u>stronger</u> than Donald Trump's picture of pillage and destruction.

Together we can create magnificent outcomes for many important issues that are dear to progressive and all compassionate citizens. Let's get started without further delay.

"Many people have brought disaster into their lives
through idle words. For example: A woman once asked me
why her life was now one of poverty, of limitation.
Formerly she had a home, was surrounded by beautiful things
and had often tired of the management of her home,
and had said repeatedly, 'I'm sick and tired of things –
I wish I lived in a trunk,' and she added:
'Today I am living in that trunk.'
She had spoken herself into a trunk.
The subconscious mind has no sense of humor
and people often joke themselves into unhappy experiences…
Fortunately the law works both ways,
and a situation of lack may be changed to one of plenty."

Florence Scovel Shinn

Our attention on being against what Trump stands for actually energized his campaign. The tremendous fear over Trump's chance of getting elected was an invisible harmonic energy that bolstered him up and over the final hurdles and into the winner's circle.

On November 9, 2016, like the majority of voters in the United States and progressive thinkers around the world, I was reeling in shock over Donald Trump's presidential win.

As I walked around New York City that day, I witnessed many conversations among Hillary Clinton's supporters that reflected my own dismay. I had been so confident of her win, and I knew that many with intuitive access were confident of it as well (and that prediction was correct: she won the popular vote).

When a stranger sat next to me on the bus and asked how I was feeling, I knew she was referring to the election results. She was filled with anger and fear. After chatting for a while, I told her to consider that if we allow ourselves to hate Trump and fear his agenda, then he has truly won. She told me that my words had helped her feel better, and the idea for this book was born.

I feel I have something of value to share, something important that will help turn this seemingly devastating situation around: I know the laws of the mind and how we create reality with our thoughts. I know how to heal from grief and tragedy. And I know how to stand up to a bully without being subsumed by his anger.

2

WHY RESISTANCE IS FUTILE

"What you resist persists."

Carl Jung

When we push back at something unwanted and try our very best to make it go away, it's as if we unwittingly waved a wand and gave the command: "Multiply!"

Whatever we resist gets stronger. It flourishes like a weed.

Don't believe me? Take a look at the war on terrorism, the war on cancer, the war on teen pregnancy, the war on drugs.

Everywhere we put our attention, the focus of our attention grows and expands, whether we consciously want it to or not.

Our evolving understanding of the mental laws means we can stop resisting, and start putting our attention and our intention on the issues that are of importance to progressive thinkers and caring people who want a better world for all.

"However, the man who is centered and established
in right thinking, the man who sends out only good will
to his fellow-man, and who is without fear, cannot be touched
or influenced by the negative thoughts of others.
In fact, he could then receive only good thoughts,

as he himself sends forth only good thoughts.
Resistance is Hell, for it places man in a 'state of torment.'"

Florence Scovel Shinn

We can feel compassion that others are misguided, that they are unaware and are still in the victimhood stage of un-awakened humanity. But compassion does NOT mean that we just go along with their program to placate their tempers.

There's a better way than resistance. We can be a new type of Freedom Fighter and attract the results we want.

A better label would be "Freedom Attractor" but I felt that since we are in transition out of fear-based thinking habits that are as old as the human race, "fighter" would be more readily understood, and allows us to contrast the techniques we'll be using against the historic methods resistance fighters have used in the past.

3

STOP ACCIDENTALLY COLLABORATING WITH TRUMP

Just because you and I wouldn't deliberately vote for Mr. Trump doesn't mean we didn't inadvertently empower his message.

If you felt fear about his proposed wall on our southern border—you aligned with the idea of the wall.

If you felt terror at his plan to create a Muslim registry—you aligned with the picture he created of the registry.

If you felt dread at the idea of his being elected POTUS—you aligned with the horrifying images of him being in the White House, of him trashing the Paris Climate Change Conference, of him starting a war by virtue of his hair-trigger temper and narcissistic sense of entitlement, of him perverting all the freedoms our country was founded on.

His agenda items are very low in frequency vibration. They are based on hate, based on striking terror into the hearts of millions of people here and abroad, based on his need to crown himself ruler of the world, with everyone quaking when he comes in view because that must mean he is very powerful and lordly.

The center of the classic narcissist's behavior is the overwhelming need to be adulated, no matter what he has to do to get the attention he craves. More on narcissism in **Part Two: Inside the Mind of a Narcissist**.

All of the shocking pictures that came into our minds and began growing emotional roots are indications that we became mentally in collusion with Trump's agenda.

By allowing our untrained thoughts to keep picturing what Trump painted, by worrying and dreading what his presidency could and would mean to the free world, we inadvertently collaborated on a vibrational level.

Let me be very clear: when I say we collaborated, it does NOT mean that we consciously agreed with his plans.

I'm not a quantum physicist, so I'll put it in the plain words that make sense to me: The "colluding" thoughts are an energy waveform connecting with matching thought forms as if they are all drawn together by powerful magnets.

All of this goes on beneath our conscious awareness. I want to be sure no one starts feeling guilty or even more upset about the election outcome.

As intuitive Sheila Gillette pointed out in a Theo webinar about coping with and understanding the election results, the purpose of Trump's threats was to manipulate and frighten. All of these issues he activated needed to be brought to the surface at this time so we can begin healing them.

Once we realize the scientific truth about energy waveforms and the fact that we are all connected, then we can move on from the shock of the election results and get to work on the issues of importance to us.

The longer we decry his presidency, the more painful the results will be, because we will be adding energy to his campaign just as if we went out in the gardens of the country and fertilized the weeds. Or, for science fiction fans, we could say that being in deadly fear of

Darth Vader (*Star Wars*' arch-villain) actually feeds Vader's energetic Dark Force, and thus his power to control and destroy.

I believe we can deliberately turn our thinking toward achieving what we want, instead of continuing to support the very things we are so against.

We become what we think about the most. This axiom of the mental laws bears attention.

As Ralph Waldo Emerson said over 150 years ago, it is vital that we learn how to "stand guard" at the portal of our minds.

We have to become more aware of the impact our passionate thoughts have, and the power of the pictures we form with those thoughts.

"Getting into the spiritual swing of things is no easy matter for the average person. The adverse thoughts of doubt and fear surge from the subconscious. They are the 'army of the aliens' which must be put to flight. This explains why it is so often 'darkest before the dawn.' A big demonstration is usually preceded by tormenting thoughts. Having made a statement of high spiritual truth one challenges the old beliefs in the subconscious,and 'error is exposed' to be put out."

Florence Scovel Shinn

Affirm: I no longer collaborate with Trump's agenda of frightening threats. I cast the burden of fear on the Super Conscious Mind, and I am free.

4

EVERYTHING WE NEED TO NEUTRALIZE TRUMP'S AGENDA

The invisible energy field we all live in, and which is "plastic" to our thinking, is neutral to what we ask it to create. If we think thoughts that stem from a deep fear and lack of security within, then we create Holocausts.

However, on the flip side, when we focus on kind and loving thoughts, we create schools and dig wells and manifest opportunities for those who lived without hope.

The quantum field of infinite possibilities is real. It's science, not magic. The law of attraction is not a game we play now and then when we wish for a new car or a fatter bank balance.

The laws of the mind are the go-between for us, like a manager who sends our messages to the boss for what we want, and brings our order back. The law of attraction is the way we access the power of creation with our thoughts.

The law responds to us whether we worriedly picture war, a wall at our southern border, wide-scale deportations based on religion, and a narcissist in the White House ... OR whether we picture broader access to education and college for our citizens, health for women and children, a protected environment, improved lifestyles for the lower and middle-class population, job opportunities, the right to the pursuit of happiness for all citizens, and so much more.

The law of attraction is not "optional" any more than gravity is. Together, we can access the power of the mental laws to create the benefits and progress we desire for ourselves and future generations.

"So long as man resists a situation, he will have it with him. If he runs away from it, it will run after him. For example: I repeated this to a woman one day, and she replied, 'How true that is! I was unhappy at home, I disliked my mother, who was critical and domineering; so, I ran away and was married -- but I married my mother, for my husband was exactly like my mother, and I had the same situation to face again.'

"'Agree with thine adversary quickly.' This means, agree that the adverse situation is good, be undisturbed by it, and it falls away of its own weight. 'None of these things move me,' is a wonderful affirmation. The inharmonious situation comes from some inharmony within man himself. When there is, in him, no emotional response to an inharmonious situation, it fades away forever from his pathway. So we see man's work is ever with himself."

Florence Scovel Shinn

5

BE A MODERN FREEDOM FIGHTER

"Never finish a negative statement;
reverse it immediately, and
wonders will happen in your life."

Dr. Joseph Murphy

Welcome, All American Freedom Fighters!

This book is a call to action for anyone who is feeling panic and dread about Trump's presidency and what he'll manage to accomplish in the next four years.

Will he start a war? Will he bankrupt the middle class? Will he endorse the white supremacists who hail him?

With an extreme narcissist like Trump, anything is possible—he's the type of man who used to be called a "loose cannon," meaning you can't predict exactly what will happen next, but you know that destruction will be involved.

Purpose: this is a call to action for people who are afraid and feel their voice is not heard and they are helpless to create desired change. It will outline how to create a vision and bring it into manifestation working together on shared goals

"I hope you'll remember that progress
isn't always a straight line. We will have to
work harder now, more so than ever before,

to keep our country from moving in
what we know is the wrong direction."

Barack Obama, January 9, 2017

Most of my life I have been the kind of person to shy away from any sign of conflict, or confrontation. I've always taken on the role of peace keeper, harmonizer, the one who smooths things over so the people get along a little better or at least pretend to do so for the sake of keeping things more amicable. I'm one of the least likely activists you're ever going to meet. And yet here I am, writing a book about how to be a new style of freedom fighter and work together for what we want America to achieve in its greatness. I felt the inspiration on the day of the news election 11 9 and I said yes I will write the book

Great opportunities are before us if we accept the challenge. However, if we feel dread, anger, worry and even hatred, then Mr. Trump and his supporters will truly win.

We cannot push against him and angrily wish for his failure, and at the same time create and manifest the important goals we desire: freedom of religion, freedom of self-expression, liberty to make personal choices about health and well-being and who we want to love. We want to achieve strides in clean energy, protect the environment and improve the condition of factory-farm animals who are treated abominably to enhance the bottom line of giant corporations.

All of these inalienable rights, and more, are at risk. That is a given, according to Mr. Trump's stated agenda of destruction and havoc. However, let's keep in mind that Mr. Trump did not buy the White House. He does not get to rename it Trump's Castle.

He is not the People's Choice.

Therefore, We the People, with the rights secured in our Constitution, have the power to change. To neutralize, to offset, and to triumph over his agenda of hate.

Love ALWAYS trumps hate.

In this book, my focus is not on detailing the manipulations, falsehoods, misrepresentations and wholesale lies spread by Mr. Trump and his team. You can research that easily for your own, but I caution you to do so lightly because if you feel anxiety well up inside, or emotions of anger, then you risk adding more vibrational energy to his agenda, instead of one of growth.

We have to be careful with our thought power. Use our emotions as indicators of where we need to turn our attention. Anger is a useful tool—it points out situations where we do not want what we see or what it appears will logically come next. But instead of staying angry and building it into a total meltdown of stress, we have to learn to shift our thinking so that we feel empowered rather than full of rage.

The old-style resistance fighter was working with a lesser awareness of the mental laws than we have access to today. They fought with the same weapons their enemies used: gunfire, sabotage, in-depth planning, and secrets whispered in darkened corridors.

Today, we can take advantage of the New Worldview which quantum physics opens a door onto. We can use the law of attraction as a much more effective "weapon."

New freedom fighters can take lessons from such iconic films as *Star Wars*—use the Force, neutralize the magnetic pull to the Dark Side. It's really important to understand the pour of that "dark side" or shadow side of our thoughts—because when we respond to hate with hate and fear, then we are aligning with what we are against, and by the laws of the universe, we make that unwanted situation even more powerful.

People who scream "Build the wall!" are not rational. They are operating out of mob mentality under the hypnotist of agitation with hate filled messages that feel empowering because of the adrenaline rush the anger generates.

These immature people are remnants of the Old Worldview that brought about such atrocities as the Inquisition, the Crusades, concentration camps, genocide, religious persecution, neighbors fearing reprisals and tattling by neighbors and within the family, and, as always, random acts of terrorism.

Safeguard yourself and your loved ones. Don't drive or walk past a mob as they cheer Trump. Take a detour even if it means being late for an appointment.

Don't allow a hate-spewing person to engage you in discussion. They have no interest in hearing your viewpoint and being the helpful Pollyanna trying to show them the path of light will only enrage such a person, and could put you in a compromising position. Don't post your personal contact information in social media.

Being a Freedom Fighter involves bravery. Yes, we learn to get ourselves out of alignment with bad things by thinking positive thoughts, but there's always the general rule: take sensible precautions.

Don't invite hotheads into your life by being careless about walking alone in a volatile crowd or known area of Trump supporters. Don't show up in the company of friends who intend to heckle the crowd at a pro-Trump-agenda rally. Make your excuses, plead a headache if necessary, but don't take foolhardy actions that can have repercussions.

Affirm: I am always in the right place at the right time.

All of the situations confronting us today can be improved by accessing the power of our thoughts at a much higher level (way up beyond the frequency of fear and worry!) and in greater numbers.

Joining together, we become an incredibly strong and powerful force for good.

While we are looking to science fiction for inspiration, remember the old phrase "Resistance is futile" mentioned earlier in this section – and understand the deeper meaning of that line of dialogue is a universal truth.

When we resist something or someone, we inadvertently energize it with our own thought power.

Therefore, at all times, keep in mind the wisdom of being FOR what you desire, and never AGAINST it.

> *"Fear is misdirected energy and must be redirected,*
> *or transmuted into Faith.*
> *Jesus Christ said, 'Why are ye fearful, O ye of little faith?'*
> *All things are possible to him that believeth.*
> *I am asked, so often by my students, 'How can I get rid of fear?'*
> *I reply, 'By walking up to the thing you are afraid of.'*
> *The lion takes its fierceness from your fear.*
> *Walk up to the lion, and he will disappear; run away and he runs*
> *after you."*

Florence Scovel Shinn

New Freedom Fighters don't do battle. We don't try to convince someone that they are wrong in wanting a Christian white society, and that we are right in desiring diversity, progress and justice for everyone.

Battling someone never leads to progress. It only leads to anger, resentments, and anxiety. When fear takes hold of us, it clings with a grip. We must loosen those barbs of fear and free ourselves to lift up into a higher, finer vibration of spiritual awareness. From that vantage point, we can have a broader perspective of the transformational times we live in, the inevitable fact that many people are still in the old mode of living and will resist and hate us for wanting to keep evolving and expanding.

America's new breed of Freedom Fighters are not defined by a specific skin color, ethnicity, age, gender, education, economic status or any other distinguishing feature. We're not a homogenized group. We are the People.

We come in all shapes and sizes and ages. What we do have in common is our desire to create a better life not just for ourselves and our immediate friends and family, but for everyone. And we want to protect our beautiful country from environmental harm. We want good health care availability for all, education, and so many more aspects of leading a high quality, enjoyable life that is fulfilling and satisfying, with malice toward none, and the unrestricted pursuit of happiness for all.

6

Special Note for Teens and Tweens

You will be the voters and campaign supporters in the next presidential election and the ones after that.

Voting is a right that we can and should hold dear to us and protect for others.

Many millions of people around the world do not experience the freedoms we take for granted in America. That is why so many people want to come to the United States and create a better life for themselves and their families with the opportunities that are readily available for anyone who is willing to set a goal, hold the beautiful vision of it firmly in mind, and steadily work toward achieving it.

> *"Success is the progressive realization*
> *of a worthy goal or ideal."*

Earl Nightingale

A cautionary reminder: Mr. Nightingale never met Donald Trump, whose definition of success is warped indeed. When Nightingale speaks of a "goal" he assumes you intend to make the world a better place.

There are countless ways to be of service in the work we do each day, whether you are being the best student possible and inspire your classmates to bring their best efforts, too, whether your goal is to serve the customers at your part-time barista job with the best coffee in town, to help others in the schools and social services at local, state and federal levels, to plan a career in science and industry to improve the quality of living, to be a writer, an entertainer, an athlete, and many thousands of other ways we bring our creative ideas into fruition.

You can start today to access the power of your own thinking to create positive change in your community, the nation and your own life.

This book will show you how, and the two books by Florence Scovel Shinn that are included at the readers page will give you wonderful examples of how people have transformed their results, along with many good affirmations you can repeat daily to retrain your thinking habits and get in charge of your life.

You are already more "hard-wired" for transformational thinking than your elders, as you have come in deliberately at this time in America to help with the transformation to a kinder and more compassionate society with liberty and justice for all.

Reader's page: evelynbrooks.com/readers-freedom-fighters

"Man has so long separated himself from his good
and his supply, through thoughts of separation and lack,
that sometimes, it takes dynamite to dislodge these false ideas
from the subconscious,
and the dynamite is a big situation."

Florence Scovel Shinn

7

QUICK LOOK AT THE ISSUES

"If you take most of the things that really matter,
they may be profound, but they are
fundamentally simple. You don't get tired of the sun,
and the sky, and fresh air, and water, and bread.
There is nothing complicated about them.
They are always there.
If they weren't, we would die.
You don't get tired of what you need."

Patricia Wentworth (from *Through the Wall*)

You are probably aware of what's at stake across so many fronts: education, the environment, immigration, religious freedom, fair wages, gender rights, health care and so many other important issues that benefit millions of citizens.

As CREDO action pointed out after the election results, "Donald Trump's bigoted attack on the diversity of our communities, including the bullying of immigrants and Muslim-Americans, was abhorrent during the election, and it will be disgraceful if he continues this behavior in the White House. His first staffing decisions show that he wants to build an administration that will use the power of the federal government to deliver on those threats. CREDO believes it is incumbent on all of us to stand up and defend those threatened by Trump."

Below is a recap of progressive issues that are at stake. My purpose in including the list is to draw attention to what We the People want to achieve, and to stimulate interest in supporting these important topics in our society. Please note that, for continuity, the brief description of each topic is taken from hillaryclinton.com/issues

At the end of this section, you'll find a few messages from organizations whose issues are under fire from Trump and his cronies, as well as a letter to *Time* magazine from a veteran who presents his point of view about Mr. Trump's agenda regarding military issues.

It must be galling to veterans and active military to realize they will have to salute a "Commander in Chief" who has zero foreign policy experience, zero military experience, and that same level of diplomatic understanding and expertise.

My father was a U.S. Army Colonel, former member of the OSS, decorated World War II veteran, and he would never have voted for Mr. Trump. No way, no how.

Economy & Taxes

An economy that works for everyone

We need to build an economy that works for everyone, not just those at the top.

A fair tax system

Making sure the wealthy, Wall Street, and corporations pay their fair share in taxes.

Wall Street reform

Wall Street must work for Main Street.

Workforce skills and job training

Every American should be able to learn the skills they need to compete and succeed.

Labor and workers' rights

When unions are strong, America is strong.

Fixing America's infrastructure

Strong infrastructure is critical to a strong economy.

Manufacturing

Strengthen manufacturing so we always "Make it in America."

Small business

We have to level the playing field for America's small businesses.

Technology and innovation

We can harness the power of technology and innovation to work for all Americans.

Rural communities

America's rural communities are the backbone of this country.

Campaign finance reform

Our democracy should work for everyone, not just the wealthy and well-connected.

Jobs and wages

We can make the boldest investment in good-paying jobs since World War II.

Paid family and medical leave

It's time to guarantee paid family and medical leave in America.

Terrorism

Combating terrorism and keeping the homeland safe: It's not enough to contain ISIS and the threat of terrorism—we have to defeat it.

Immigration

We need comprehensive immigration reform with a pathway to full and equal citizenship.

National Security

With policies that keep us strong and safe, America will lead the world in the 21st century.

Quality of Life

Social Security and Medicare

We must preserve, protect, and strengthen these lifelines.

Veterans, the armed forces, and their families

America must fully commit to supporting veterans.

Poverty

No child should ever have to grow up in poverty.

Housing

We need housing policies that connect working families to opportunity.

National service

Do all the good you can.

Health

Health care

Universal, quality, affordable health care for everyone in America

An end to Alzheimer's disease

We can prevent, effectively treat, and make an Alzheimer's cure possible by 2025.

Mental health

We have to address the mental health crisis in America and end the stigma and shame associated with treatment.

Autism

Millions of Americans live with autism—and we've got to do more to support them and their families.

HIV and AIDS

We have reached a critical moment in our fight against HIV and AIDS.

Addiction and substance use

Through improved treatment, prevention, and training, we can end this quiet epidemic once and for all.

Criminal Justice Reform

Our criminal justice system is out of balance.

Gun Policy

We can—and must—end the epidemic of gun violence.

Military and Defense

We should maintain the best-trained, best-equipped, and strongest military the world has ever known.

Environment

Climate change

Taking on the threat of climate change and making America the world's clean energy superpower.

Protecting animals and wildlife

The way our society treats animals is a reflection of our humanity.

Human rights

Voting rights

We should be making it easier to vote, not harder.

Disability rights

We must continue to expand opportunities for Americans with disabilities.

LGBT rights and equality

Lesbian, gay, bisexual, and transgender Americans deserve to live their lives free from discrimination.

Racial justice

America's long struggle with race is far from finished.

Campus sexual assault

It's not enough to condemn campus sexual assault. We need to end it.

Women's rights and opportunity

We need to break down barriers that hold women back.

Education

K-12 education

Strong public education is the key to preparing our children for the future.

Early childhood education

Every child deserves the chance to live up to his or her God-given potential.

Making college debt-free and taking on student debt

Hillary will make debt-free college available to everyone and take on student loan debt.

> *"We encourage you to make peace with everyone*
> *who opposes you and with everyone whom you oppose,*
> *not only because you cannot insist on their yielding*
> *to your perspective but because their opposing perspective*
> *is of tremendous benefit to you.*
> *You see, because of your exposure to what you perceive as*
> *their wrong or bad or unwanted behavior or perspective—*
> *you have given birth to an improved situation.*
> *And just as they helped the problem side of the equation*
> *to come into focus, they helped the solution side*
> *of the equation to come into focus, also;*

and that solution waits for you in
your Vortex of Creation."
Abraham-Hicks

A Message from CREDO

November 10, 2016

"It's happened. A candidate who ran on a platform of hatred, racism and misogyny was just elected president of the United States.

"While a Trump presidency will attack and assault every progressive value – from defending the environment to reining in corporate greed, from defending civil rights and the social safety net at home to promoting peace and human rights abroad, it's important never to forget that his agenda and rhetoric put some people more than others at very real and very terrifying risk.

"At CREDO, we are horrified by yesterday's results, and we're gearing up to stop the fascist who is about to become president and the Republican extremists who enabled and endorsed his racism, xenophobia and hate. But first, and most importantly, we want to make it clear that we stand in solidarity with the people who have the biggest stake in this fight.

"No matter what, we will always stand shoulder-to-shoulder with every community Trump has attacked, threatened and marginalized in his campaign of hate. We will not be silent, and we will not back down."

A Message from Defenders of Wildlife

November 9, 2016

"The election is over. We know the outcome. And now, more than ever we have to pull together to protect the wildlife we all love.

"At Defenders of Wildlife, we will continue to do what we do best. We will double down and honor our mission of conserving wildlife and wild places. Your support – and your engagement – is now more important than ever. It is essential that we work together to be the voice for the animals that cannot speak for themselves.

"Today, we renew our passion and intensity to speak out for nature.

"Wildlife is depending on us – and we will not let them down. Our children and grandchildren are depending on us to ensure a healthy planet for their future – and we will not let them down....

"We can do this. And we will do this together."

A Message from Greenpeace

November 2016

"Fear may have won this election, but hope, action and perseverance can overcome... Together, we are stronger than Donald Trump will ever be."

"Averting climate catastrophe has just become harder, but not impossible. President-elect Donald Trump may be the world's most infamous and powerful climate menace but we will not give up. We will work even harder and invite more and more people to join this powerful movement. The stakes for current and future generations are too high and time is too short.

"We will not allow a Trump administration to distract the world or rob it of the growing momentum towards a clean energy revolution and all of the benefits that brings for the climate, public health, jobs and global security.

"The renewable energy transformation is unstoppable. China, India and others are racing to be the global clean energy superpowers, and the US, as Donald Trump will learn, does not want to be left behind.

"People around the world will intensify their work with the many climate champions in the US: senators, members of Congress, governors, mayors, CEOs, citizens and in the Republican Party. Greenpeace will continue to work with the millions of people around the world who believe a greener, safer, more peaceful and just world is possible."

A Message from MoveOn

December 2016

"We're all going to be needed — to be powerful enough to stop a Trump presidency and GOP-held Congress from tearing our country apart."

A Message from The Nature Conservancy

December 2016

"Protecting nature, for people today and future generations. The mission of The Nature Conservancy is to conserve the lands and waters on which all life depends. Our vision is a world where the diversity of life thrives, and people act to conserve nature for its own sake and its ability to fulfill our needs and enrich our lives."

A Message from NRDC [Natural Resources Defense Council]

December 2016

"We already know what Donald Trump has planned for our environment come January. He has told us.

"He intends to withdraw America from the landmark Paris climate accord … approve the disastrous Keystone XL tar sands pipeline … throw open our public lands and coastal waters to rampant oil development … kill President Obama's Clean Power Plan … scale back support for wind and solar … weaken fuel economy standards for cars and trucks … and unleash big polluters from strong environmental regulations.

"The consequences are truly unthinkable. …

"Never forget: NRDC has a long and storied history of taking on the toughest, uphill battles – and prevailing."

A Message from Planned Parenthood

December 2016

"It's going to be a challenge of epic proportions. And it's going to be up to us – those who consider reproductive rights precious….

"The way ahead is fraught with danger, as powerful forces align to eliminate a woman's right to make her own choices and to reduce access to quality reproductive health care….

"It's painfully ironic that, in Planned Parenthood's 100 Years Strong anniversary year, we are facing opposition that would feel familiar to our founder, Margaret Sanger, who campaigned for the rights of women to have access to contraception and was jailed for her outspoken beliefs!"

A Message from a Veteran (former Marine)

Donald Trump Undermines Everything Veterans Have Fought For

by Dan McCready at Time.com July 26, 2016

"We fought for the safety of our country, but Trump would make us less safe. He has no foreign policy experience. By his actions and his words, he has shown himself to be self-serving and impulsive. A man who says: 'I know more about ISIS than the generals do... believe me,' despite not spending a day in the service of his country, should not have the power to order one American into harm's way, let alone launch a nuclear weapon.

"We fought for democracy, but Trump promotes tyrants. He has praised Vladimir Putin. He suggested our NATO allies might be on their own if Russia attacks them. He minimized Saddam Hussein's throwing 'a little gas' (i.e., chemical weapons) on victims that included women and children.

"We fought for the man or woman serving alongside us regardless of their background, but Trump turns our fellow citizens against each other. He speaks the language of fear. Among 'second and third generation' Muslims in the United States, he falsely said: 'there's no real assimilation.' He has not just derided Muslims, but also immigrants, African Americans, and women. He even denigrated the service of a patriot and former prisoner of war, Senator John McCain."

"It takes a very strong mind to neutralize a prophecy of evil.
The student should declare, 'Every false prophecy
shall come to naught; every plan my Father
in heaven has not planned, shall be dissolved
and dissipated, the divine idea now comes to pass.'
However, if any good message has ever been given one,
of coming happiness, or wealth,
harbor and expect it, and it will manifest sooner or later,
through the law of expectancy.
Man's will should be used to back the universal will.
'I will that the will of God be done.'

It is God's will to give every man every righteous desire
of his heart, and man's will should be used
to hold the perfect vision, without wavering."

Florence Scovel Shinn

PART TWO

INSIDE THE MIND OF A NARCISSIST

"If you hate and resent a situation, you have fastened it to yourself,
for you attract what you fear or dislike....
History will repeat itself until you think you are cursed
with misfortune and injustice. There is only one way
to neutralize it. Be absolutely undisturbed by the injustice,
and send goodwill to all concerned.
Affirm: My goodwill is a strong Tower around me.
I now change all enemies into friends.
All inharmony into harmony.
All injustice into justice."

Florence Scovel Shinn

My Experience with Narcissists

First off, I want to be sure you know I'm not a psychiatrist and I haven't done any special research for this section of the book. You won't find footnotes and a bibliography at the end. Unfortunately, I didn't need to look up information about narcissism because I experienced the shock waves of it firsthand, year after year, while I remain trapped in a series of abusive relationships with narcissistic men. I felt helpless to change what was going on, and embarrassed to have anyone find out. After all, who would willingly stay with an emotionally abusive narcissist?

Most of my life, I lived in total people-pleaser mode as if someone had activated a switch and I was a robot with one setting: placating

111

mode. If someone was angry, I did my best to smooth things over, minimize the potential damage, and head off their imminent eruption.

"Keep the peace" was my daily mantra for far too long, until finally the price of that peace became too high, and I sought a better way to live, a freer way to enjoy my life and bring my gifts to the world.

My experience with narcissists is one of the reasons I am writing this book: to show other people-pleasers and amiable people that it is possible to stand up, to speak up, to fight back and not bow down to anyone's rage out of fear of retaliation.

Following are my observations after many years of interacting at a close level with narcissists. You may recognize someone you know, and you will surely recognize Donald Trump, who is an extreme narcissist.

Please note that I've avoided the awkward use of he/she throughout, but I'm not implying that only men can be narcissists.

What Is a Narcissist?

Like any topic related to the human personality, narcissism can be complex. The person may display different levels of narcissistic behavior under different conditions, and some people may never go to extremes with their narcissism.

I believe the more moderate, controlled level of narcissism occurs when the person's family and friends buckle under and give him all the attention he demands, so he never has to display his full capabilities of cruelty to get his way. He doesn't have to make them understand how serious he is about being the only important person in the room, because they already grant him that privilege.

Deep within, so well-hidden that it might not be obvious, a narcissist has a tremendous lack of self-confidence and self-respect. It is that void which prompts the narcissistic behavior in the first place.

The classic narcissist looks outward for approval, praise and adulation in order to feel better about himself. His insecurities are so deep that he cannot bear to look within, and the concept of self-reflection is abhorrent. He doesn't dare look inside because he knows what he will find: *nothing.*

The emotional immaturity of a narcissist is one of the first things one might notice. At times you may observe these three "ages" or "life stages" in a broad way, as noticed in a spoiled child who has never been given limits or held to even a small level of accountability:

1. The tantrums of a 2-year-old,
2. The cockiness of a 10-year-old,
3. The arrogance of a 16-year-old.

In my experience, the true narcissist never matures beyond the level of a spoiled teenager whose attitude is: *Whatever. I'm in charge and nobody dares take me down.*

We've seen those teens in the news for despicable crimes. How many others indulge in bullying, gang rape, vandalism and more, without being held accountable?

And as they grow up, their unchecked actions get even worse.

They are smirking now, post-election 2016, those other narcissists, the ones who were warned by teachers and parents that they would never get anywhere in life without a change of behavior.

Traits of a Narcissist

It may seem that the narcissist is coming out on top, but there will come a day of reckoning. In my many years of experience with narcissistic men, I recognized the irony that the narcissist believes that he practices the Golden Rule as his motivating principle. He apparently cannot see the disconnect between his actual behavior and the high ideal he has convinced himself he adheres to.

> *"The law of laws is to do unto others*
> *as you would be done by;*
> *for whatever you send out comes back*
> *and what you do to others will be done to you."*

Florence Scovel Shinn

If you feel confused about whether someone you know might be a narcissist, I believe this is the "litmus test": a narcissist looks out for his own interests no matter how many others are hurt, and when called to task will always have a scapegoat handy.

Angry All the Time

The narcissist has a deep inner sense of rage at the world for not giving him the love he desperately needs to fill that void within. He loves to have the upper hand in every relationship and feels satisfaction when others leap nervously at the crack of his whip.

A narcissist can be an ordinary salesman, an unemployed widget maker, the head of a big corporation, or a perpetual student evading the need to get a job. The underlying anger is always present, but can be readily masked with a lot of jolliness and camaraderie that fools people he's such a great guy and so cool to hang out with.

Bullying Braggart

In general, narcissists are the bullies of our society. They are confident the rules don't apply to them, and they don't care who they hurt in their climb to what they consider the top.

Narcissists do not express compassion, empathy, or kindness, unless there is a self-serving reason to fake it.

The bully bullies to cover up his insecurities. He stomps around like an emperor to disguise his secret lack of self-respect.

He frequently acts and sounds like a furious two-year-old who has just been told he must share his toys, or some other limit to the un-reined freedom he feels entitled to.

If you want to be in his circle, you'll have to play by his rules, and his rules alone.

He gets a visible thrill from lambasting people from another culture, ethnicity or background than his own. His family, employees, and people who recognize his behavior for the sickness that it is, learn to observe his mood and stand back as he winds up to trash somebody. Each time he gets away with this behavior, he feels more entitled to step up his game.

Coward

Bullies are cowards, and they surround themselves with other bullies so that they can feel important and powerful. Their hate-based tactics are to dominate and control with threats of injury both physical and emotional.

When we learn to stand up to bullies, we take back our power.

Cruel despot

"A man may smile and smile,
and be a villain."

William Shakespeare

A narcissist is easily recognized by his treatment of those he sees as inferior to him. When it's "safe" to do so, he'll belittle and mock them, or worse.

If he is in a position to hold the purse strings, he will be very stingy with wages as often as possible, but reward his cronies with massive salaries that keep them loyal to him—he needs people in power who are willing to turn a blind eye to his cruelties and his contemptible treatment of others.

He delights in saying things to humiliate people he considers inferior to him. He's careful when choosing a target because it must be someone he's confident will not rear up and fight back.

He can turn this mode of attack versus charm on and off like a light switch.

At first, when you learn about narcissism or think you might be dealing with a narcissist, you think he's just in anger-mode all the time and can't control it. You may even feel sorry for the poor guy that he's got such a bad temper.

But when you step back a bit, and start watching for the pattern, you'll notice he can indeed pick the time and place when he erupts.

If he is ready to blow off steam and you aren't doing anything in particular that he can point to as the reason for a rage, he'll simply grasp the trivial or invent something. And if you don't know you are dealing with a narcissist, you'll go on the defensive and try to figure out why on earth he'd be so upset about your offering him a sandwich for lunch, for example, only to have him rage that you are trying to poison him with leftovers.

Playing the master of the house allows the narcissist to see himself as a wonderful person, and it provides inner proof whenever a little voice within may dare to scold him for being cruel.

Devious

A narcissist is focused on having his needs met no matter what it takes to make that happen. He has to surround himself with glamour, with signs of importance so that others will be fooled about his power. The saying "The end justifies the means" was probably coined by a long-dead narcissist.

For a narcissist, life is all about doing what needs to be done to survive inside the daily hell of the narcissistic mind where self-contempt rules and must be hidden from view.

Easily Bored

The narcissist cannot abide being alone, so he always finds someone who is willing to do anything to try to appease that anger and not inadvertently set off his rage. A power-hungry narcissist is never satisfied, no matter how many doormats he amasses to wipe his feet on.

He hates to be alone because he might have to confront that emptiness inside, so he surrounds himself with noise, people, TV, music (not soothing classical, but anything that has a loud beat to keep his adrenaline jumped up).

He adores being the life of the party, the center of attention, and can usually charm his way into any circle as long as people are willing to let him be the star.

The narcissist seeks out entertainment and conversations and a crowd. He needs all that chatter and activity so that he is never forced to endure solitude, something he inherently dreads and fears.

The narcissist cultivates a circle of friends and admirers who can be relied on to dismiss any sign of temper and overlook any lapse. With this crowd, he can be at ease and dazzle everyone with his cleverness, since he can count on them to look at him with starry eyes and no criticism.

Easily Offended

If you've ever had a conversation with someone who blew up at you over a mild comment you had made, and you found yourself scrambling to try to explain that's not what you said (and believe me, it was probably something innocent and minor), then you've had an encounter with a narcissist.

A narcissist perceives insults and put-downs at every corner. Odd that he deals them out so much to others, and can never seem to notice that what he does to hurt others is the same thing he imagines others are doing to him. That "quirk" is an integral part of the narcissistic character.

Entitled

The classic narcissist is puffed up with his own self-importance and deep sense of entitlement. His ego is over-inflated in order to hide the terrified little boy inside who has never been able to feel or give love, and is seeking something, anything, that will make him feel better about himself. Feeling superior to others helps him feel better for a little while.

A narcissist feels fully entitled to get what he wants when he wants it, if not sooner.

He feels entitled to take what he wants, without any protest from others. Students of history may think at once about feudal lords and the behavior they insisted was theirs by right. Sexual harassment is the arena of the narcissist, who feels he can do no wrong.

He feels entitled to keep others waiting. Feels entitled to take off his shoe and slam it on the conference table to make his point.

Every narcissist, no matter how poor or rich, successful or not in his own neck of the woods, finds a platform where it is safe enough for him to rant without boundaries. It may be behind closed doors with his family. It might be in the back room of a business he owns or manages.

Hair-Trigger Temper

The overweening need for supremacy over others means a narcissist lashes out with fury at any obstruction (perceived or real). He covers up his own deep-seated insecurities by quickly shifting the focus away from himself and out at others, such as with a wild accusation that will make the other person feel off-balance and defensive, and take the heat off the narcissist.

He's easily goaded into blowing up.

He erupts in a rage when he perceives an insult. He frequently acts and sounds like a furious two-year-old who has just been told it is time to take a nap, or some other limit to the un-reined freedom he feels entitled to. He hates to share the sandbox.

He cannot tolerate being made to look foolish. He has no motivation to change his habit of blowing up for no reason at all, because in that moment of rage, he feels an inner sense of release. It is the closest he gets to what the rest of us call inner peace or serenity. For a little while, all the tension that has been building tighter and tighter suddenly uncoils in a huge wave of relief.

And then the coiling up process begins again, until he finds any excuse at all to blow up yet again. And so, the cycle continues, uninterrupted.

Hates Looking Foolish

He cannot tolerate anyone mocking or teasing if the subject is a sensitive one. To him, that is disrespectful, and he'll likely blow up in your face and make sure you feel his displeasure at your ill-advised treatment of him.

If you get too close to a deeply sensitive area with your teasing jokes, he'll slash back and cut you to ribbons, far out of proportion to the joke you made, such as a comment about his latest outfit or something that he perceives as a moral judgment against him.

He hates to be laughed at or made to look foolish. He has an internal "offense gauge" that is set to super-sensitive so that he'll go from mellow to yell-out in a split second if he suspects someone is being disrespectful.

In fact, although he is extremely sarcastic and cruel to others, if the tables are turned, he reacts as if deeply wounded by the mildest of teasing.

It's Personal

For the narcissist, everything is personal. The daily ups and downs of life that the rest of us take in our stride are seen as personal affronts by a narcissist: *How dare that driver cut me off! How dare this road have a pothole! How dare that server keep me waiting!*

The overall attitude is as if they are constantly thinking, "Don't they realize who I am?"

A narcissist once assured me that he could go as fast as he wanted on the freeway because any cop who saw the expensive car he was driving would realize he must be someone important, and wouldn't stop him. He wasn't kidding. We were on the freeway at the time, going 90 mph in broad daylight.

The narcissist is frequently exhausting to be around because it's all about him, all the time, and he truly hates to share the spotlight.

His odious behavior is sometimes startling because it is so outrageous it seems impossible anyone could seriously walk around acting like that … and get away with it.

Jealous

He's quick to react to perceived slights or to the hint that someone is encroaching on his territory, hence is swift leap to jealousy in the most innocent of situations. Randomly accuses spouse or girlfriend of cheating on him despite any lack of evidence. This serves two purposes: keep her off-balance and nervous about him, demonstrates his power to keep her under his thumb as she pleads with him to stop even thinking she would ever cheat on him.

Wildly jealous of other men's attentions even though paradoxically very proud and possessive of her input ice because an attractive mate makes others envy him., he sees wife and children as possessions in the same class as his car, home, and other material goods, he sees any sign of discontent as betrayal and will punish the offender.

Jekyll-Hyde Personality

His impulse control is minimal. When provoked, that Mr. Nice Guy demeanor (Dr. Jekyll) twists into the snarling Mr. Hyde whose verbal abuse is legendary.

Usually, presenting an amiable face to the public is important to the narcissist so he can be treated like a great guy and admired for how jovial and easygoing he is. Ironic, when often that same man is a like a demon to those closest to him. In fact, there's an old term to describe the narcissist: *Street angel, home devil.*

At a glance, victims of a narcissist's behavior may think they triggered what he did and said, and they walk on eggshells trying not to "set him off," however, he doesn't need anything special to indulge his appetite for raging.

If you don't cooperate by providing him with a topic, he'll invent one. And after he's raged, he feels a sense of peace inside.

Rarely will a narcissist apologize for his nasty behavior. Instead, he simply acts like nothing happened. For him, it is business as usual, and woe betide the hapless family member or witness who speaks up and tries to bring up his rant for discussion and behavioral modification.

If he's got his family well-trained not to leave him, the narcissist can indulge his temper at any time he pleases behind closed doors, and feel safe that his secret remains hidden from friends and colleagues who might not think so highly of him if they found out.

He is frantic for adulation, and may be seen charming strangers with jokes and anecdotes so he can fool himself that he is well-loved by all who meet him. This tactic is called "earning narcissistic supply" because he has to keep that supply of compliments ready at hand to not feel so unlovable and unloved.

He'll often be extremely generous with showy gifts, and basks in the praise others give him for being such a caring husband or boss.

He may be the gentleman bully who only reveals the steel beneath the velvet glove when alone with his family, or at the other end of the spectrum, someone who is so deep into narcissism that he doesn't care what others think and will rage freely in public, feeling fully entitled to be as cruel and heartless as he pleases.

The narcissist can be affable and expansive—even jovial—when he's feeling sated with power, as if he has an internal fuel gauge which alerts him when he's got enough in reserve to put down his whip and play at being the benevolent master for a while... until the glow of his narcissistic supply begins dwindling, and the cycle continues.

Lack of Empathy

If you want to be in his circle, you'll have to play by his rules, and his rules alone. Get used to having your needs ignored. The narcissist has a complete inability to see life from the perspective of anyone else. It is always all about him, all the time.

A narcissist sees the pain that others are experiencing, and is indifferent to it.

Unlike a true goal achiever – someone who has a big dream for success and finds ways of being of service to others – the narcissist wants to be king of the mountain without having to go through the steps others take. They want to reach the top to be admired. A narcissist doesn't care how many people he steps on to get ahead. The narcissist schemes to make money no matter what it does to the people are making his income possible.

Liar

The narcissist feels no compunction to tell the truth or to honor agreements unless it is convenient to do so and/or is for his benefit. He always looks out for his own interests first and foremost.

A narcissist can look you right in the eye without blinking and tell a bold-faced lie.

He's glib. No hesitation, no shifting eyes, no glancing away. In that moment, he believes what he is saying. He cannot see the contradictions between truth and his own words.

From his viewpoint, he wasn't telling a lie, he was simply telling his version of what life ought to be. And if that takes recasting the entire scenario to fit his illusion, so be it. He'll never admit to being a liar, even if his pants catch fire from the habit.

It's deeply engrained in his mindset that he doesn't have to follow convention, so lies don't even count.

The narcissist believes his own lies. He has to, or else he would implode with self-disgust.

No Sense of Inner Value

The narcissist must feel very lonely inside. He clearly has no sense of self-worth, of spirituality and contentment. If he did, he could never treat others with the contempt that he does.

His view is generally materialistic in nature.

He takes pride in being a good parent or employer when it comes to bestowing material gifts or things that others will admire and envy. No matter what his income level might be, a narcissist's measuring stick for love is frequently based on materialism.

He feels loved if people took time to select a gift that cost more than they could afford. He feels he is a loving parent or spouse when he can say: *"I paid for their food and clothing and housing, I paid for their schooling, I paid for ..."*

Outspoken

The narcissist has no filter on his mouth. No control over what comes out. If something pops into his mind, he says it.

He must always have the upper hand and talks over others who are saying something he doesn't want to hear. He'll often make "speed it up" gestures when others talk. Along with this comes the habit of interrupting other speakers because he doesn't it like it that the attention is on them, and a total disregard for manners.

If confronted by an egregious error or lapse in judgment, he'll put a spin on it and claim he was joking and the fault lies with others for not being able to tell when he was "just kidding."

He can talk for hours about nothing, and he loves to cut people off to further his own agenda, to call the other person names, and to ruin the punchline of a joke and get the spotlight back onto himself, where, in his opinion, it belongs all the time.

Paradoxical Beliefs

The narcissist can hold seemingly incompatible ideas at the same time. This results in the many inconsistencies seen in his behavior.

He can label someone else as a danger and threat, turn around and behave in a way that matches those definitions, and yet label his own behavior as benevolent and necessary.

This type of thinking is like the despot who demands that the citizens must tighten their belts and sacrifice for the good of their country, while he feasts in his private banquet hall.

Racist

No matter what the color of his skin is, the narcissist has an inner belief that he is superior to anyone who is of a different race. His contempt for the race as a whole may be expressed in snide comments to a stranger, a loudly told racist joke in a public place while surrounded by his safety net of people he can count on to laugh or at least not call him to task, or a muttered insult at the television when someone of the despised race appears.

Paradoxically, that same person may have an employee, house cleaner, mechanic, or handyman who is of that despised race but provides a necessary service—to that individual, he'll be full of praise about their work when others are around to witness his joviality. He may give large tips or spontaneous gifts, and then bask in their genuine affection for him as the benevolent lord of the manor, whether it is a yuppie mansion or a tract home.

Self-Absorbed

Narcissism goes far beyond vanity, beyond an inferiority complex, beyond temper tantrums and into the realm of mindboggling self-absorption.

The narcissist has no empathy—no ability within that cold heart to look at others with compassion and reach out to offer assistance.

Any offer of help will always be self-serving.

The narcissist looks at life from the perspective of personal gain. He is ruthless in getting his way all the time, even over trivial matters ("Who took the garage clicker!") that you would think wouldn't be important to get in such a rage about.

His view of life is "Gimmee, gimmee, gimmee"—although he feels undeserving deep inside, on the outside he grabs as much as he can as if that proves he must be special.

He is always looking for an angle to come out on top of everyone else.

Every situation and relationship is about control. It must be an "I win/you lose" outcome. It's never about win/win or working together for a common good.

His ego is so distorted that he cannot see any advantage to being the sort of person about whom a kindergarten teacher would say "plays well with others."

He makes it clear when he's unhappy with your choice of a TV show, movie, restaurant, and any other activity – – it becomes easier to not have to go through all that rigmarole just to go out and have what you thought would be a pleasant evening. So you cave in time and again until it is so automatic that you do it without conscious thought, and in fact circumvent the whole issue by only suggesting activities he has already marked with his seal of approval. You cater to the narcissist and he wins on a regular basis. This inadvertently feeds his sick behavior so that it grows stronger and deeper roots.

Think twice before asking him to compromise, because to a narcissist that is the greatest insult. "My way or the highway" is the attitude most often demonstrated, unless he's already dismissed the importance to him of the issue you want to compromise on. If so, he'll "let" you win as if tossing you a crumb and pretending he doesn't care or doesn't have time to deal with your whining.

Be wary, however, because the value of that crumb will suddenly go up when he wants you to compromise—he'll expect you to give him 100 times the value of that concession he grudgingly agreed to earlier.

Skewed Perception of Himself

The narcissist is proud of his excesses. He often has a keen interest in being well-groomed at all times and well-dressed so that no one can find fault with his appearance.

If he is of modest means, the narcissist will not care what the rest of the family must sacrifice for his clothing budget to be indulged. And yet, he will turn on them in a fury if he feels the way they are dressed is an embarrassment to him. He sees himself in a distorted mirror that tells him he is the greatest in the land and no one can compare.

He creates messes and leaves them for others to clean up.

As a child, that might have been the task of an overworked or exasperated parent who kept hoping things would change. As an adult, the messes have grown much larger and more threatening to the welfare of others, but he still looks to others to clean up the mess and keep him out of trouble.

Toxic Behavior

When you witness a narcissist in action, you may stare, your mouth agape, wondering how he gets away with what he does.

His attitude is: I can do and say whatever I want (everyone else be damned), rinse, repeat.

When you are involved with a narcissist, the fog of denial seeps over you on a regular basis because he's so good at stonewalling you and simply pretending that he never said what you know he said, and that he never did what you know he did.

Unmasked

A narcissist craves adulation. He lives with the secret terror that someone will discover he is a total fake. The narcissist is driven from within to pass himself off as a success and prevent the annihilation of being unmasked. That is why the outward trappings become so important—the narcissist may pay a lot of attention to his appearance, clothes, hair, jewelry and status symbols, even if he can only afford the knock-offs.

Although narcissism is not just a case of being a little conceited, the vanity that is under the surface drives a lot of resentment toward others he fears may be or have more than he does.

The narcissist has been a stock character in plays and films time out of mind. He's easy to spot—look for the one strutting like a peacock in full display. And watch for the one who is charming until thwarted, at which time his wrath explodes on the hapless folks in his orbit. In a romantic comedy, he'll be the guy we hope our sweet heroine will jilt at the altar because she has come to her senses and realizes what a jerk he really is.

Trump's Extreme Narcissism

Trump's television celebrity made it "safe" for him to explode at will, and get admired for how nasty he could be as he crushed people under his heel.

It's never a good idea when dealing with the narcissistic personality disorder to let the person go on a rampage. It may appease him momentarily as he gets the inrush of feeling powerful, but soon the emptiness returns and he craves more and more attention, more and more power.

The country, indeed the world, needs to get better informed about what it's like to have a narcissist in charge.

A narcissist is determined to get what he wants when he wants it, and you'd better not thwart him.

The narcissist is 100% positive that the rules do not apply to him, because he's special. Rules are made for lesser people, not for his highness. Any parent who has raised a toddler will notice the similarity between a toddler's tantrums and those of a narcissist; however, of course, the narcissist in a position of power can do far more damage than a two-year-old kicking his heels in the air and screaming to relieve his frustration when things don't go his way.

Like an overgrown toddler, furious with contempt and outrage for anyone who stands in his way, the adult narcissist spends a lot of energy on punishing those he sees as enemies. The child yells out "I hate you!" to his parents. The adult narcissist takes stronger measures than just a few words of contempt. He is superior to everyone, and demands the adulation that goes with that superiority.

Our popular culture praises, applauds, aids and abets the narcissists in many ways with our lopsided love of celebrities.

But with a narcissist, that moment will not be something to examine and grow from –instead, it would be seen as the slug under the rock, something ugly and unwanted to stomp on and push away because the feeling of unworthiness is not congruent with his inflated ego.

Everything going on around him is a perceived threat to the narcissist. He walks through life on alert, ready to pounce on an idle comment that someone makes which he feels was an insult. Seeing a homeless man will evoke terror that it might happen to him, so he has to do what he can to push away those uncomfortable feelings inside, such as yelling out to the man, "Get a job!"

An extreme narcissist wreaks havoc in the lives of everyone around him and yet seemingly feels little or no remorse. His sense of entitlement (pumped up by the groveling praise from minions) assures him that the rules don't pertain to him.

In his mind he's far above the ordinary man who must bow and kowtow to the demands of society and family. He sees empathy as weakness.

The out-of-control extreme narcissist is the one who has left those closed doors behind and feels entitled to act how he pleases, wherever he wants. He rages in public, at the drop of a hat.

He is confident he can get away with this outrageous behavior because he's been applauded for his abusive comments. He knows he can do as he pleases and say whatever pops in to his head without losing the support of loyalists who overlook his excesses of anger and overweening pride.

Trump: A man who brags that he doesn't pay income tax because he "doesn't have to" and yet complains bitterly that he is inconvenienced by taxpayer-funded roads that need repair.

Trump: His team members decried his snide comments about groping women—and yet stood by him anyway. We used to call that being a "hypocrite" but apparently now it's just considered by the Republican party to be "business as usual."

Trump in response to a comment about his total inexperience with foreign policies and as an international diplomat: "I've been places!"

This seemingly paradoxical phenomenon is actually part of the web that a narcissist casts, where people join up in alliance with him for their own gain and simply turn a blind eye to his faults and lack of experience as if he's got a bad tic that he shouldn't be blamed for.

Trump and his team capitalized on his reality TV fame and managed to pull off enough entertainment for enough people to be fooled that "celebrity" must equate "ability."

He is the least qualified candidate ever put before the American voters, and yet…he was given the presidency. Historians will interpret this to the best of their ability—and I wish them luck in identifying the lack of awareness in a voting public that couldn't see the difference between electing a progressive thinker with many years of experience in diplomacy and Constitutional law, and someone who rants and raves when his least whim is thwarted.

It's important to understand just who your foe is and what principles they represent. We label people "paranoid" if they walk around flinching at shadows, because we can see their thinking has become dis-eased and they see threats everywhere, even when the enemy is truly the mind within.

An extreme narcissist sees only his own needs and glory.

Trump has made it abundantly clear that the frightened little boy inside would delight in forcing the world to its knees and then crown himself emperor.

If you ask a narcissist to do something that he doesn't want to do— because he's afraid it will weaken his position or diminish the esteem people hold him in— he simply digs in his heels and finds one excuse after another no matter how implausible.

The key to working with a narcissist is to find ways to show him how this new plan you are suggesting will actually benefit him in some way. He has to see that he will be admired if he agrees to it.

When dealing with a tyrant you have to be aware of his ego-driven motives, and work with those needs instead of trying to push against him, or make him see reason.

Attempts to show a narcissist why his thinking is "wrong" will simply result in his taking an even firmer stance and gathering in the forces he needs to support his position.

PART THREE

ALPHABET SOUP TO STRENGTHEN & INSPIRE

"The divine design of my life now comes to pass.
I now fill the place that I can fill and no one else can fill.
I now do the things which I can do and no one else can do.
I am fully equipped for the Divine Plan of my life;
I am more than equal to the situation.
All doors now open for happy surprises and
the Divine Plan of my life is speeded up under grace."

Florence Scovel Shinn

At this time, in the wake of Mr. Trump's election, the majority of voters in our nation are feeling sick with fear and dread. I suspect many thousands of people who voted for Trump are now beginning to understand what the fuss was all about—earlier, when voting, they lacked awareness of his agenda and simply went along with the Republican ticket as usual.

Regarding our physical health, it's common to eat soup when we are ailing and fear we'll never get better. In many cultures it's even a tradition to prepare and offer a special bowl of hot, nourishing soup.

Soup is comfort food. It warms and delights us, and reminds us of childhood when we trusted that our parents would take care of us or that someone would magically make us feel better.

Even as adults, when we are the ones opening a can for ourselves or buying a cup of deli soup, we access genetic memories of countless times throughout history that a bowl of soup provided nourishment, sustenance, and a powerful reminder that we are, indeed, still alive and capable of making choices about our health and our direction in life. And furthermore, that we <u>will</u> get well, and thrive once more.

For your consideration, in this section of *America's New Breed of Freedom Fighters*, I respectfully offer an "Alphabet Soup" of inspirational, motivational and spiritual advice and techniques to support our mutual desire for progressive change in the world.

The soup contains 26 topics for your discovery and, hopefully, edification on ways to create the results you desire in your own life, in our nation, and in the world as a whole.

Let us also commit now to a connectivity in which we nourish each other, and share our vision of progress, liberty and justice for all, in every thought, word, and deed. Connect with me at Facebook.com/evelynbrooksauthor

Within each topic, you will find quotations from two of Florence Scovel Shinn's books on using the power of the mind: *The Game of Life and How to Win It,* and *Your Word Is Your Wand.* Ms. Shinn (1874-1940) was a New Thought spiritual teacher and also a writer whose books remain popular today for their accessibility in understanding the laws of the mind and how to use them.

She is one of my favorite inspirational authors. I have read all of her books many times over the passing years, and I dip into her books on a regular basis for insight and upliftment. I think you will find her way of explaining matters very easy to follow and apply to your own life.

Gift: Both of these books by Ms. Shinn can be read or downloaded in PDF format at your reader's page: evelynbrooks.com/readers-freedom-fighters There are other gifts for you there as well.

Enjoy your soup!

1

ALIGN WITH GOODNESS

In every waking moment of every day, we are choosing (whether consciously or unconsciously) to align with either good or the lack of good.

It may feel impossible to do, but we must celebrate life and be thankful in advance for the results we want in issues of importance to progressives and liberals.

Emotions like fear, terror, anger, worry and anxiety actually empower any agenda that is on that same low-level frequency.

The laws of the universe cannot bring to us good (high frequency) results when we are thinking unhappy (low frequency) thoughts—that would be in violation of nature and the way things work.

It would be comparable to someone being able to coax the law of gravity into giving them a much-needed break by making a heavy package lighter to carry.

In order to change the results we dislike in our lives, we must systematically up-level our thoughts. We need to go high, as high in our vibration as we can every day from now on.

You can gauge how you are doing with the alignment process by noticing how you feel. If you feel happy, you're doing great! And in contrast, of course, if you're discouraged, upset or anxious, that is a signal from your inner self that you are aligning with the type of results that reside on a lower frequency in the universe, and if you don't make a shift in your mood, those things are going to materialize in your life.

It's as if we need to be tuning forks, and get really good at always running on "High C" so that everything way up on that frequency of love will come dancing happily into our experience with ease and grace.

By coming together now as Freedom Fighters, we can encourage, support and lift each other in as we bring about this manifesto of progressive peace.

****

2

BECOME CONGRUENT IN ALL YOUR AFFAIRS

Have you ever made a New Year's Resolution?

What happened? Did you keep it? Did you go to the gym every day like you swore you would? Did you start picking up after yourself and keep your desk more orderly? Hmmm, what else did you promise?

The reason we "break" our resolutions is not that we are bad people, or lazy or stupid.

The entire reason is lack of congruency.

The person who goes to the gym every day—what is that person like? What do they do besides workout at a gym? Do they also eat more healthily than you do, drink more water, perhaps take supplements and watch their intake of sweets?

While it is important to keep our big goals closely guarded from criticism or skeptical comments from others, there is also a time for stating clearly what we are doing with our lives.

It's like creating a mission statement for your own life, as if these years you are here are for a specific purpose. This purpose can be broad, with a single goal, or a whole array of things you want to accomplish.

You might end up with a general statement and then bullet points or what I like to call "butterfly points" beneath it, because bullets kill but butterflies make us smile.

Example: I intend to bring more joy in to the world, and I do this by being a good friend, loving parent, romantic spouse and person of integrity in the work I offer in exchange for money or other goods.

Find ways to be congruent with the kind of person you want to be, and when you practice those traits in advance, you begin to inhabit that personality, and sooner than you might think possible, you will actually be living that person's life. That person you described will be you.

***

3

CULTIVATE YOUR PASSIONS

Think about what makes you feel excited in life. What makes you come alive?

What activities and relationships bring you great joy?

Then realize that everything in your life right now, every one of the smallest relationships to the most important ones, present opportunities for expansion.

If you're in a hurry, does it seem excusable to cut someone off in traffic, to ignore the cashier who told you to have a nice day, to shrug off a compliment? We all do these things, but when we remain unaware of our behavior, it's as if we wander through life in someone else's screenplay.

We get into what I call a "zombie rut" of simply going through the motions, doing our job, taking care of errands, getting together with friends, moaning about relationships, complaining about the boss or the neighbors or the spouse and sympathizing with our friends' complaints about their lives.

What if you started today to shift that energy over into creating more of what you do want instead of additional things to complain about?

The choice is yours.

It requires a different sort of discipline than most of us learned in school. Growing up, discipline was often equated with punishment in most families and classrooms.

But true discipline means learning to control the pattern of your thoughts so that you spend more time thinking about being of service in your life and the lives of others, and less time allowing yourself to react mindlessly to what is on the news, what angry people are yelling about, and what latest disaster is being predicted.

When you discover and cultivate your passion, you'll be in harmony with the creative force of the universe, and everything will begin to shift. Opportunities will arise, doors will open, and you'll feel happier and more contented. It's a great way to live.

***

4

DECIDE TO LIVE WELL

Someone said, "Living well is the best revenge."

What is it that you would really love to experience in life? Are there dreams you put on the back burner so long ago that the fire went out, the pot is cold and gathering dust?

Do you have a friend or family member you often provide a listening ear for? Or perhaps you are the one in your circle that others go to for advice on relationships because you are demonstrating happiness in your own marriage.

Spread that circle outward.

It's easy to tell ourselves "tomorrow" I'll do better at this, and then the next day we act in the same way and shy away from taking the big leaps into the unknown territory where our dreams are fulfilled.

We always have a choice, often it feels as if we are a victim of our own thoughts and feelings. And each instant we can ask ourselves: *Am I aggravating the problem, or am I helping to resolve it?*

We always have the option to take a different path.

Instead of responding in kind to Trump's hate-filled messages of building walls and dissolving hard won rights, and overturning environmental support, let us use our immense energy to neutralize his power, and create more good instead.

When we live well, we wake up feeling refreshed and rejuvenated, ready for the new day to begin. During the day, we bring our gifts into our waking hours as we work, go to school, care for children and the elderly. Everywhere we go, we can offer kindness to others, we can live from a central core of love and compassion, we can take steps toward our personal goals and dreams.

If you feel that your life is in a frenzy and out of control, take time to reflect on what you hope to accomplish by all that rushing around. It's easy to get caught up in the whirlwind that society seems to be saying you should want. It takes more thought effort to examine the options and make a decision for yourself of what lifestyle brings you the most joy and satisfaction.

> *"It is not enough to be busy.*
> *So are the ants.*
> *The question is:*
> *What are we busy about?"*

Henry David Thoreau

Living well means that you feel you are growing and expanding in joy and creativity. It's not about a bank balance, it's about the balance you feel in your calm heart.

***

145

5

EXPRESS ONLY YOUR HIGHEST THOUGHTS

We all have strengths, even ones that we dismiss as not very important because we learned at an early age not to boast. Now is the time to dust off your gratitude for the very strengths that make it possible for you to create a better life for yourself and others

What might these strengths be? Often, if we're asked to name what we are good at, we tend to mumble something about being good at baking or a certain sport, or good at using new software or tech gadgets. But our strengths go far beyond the classification of "life skills."

Take time to finetune your natural ability to create and manifest results you want—and minimize the unwanted experiences.

If you're finding this a challenge, ask yourself this question: *What's going on inside?*

The answers will arise from your inner self. Anxiety means that you are fearful about something. Fear is always about the future—it's peering ahead in your imagination and being scared what will happen next. Fear is a signal that you are projecting your thoughts ahead of you, and anticipating unwanted results in any and all areas of your life.

Humanity's history of fear-based thinking is evidenced in thousands of limiting proverbs and axioms such as "It's better to be safe than sorry"—what about "It's better to give it my all and make the results I want happen!"

When we allow our minds to remain untrained and wild with thoughts of fear, anxiety and dread, we become inadvertent collaborators with Trump's agenda.

Even though we tend to complain that the law of attraction doesn't "work" because when we do our success or health affirmations, nothing much changes—that's not the fault of the law.

The fault lies in our thinking habits.

Think about ways you can express only the highest level of thoughts throughout the day. That means developing a new habit where you pay attention to how you are feeling and thus what you were just thinking about.

When we turn our attention to examine the results we have in life, such as frequent colds, money problems, relationship issues and so on, and we see how those results relate to the law of attraction, we can more readily see that we do indeed create our experience.

That time lag between asking and getting is a good thing because otherwise the moment you thought of something, it would manifest. At first that seems like it would be wonderful—think about wealth and your bank account magically grows, think about health and you are totally rejuvenated on the spot. But the reverse is true as well— worry you'll get in a car accident and BAM! one collision, as requested.

So, when we intend to create positive change, such as affecting the outcome of progressive issues, we need to be aware of that underlying stream of thought power.

The reason we end up with so many unwanted things is that 1) we are thinking about what we don't want, 2) we expect bad things to happen, and 3) we don't doubt bad things will happen.

If the answer is to think about what we do want and wait for it, then why do we still experience the frustration of not getting our desired results?

The answer lies in the word "highest belief" – if your highest level of belief in the recesses of your mind is along the lines of "I sure wish for this, but I probably won't get it" then that doubt is causing the delay.

To up-level your highest thoughts, notice when you are affirming what you want but at the same time you secretly don't believe you can get it or deserve it.

Keep affirming your desires again and again, not just once or twice a day. Retrain your thoughts with the repetition of positive statements.

We often give up when we don't see immediate results. It's important to learn to recognize the clues that your manifestation is on the way. If you are magnetizing financial success into your life, for example, and you find a quarter on the sidewalk: that's a clue. If you get an unexpected monetary gift or refund check, that's a clue. If you get a bonus at work, or a gift card from a friend—those are clues. The problem is that we think the clues are the final answer.

If you spot the clues and dismiss them with scorn for not being what you wanted, then the doubt and discouragement yank down your high vibration just before the manifestation would have materialized. That back and forth frustration can feel upsetting, because it seems you're not getting anywhere.

From now on, watch for the clues, keep your vibration high and fine and strong and steady.

Imagine your manifestation is inside a box kite high up in the sky and you hold the string and the reel. You wouldn't cut the string, would you? You wouldn't drop the reel just because the kite has gone behind a cloud. Keep that string of belief nice and strong, expect your good to come to you, and reel that kite right into your life.

***

6

FOCUS ON WHAT YOU WANT TO HAPPEN

S pirit cannot overcome inertia. We have to take action, and for most of us, we need some kind of "fuel" to get up and get going. That fuel is our motivation or inspiration, and there are countless places to find that. You may feel motivated by the desire to provide a better life for your family. You may feel inspired by the achievements you have seen others create, and want that for yourself.

What perspective can you work on in your own life? Do you have ongoing problems at work or in your family?

Step aside and be the observer in your life for a while.

Take a look not only at what others are saying and doing, but see if you can figure out what they must be thinking and feeling in order to provoke that kind of behavior.

Are they feeling threatened, and lashing out because they are scared their life is getting out of control? Are they worried over money and fear is pushing them to snipe at your success or undermine your work to bring you down to their level?

All of us behave the way we do because we have a very complex mindset made up of thousands of beliefs, experiences, judgments and assessments of our life up until now and our anticipation of the years to come.

After you spend some time looking on what others focus on and what they are trying to get out of life, turn that same curiosity toward yourself and see where your behavior reflects ideas and memories that aren't helpful at all, and in fact may be sabotaging your best efforts and producing results you are unhappy with.

When we come from a motive of loving interest in our growth and the growth of others, we can step up to a higher level of awareness, and see so many beautiful opportunities to make this world an even happier and better place for all to live in.

***

7

GO BOLDLY WHERE YOU HAVE NOT GONE BEFORE

Where haven't you gone yet? Do you have a wish list or bucket list? And if you don't, why not? Even if the list isn't written in a journal, I bet you could sit down and write at least ten places you want to visit or events you want to attend or restaurants where you want to dine. Now start adding material things such as that new TV you've had your eye, a new car, new furniture, and the list quickly expands.

But what about the non-tangible places you haven't been to yet, or that you have visited briefly and would like to enjoy again? I'm talking about peace of mind, serenity, and a sense that "all is well" in your world.

Unless we deliberately seek out ways to invite calmness into our daily lives, it is pushed away by our frantic busy-ness, as if there's a magical day on the horizon where we'll finally have time to relax and enjoy the sunset.

Take time now to delve into that kingdom of joy where you have not gone before, and start exploring ways to seek out those new ideas, those new friendships, those new dreams to build for you, your family, and to improve the world.

If you're feeling nervous about being an adventurer, a quick way to calm your emotions is to relax your shoulders, breathe slowly in through your nose to the easy silent count of 1-2-3, pause briefly, and then exhale slowly to the silent count of 3-2-1.

Repeat this "mindful breathing" exercise several times until you feel the tension leave your muscles and your body is more at ease. We hold a lot of tension in our neck and shoulders, so do a few shoulder shrugs and head rolls to ease that area of your body. Use the mindful breathing like a relaxation mini-break throughout the day, or any time you are feeling stressed or upset.

When we are tense with worry or fear, we actually invite dis-ease and bad experiences to come into our lives.

It's vital to learn how to calm yourself, and stop reacting to everything others are doing that are not in alignment with the greater good.

**

8

HONOR YOUR CORE VALUES

What is your truth? What do you really believe in? I'm talking about the things that YOU believe. Most of us don't know what we believe. We grew up parroting what parents and grandparents and teachers told us we should believe, and we practiced saying it long enough that we fell in step with them and nodded: *Yes, I believe all that, too.*

Everyone has core values. These values are at the heart of our lives and the choices we make.

Core values are those solid beliefs that help us make sense of our place in the world. Not all of these values are good or helpful. Many are, in fact, damaging to the individual and deadly to the rest of the world.

When someone's core value is to put himself first at the expense of the rights and needs of others, he reveals himself as an egomaniac, a danger and a threat to freedom and justice. A narcissist lives by the core value that his needs come first and everyone else is on earth to serve him and make sure he gets what he wants.

If your core value is to grow and prosper and help others do the same, then make sure that everything you do in life honors those values. People will say things like, well I hate dishonesty but my job requires me to lie to customers about the freshness of the goods or where they were made. That person needs to change jobs or the steady drip-drip-drip of being out of alignment with their stated core values on a daily basis is going to create real problems for them.

We have to be more vigilant about being in harmony with what we say we believe in

***

9

IMAGINE EVERYTHING
WORKS OUT GREAT

Y ou may have watched "The Secret" film and then decided to try to use the law of attraction to improve your results.

Many people gave up quickly, saying it didn't work, as if the law of attraction is some option we can choose to use or discard.

Actually, it's always with us, every moment of the day, and it is always in action. Our thoughts direct the law of attraction to bring to us, or attract in, those things, people and events that are in vibrational harmony with our thoughts.

Have you ever noticed that if your day started off poorly (and you didn't do anything to change its direction), that more often than not, the whole day goes from bad to worse?

That's the law of attraction working in your life. It is a neutral force, simply responding to our thought requests.

Our challenge is that we've gotten the idea that what we "Say" or "Affirm" is what we are ordering the law of attraction to bring us. That does work, but only if what we are saying and affirming matches what we believe we can receive and what we expect to get.

That's where things start falling apart, as if you walked up to a take-out counter and could order whatever you wanted, but the clerk heard a garbled version and you're annoyed when they give you something totally different from what you were sure you ordered.

Without awareness of the crucial part our thoughts play in this creation process, we end up feeling discouraged, in debt, out of luck, out of love, and quite often more than a little miserable.

We end up with results we don't like or want, not because we are being punished but because we didn't follow the rules of the mind game.

If you clearly imagine what you want, it's not enough to be able to picture it and be excited about having it or really wishing for it night and day. You have to be in a state of mind where you <u>believe</u> the result or experience is already yours. That inner belief is the key.

***

10

JUST KEEP GOING

Many battles have been won in our history by the victor simply wearing out the other side's resistance. They cut off supplies, food, water, heat and power and make life so miserable that the ones under siege finally surrender in defeat, not knowing what else to do.

Just as there are desk calendars and digital apps that give you a new dictionary word each day to stimulate your understanding and encourage expansion into a broader vocabulary, we can do the same thing with our thoughts. Let's find ways to expand and to question the status quo.

First, choose who and what you want to collaborate with. It's our inadvertent collusions that get us in trouble in life, because without understanding the universal laws, we allow ourselves to be drawn into the mental force field of negativity, and thus create unwanted outcomes.

The kind of collaborating we're looking for here is in support of issues and rights that are dear to the heart of progressive thinkers. You may wish to take another look at the Issues section in Part One to get ideas and inspiration on where to start.

Perhaps you enjoy working with children and teens—looks for ways to collaborate on the issues related to education. Perhaps coach a team on weekends and after school. Teach an arts and crafts class in an after-school program. Get involved in your local PTA and let your voice be heard.

The worst thing we can do is come to a halt, like a stalled car on the freeway. It's a waste of our opportunities; it's a waste of the gift of life. If you are feeling stuck, start with one small action every morning that makes you feel good.

By creating happier feelings inside, we attract more happiness for ourselves and others. Soon, ideas will pop into your mind for something that you'd enjoy doing, and it will seem magical how everything comes together quickly in support of your new dream.

***

11

KEEP YOUR SPIRITS UP

When we get on the anger wavelength and stay there, more things to be angry and fearful about come into our experience, magnetized by the fear.

It is vital for your own health and wellbeing, and the wellbeing of our nation, to make a conscious decision to focus on uplifting thoughts and images.

When you feel your emotions flagging, that's a sign that you need a boost up! Find ways to enliven and re-energize yourself. Put on happy music (I love Pharrell Williams' song "Happy" for this very purpose) and dance around. Who cares if you know how to dance? Somebody made up those steps, so why not make up your own, too, and enjoy yourself?

Look for ways to bring nature into your life on a daily basis, whether it is putting a houseplant on your office desk or by the kitchen sink, adding floral print pictures or throw pillows to your décor, looking at spectacular images of landscapes and naturescapes around the world, or enjoying the antics of your family pet.

Being in nature always has the potential to calm and uplift us. Take advantage of a half-hour evening stroll or morning walk to get yourself centered spiritually. We get so busy with our crammed schedules of appointments and errands and To Do lists that we shortchange the very joy that life on this planet offers us—and that we came here on purpose to experience.

Oh, did you think you arrived here randomly to be part of the transformation to a higher level of human awareness? That's not how it works. We are all eternal beings and we came to Earth at this time on purpose.

Your higher self knows all about your decision to be here right now—and you came with the full knowledge that it would be challenging to stay positive in the midst of so much terror and fear. But you wanted to help, you wanted to be on the leading edge of change, and you said, "I'm in!"

Keep your hopes up. Become aware of your feelings and the thoughts that preceded them. Thought always comes before the image and then the feelings follow that, but our mind reacts so swiftly that we often assume our feelings come first in the chain reaction.

When you realize you are feeling down or doubtful or discouraged, glance back to your thoughts in the last few moments or days—did you open a big bill and worry that you can't pay it? Even if you immediately countered that with a rote affirmation "Thank you, this bill is paid! Thank you for my prosperity! I now attract all the wealth I desire and require!" if those words stayed on the surface and didn't permeate your inner belief system, then your worry about money has been affecting you, and now you feel stressed.

With our Old Worldview, the idea of counteracting that feeling of stress would be to quickly make an action plan to make more money to pay that bill. But when we leap into logical steps without first paving the way with a deep conviction of worthiness to receive prosperity, those steps won't help. And when the action plan works only a little bit or not at all, and the reaction to that failure results in more stress, it can appear to the rational mind that all of that law of attraction stuff is just useless and what's the point of even trying. Might as well get used to always having too many bills and not enough money.

Can you see how quickly that slippery road down can take you from worry to being totally stressed over money?

Switch those emotions around, keep your spirits up and your dream right in front of you—allow that picture of what you want to pull you forward and keep dancing to lift you right up to the frequency where your dream resides, so you can meet it there.

**

12

LOVE YOURSELF AND EVERYONE ELSE

Studies have shown you end up making about the same income as your six closest friends do. That's because we come into alignment with the people around us and subconsciously agree not to outshine them.

However, when you want to grow and expand and do more with your life, often times that same group of friends can be detrimental. If they don't support growth, if they disagree with your ideas, it can quickly become unpleasant. The most common reaction is to surrender, to give up on your plan and get pulled back into the circle. After all, it's far more familiar than the strange new country you had dreamed of visiting.

Now's your time to get out of a rut.

For example, if you have already made up your mind about someone, say to someone at work you don't particularly care for, and then someone else tells you a nice thing about that person.

What is your first reaction? I'll bet it would be to dismiss this new information as being unlikely, perhaps even a lie to try to change your opinion.

Depending on how open-minded you are and how fair you strive to be in your life when you are provided with a new concept to think about, you will either entertain this new idea about the other person, look at them in a different way, and question your own judgment of them – or else, you will simply dismiss the new information as being untrue, and congratulate yourself on sticking with what you see are the facts.

But the real fact is that you are operating from hidden beliefs that make it easy for you to keep going down the same road again and again instead of opening to a broader perspective.

From childhood, we're trained to nitpick. Most of us learn the criticizing and fault-finding habit easily. We start practicing it as soon as we are aware of it, and join in the fault-finding of our parents, siblings, teachers and neighbors.

It's what we do as humans, but only because it's what we learned.

You see someone walking toward you on the sidewalk and your mind instantly makes dozens of judgments faster than a spark of light. *Her dress is too tight, I hate that hair color, she's got on too much lipstick, what an idiot, she looks like a cow chewing her cud, didn't anyone tell her she should never wear stripes….*

What's that all about, anyway? It's the result of the fault-finding habit, which has no love in it.

It is learned behavior that you can change. You'll have to be strict with yourself to notice what you're thinking and deliberately choose a more pleasant thought.

Try it out and watch how much better you begin feeling. Love will pour through you and spill over to everyone around you, while lifting you up into a more glorious way of living.

Okay, let's pretend that exact same woman is walking towards you, chewing gum, wearing the same outfit. She hasn't changed her makeup and is still talking on the phone saying something you think is really idiotic.

Your old habit starts in immediately: Looks like she put on the lipstick with a trowel...

But because you've made the intention to find good everywhere you go, you catch yourself with that snide judgment, and you switch mental direction.

This doesn't mean you try to force yourself to admire the things your instantaneous judgment is saying "I don't like..." about. That would be false, and the resistance you'd set up inside would defeat the whole point of the exercise.

Instead, simply find something easy to compliment: Her hair is so shiny, what a pretty color blouse, I like her shoes, she has a nice smile...

Keep practicing until it becomes a habit to be a good-finder everywhere you go, with everyone you know, and the many billions of strangers whose names you will never learn. Don't stay on the surface as in the example above—find good in the actions of others and in things they say.

Part two: start paying compliments. When your eyes light up seeing a stranger's cute hat or sweet child, in passing (not in a creepy way like you are now BFFs), say, "I couldn't help noticing how great that hat is on you!" Again, don't feel you need to stop the person and try to strike up a conversation—think of yourself as a butterfly dispensing joy everywhere you go.

And watch how the joy in YOU grows.

***

13

MAGNETIZE JUSTICE FOR ALL

#1 Rule for the New Breed of Freedom Fighters: Stop collaborating with the opposition!

Some people laughed at Hitler—that funny little painter from Austria. I've read contemporary reports of ordinary people who attended one of his massive rallies and came away enthralled by the energy he raised with his rants, and yet found it puzzling that they couldn't recall anything specific he said that would inspire such excitement. One woman said that all she was sure about was that she felt excited that Germany would be "great" again. Sound familiar? It wouldn't have surprised me if Trump had begun sporting a bottlebrush moustache during the election campaign, but then maybe that's my dark sense of humor coming to the fore.

Students of world history know that the saying "history repeats itself" isn't an idle comment. We see the boot marks of Trumplike behavior marching across the years of the human race, leaving pain and destruction in its wake. And, oh yes, in case you didn't know this factoid: Hitler was elected. He later was given full power, but first he was elected.

When justice is threatened, in our own lives and on a larger scale, it can feel overwhelming. What can we do about this situation? If we feel helpless, then the strong energy of hate and destruction will roll over justice like an army of tanks.

Magnetizing justice means contemplating what it means to us to feel that justice prevails in specific situations and also as a rule of the land, and then imagine that our heart center is actually a strong pulsating magnet that pulls in the quality of justice so that it can manifest.

If there is a situation in your life right now that feels unjust, such as something going on at work, use that as your focus. Breathe mindfully to relax your body and get into a calm state of mind. It's no good doing this when you're feeling frantic and upset because that is the frequency of fear, and the light can't come in and blend with us when we are that low on the vibrational scale. Allow yourself to relax and allow thoughts to simply drift by like dry leaves on a breeze, without paying attention to them. In that relaxed state, ask light and love and justice to come in at a higher level than ever before. Believe you have this power. Feel the light inside you growing brighter and responding to your request for more justice.

Enjoy the feeling, and breathe mindfully again to end your mini-meditation and come back to everyday awareness of your surroundings.

You have just magnetized justice for all. You have created more justice than there was before, and now you can radiate it outwards as you go about your day.

***

14

NOTICE HOW YOU FEEL INSIDE

Many athletes get far better mind training than the rest of us. They are drilled in mental exercises to focus on the outcome they desire, to visualize themselves achieving that specific outcome, to seem themselves winning, to "be the ball"!

Meanwhile, the rest of us flounder around with the Old Worldview thinking habits that were still in use when people believed the world was flat and the sun went around the earth.

With our poorly trained thinking habits, instead of recognizing a fearful reaction to someone like Trump as soon as he opens his mouth, and realize our emotions are warning us we are going in the wrong direction if we keep paying attention to him, we collectively got more and more fearful – egged on by two factors: 1. Trump's rants and the gruesome vision he painted of a godless country ruled by a despot interested only in his own extreme agenda, and 2. Hillary's downward spiral in the marketing area of campaign emails and announcements. To the point, email subject lines similar to this: "I'm terrified! Trump is outspending us!" The subject lines alone rang the death knell for her campaign to be elected.

Those negative affirmations that one supporter after another read and absorbed and came into harmony with mentally were deadly to the desired result of Hillary's winning the presidency.

We can learn from this lesson, so that it won't happen again. When our feelings are in the lower range of fear, anxiety, worry and dread, that means our thoughts are in that lower range, too. And from that standpoint, the only things we can attract and manifest will also share that low frequency. Hence, the election of a man who is a racist, bigot and extremist with avowed white supremacist supporters.

Notice how you are feeling—our emotions are the pure indicator of our thought patterns. When we feel upset, since most of us never learned the laws of the mind and how to use them properly and effectively to improve our lives, we get the bright idea that we need to force ourselves into a happy mood.

Can't be done. Force negates. Oh, we can paste a smile on and pretend we're doing okay. I know, because for many years of my life I kept on smiling, but the smile was false. I was trying to cover up my fear and anxiety over a really bad marriage, and put a good face on it. Read that again—do you see what I said? It's what we've been taught: cover up, put a good face on it. But we can't cover up fear by smiling—that emotion of fear beneath the surface is driving our results.

Be calm in the face of hatred. It appears to be directed at you and all you hold dear, but when we realize what is going on with the other person, we can see they wouldn't be so hateful in their messages to others if they felt any love for themselves.

While we can and I believe should feel compassion for even Hitleresque people, it doesn't mean we roll over and let them trample over us.

The reason I feel we must emphasize having compassion when being a modern-day Freedom Fighter, is that if we act hateful, if we spew angry messages in response to Trump supporters, then all that retaliation on our part means we have aligned with the very "Dark Force" that we wish to eliminate.

Allow the rage-aholics their own experience of being fear-driven, but detach yourself from joining in on that vibrational wavelength.

"Calmness of mind is one of the beautiful jewels of wisdom.
It is the result of long and patient effort in self-control.
Its presence is an indication of ripened experience,
and of a more than ordinary knowledge
of the laws and operations of thought.

"A man becomes calm in the measure that
he understands himself as a thought-evolved being,
for such knowledge necessitates the understanding
of others as the result of thought, and as he develops
a right understanding, and sees more and more
clearly the internal relations of things by the action
of cause and effect, he ceases to fuss and fume and
worry and grieve, and remains poised, steadfast, serene."

from *As a Man Thinketh* by James Allen

You can read the full book by James Allen at your reader's gift page: evelynbrooks.com/readers-freedom-fighters

As a whole, we do much better obeying traffic signs than we do the signs our emotions helpfully offer us. For instance, what would your reaction be if you were driving along and came to any of these signs along the roadside or on a freeway lighted panel: *Wrong way, do not enter, turn around, go back, bridge out, yield, stop.*

Notice the signs your feelings offer, and ask for guidance.

Affirm: In the morning, I will know just what to do

***

15

OPEN YOUR MIND TO POSITIVITY

A closed mind gathers no insight or growth. People who refuse to look past the beliefs planted in their minds as children will leave this lifetime with a wasteland of missed opportunities behind them.

The power of modern communication gives everyone with access to the internet an instant platform to share their worries and negativity with countless others. There is a reason that "CNN" is known in the personal development world as "Constantly Negative News."

In the future, hopefully not too many generations hence, there will be more balance in what is called "news" and topics will be presented with possible solutions offered at the same time.

No more browbeating the populace with one disaster after another in exhaustive detail, while 99% of the rest of life is actually running along pretty well. Seriously, how many times today did you get confronted by an armed terrorist? And yet, if you watch the news or, worse, are a news junkie and have it on all the time as a background to your life, you have affirmed thousands of times a day that you believe in fear, terrorism and hatred.

Those beliefs don't sit on the surface of your life like a harmless hat you can toss on a chair. Fear walks right in and sits down and gets cozy in the driver's seat of your life.

Every result we have in our individual lives is something that "driver" (our subconscious mind) has brought us to.

Affirm now: I attract only good into my life.

That affirmation will help change over the belief that your "driver" holds and you will magically find yourself missing accidents that happen to others, walking out the door in time to see a rainbow, turning a corner to meet an old friend or to give a stranger much-needed directions.

Your life will become more joyful. It's all a matter of shifting those negative beliefs into empowering ones.

Yes, there's far too much negativity in our society, but we aren't powerless. We can change that, if we want to, and if we are willing to access the power of our thoughts to create something good on purpose.

Let's be more deliberate about setting our goals and imagining them into manifestation.

A quick way to get more in tune with positive thinking is to invite inspiration to come into your life every day. If you've gotten stuck and feel overwhelmed with bad feelings about yourself and loss of hope in the future, you will probably need to practice this many times, rather than making a one-off wish.

The reason affirmations "don't work" isn't because they aren't positive enough. It's that we say them on the surface, like paddling around on a boat, while underneath, that deep current pushing us down the river is our thought system or paradigm: all those hidden beliefs about ourselves and what we can achieve.

To change our beliefs to be more positive and creative, it's necessary to retrain our thinking, notice how we feel, keep up the self-chat with good affirmations.

You might be surprised to realize that all things we say to ourselves and others are "affirming" something that is either in support of our dreams or working against them.

Affirm: I now open to the delightful world of inspiration. Wonderful ideas come to me on a regular basis.

Inspiration comes to us in a flash. The nature of the idea is in congruence with the habitual thoughts we think. Therefore, inspiration to a man like Trump would be the idea: *I want to be ruler of the world and take whatever I want!*

Inspiration to me, since I write personal development books and constantly think about ways to express my understanding of the mental laws so that others can access and use them more readily, was: *I want to write a book that will uplift millions of people and show them how, together, we can be the new breed of freedom fighters and create more good in the world!*

What flash did you have when you woke up this morning? We all wake up with an idea in the forefront of our thoughts, but unless we give ourselves the bedtime command for greater good in our lives and the lives of others, that thought might be along the lines of a groan that it's another day and how boring that is.

If you are bored with life, apathetic about your future, it merely means that you have been using the laws of the mind to attract boredom and failure into your life.

In my law of attraction book *You Were Born to Triumph: Create a Five-Star Life in Your Quantum Kitchen*, I get into this topic more, and teach how to keep T.A.B.S. on your mind retraining – T.A.B.S. stands for "Tell a Better Story." It's a reminder to watch what you are saying about yourself in conversation with others, under your breath when you're annoyed with yourself, and in your head while you're doing ordinary things. That inner dialogue between you the personality and You the higher self is generally one-sided. We've learned so well how to put ourselves down that our higher soul can't get a word in edgewise.

In effect, we've all been brainwashed to belittle ourselves and imagine that we aren't entitled to our big dreams. We set goals that look reasonable enough to achieve, and reset them as needed to lower the bar instead of raising it.

All it takes to get one good idea to improve your life is to open to changing your thought habits. When we start thinking better thoughts and telling a better story about our own lives and the wellbeing of our country and our world, then the quality of ideas gets better and better.

***

16

PURSUE HAPPINESS

Focus on what makes you feel happy each day. Pour your energy into doing what you love. You'll feel the difference first. Enjoy the feeling of inexplicable happiness, laughter and joy.

Let happy emotions carry you along, and ignore the doubts that want to yank you back into the muck of negativity where most people continue to live from lack of understanding there is a better way.

Just as you may have reached critical mass as far as fear and dread go, you can shift that around, and soon reach critical mass for happiness meaning it will be a bigger part of your day in every way.

Being a happy person doesn't mean you skip through life in a foolish, happy-go-lucky way, but it does mean that a deep sense of contentment abides in your heart, and you can withstand anything, including things that used to rock you off your foundation.

As a society, we are bombarded with negative affirmations night and day, and like well-trained schoolchildren, we repeat the essence of fear in every waking moment. How do we do this? By talking about and thinking about what we don't want. Cancer, divorce, accidents, financial disaster, job loss, and the election of Donald Trump, an extreme rightist with delusions of grandeur and power.

Untrained thoughts are similar to a distracted gardener haphazardly tossing fertilizer pellets in the garden: some goes on the sidewalk, a handful goes on the weeds, and then a little of the food actually lands in the flower bed and helps the roses bloom.

Untrained thoughts say: "Oh no, they're predicting rain on Saturday—we'd better call off the picnic. Too bad, the kids were all looking forward to it." Trained thoughts counter that with: "Hey, let's predict the weather we want… the outcome we WANT!"

Your Mind Is a 3D Printer –everything you think with enough emotion and interest is something that then "outpictures" in your reality.

Start taking more care in what you imagine. Make those pictures about things you love and experiences you want to imprint on your subconscious mind to create in the physical world. As above so below—that ancient saying means as we think (above) so it turns out in life (below).

When you are pursuing happiness, understand it is not a set goal you hope to achieve. First be in alignment with the emotion of happiness that you have already received all that you desire, and believe that your wish is already fulfilled. Enjoy that feeling, and enjoy the happiness in advance. That is the true power of being a happy person, with the unshakeable belief that all is well.

***

17

QUESTION YOUR POINT OF VIEW

"I followed the pavement a little over a mile
and then turned left again onto a dirt road.
It was as narrow as a bigot's mind, and
I got in the ruts and stayed there.
My lights showed me nothing but
the still bare branches of trees and
shrubbery close on both sides."

Rex Stout (from *The Red Box,* a Nero Wolfe mystery)

We start making our preferences known as infants, and keep going from there. Anyone who has ever tried to get a toddler ready to go out for a walk or get to grandma's house on time knows that child has a firm idea of what he is or isn't going to put up with wearing or doing in order to make that timely exit possible.

It's not that the child is being deliberately ornery, although it can seem like it. At that stage of development, it is important for each of us to begin formulating a healthy sense of self.

As the years go by, our preferences and beliefs solidify into a perspective of life that feels very real and true to us, even though so many of those beliefs would not hold up to questioning in the light of day.

A bigot learns early on that he is superior to others for one reason or another that his parents, teachers and society teach him, or that he learns from peers and latches onto. It might be his skin color, the shape of his eyes, the part of town he lives in, or the family name. Since the feeling of superiority is deeply rooted, the bigot's actions are automatic—he runs on auto-pilot driven by an innate belief in entitlement.

But what about the rest of us? What about our perspective on life, and on the people we meet? We run on auto-pilot too, generally from a broader base of awareness than the bigot's narrow mind, but we too have hidden beliefs that simmer below the surface of conscious awareness and that drive our behavior.

"Walk a mile in his moccasins." What does that old saying remind you of? Of course, it's that little nudge to take a look at the other person's perspective, to try on the situation from their vantage point.

Many times when we broaden our perspective and think about how our bright idea would impact others, we readily find ways to compromise, to add a little here, delete a little there, and come up with something for the greater good of all concerned.

That is diplomacy. We were taught the rudimentary traits of a diplomat in pre-school or our first toddler play dates. Many of us kept going with the art of compromise. Bigots don't. They stall in the me-stage of superiority to others. It's unfortunate and sad, but the best help we can give them is to be an example of people with a higher level of awareness.

If you lower your perspective to examine the bigot too closely and wonder how they got that way, be sure to shake off that vibration and get back up on your Joy Channel.

You don't want to risk being so sympathetic to a low level of perception that it rubs off on you. It's not that you risk becoming a bigot yourself—rather, it's the thought frequency they inhabit that could bring you down and cause you to attract into your life troubles that are on that fear-vibration.

When we think about what bigots do and say, or might do next, our ever-helpful memory immediately activates dormant thoughts, flooding our minds with images and stories related to racism and bigotry.

You may find yourself delving into the subject more, reading blogs and true accounts online of what people have experienced on the receiving end of that kind of hatred.

Although it is important for us to recognize problems in our society so that we know where there is room for growth, room for improvement and opportunities to be of service to the downtrodden or abused, it is equally important to monitor our own emotional health and not get so caught up in the stories of abuse that our feelings plummet, and with those feelings our power to attract good into our lives actually plummets, too.

I use and advocate a type of detachment, not the same kind of "I don't care what happens to you" that is typical of a narcissist, bigot and the like, but the type of stepping back, and stepping up to a higher vantage point so we can recognize how to be of the most value to those who need assistance.

If your friend fell into a swamp, she would probably prefer for you to stay on dry land and toss a rope, rather than jump in with her out of misguided sympathy, and yet that analogy describes exactly what we do when we go too deep into feeling the feelings of fear, discouragement and depression that targets of abuse experience.

When we give up being overly stubborn about our personal beliefs, it means we open up a space in our mind to allow new ideas to come in where we can sample and taste and get to know them, and perhaps even decide we like how we feel when we look at life from that perspective.

Keep track of your point of view, notice when you are holding too tightly to the reins of old beliefs—question those beliefs and release them when you realize they are no longer serving you.

Affirm: I now enjoy a higher perspective from which I view the long term road of human evolvement, and I happily step onto the path of progress.

***

18

RAISE YOUR OPINION OF YOURSELF

Most people, in my opinion, walk around with a very low evaluation of who they are.

We learn early on that it's wrong to boast or brag about our accomplishments, and of course our parents were trying to teach us to be polite and not become a show-off to the point of making others uncomfortable around us.

However, in the process of learning some manners, far too many of us absorbed the erroneous concept that we don't matter, that we're nothing special, that we're pretty darned ordinary in fact and the world would hardly miss us if we vanished inexplicably.

Did you know that the universe could not exist without you? You would leave a void so massive that life as we know it would not continue.

Are you familiar with the holiday classic film *It's a Wonderful Life*? In this movie, George Bailey (Jimmy Stewart) encounters one disaster after another in the family business. In despair, certain the world would be better off if he had never been born, he contemplates suicide. However, in response to prayers from his family and friends, an angel-in-training named Clarence (Henry Travers) is sent from heaven to help George see what his town would be like if he had never existed.

In the movie, George soon sees the impact his day-to-day kindness and compassion had made in the town, because now there is darkness, despair and lack of love everywhere he turns. He begs to go back and rectify the situation.

Look at your own life and see how much good you do. You may not have a huge circle of friends, but you have interacted and affected many people in your lifetime, from early classmates and playmates up until today's coworkers, employees, neighbors and friends.

If you don't think you've made much impact of a positive nature, then ask to be inspired for ways that you can change that.

Understand that no matter what your list of accomplishments, the acts of the heart are always the most powerful ones. You're not a "big nothing" or a "total failure" and if you use language like that in your self-chat you are making matters worse with all that negativity.

Affirm: I am a beautiful eternal spirit, here in this earth-suit to grow in love and creativity and help others do the same. I am worthy of all I desire.

***

19

SPEED UP YOUR LIFE PLAN

W hy are you here? I don't mean "here" as in reading this book, but here on Earth. Here at this time in the 21st century when the most powerful nation in the world is teetering because of the results of election 2016.

Not knowing or recognizing why you are here tends to lead to discontentment with all aspects of your life from work to relationships, from satisfaction to self-esteem. Confusion over your life purpose can make it seem your life has stalled or is in a rut.

What if this is the best opportunity for growth that we needed in this country at this time?

What if there is great good that can come out of this seeming disaster and travesty of justice?

What if all those people filled with hatred and fear and demanding that walls should be built can be led to a higher level of awareness of who they are and that love really does trump hate?

It takes bravery to be a Freedom Fighter. But don't back down just because you think you don't have it in you. We aren't born with courage, we develop it by acting as if we already have it!

Ask for good things. Ask for love.

Tell yourself over and over again, I love myself and I appreciate myself.

That's not being conceited or vain. It's healthy. Saying good things to and about yourself sets you at a higher vibration. You should love yourself.

Without a good solid base of self-respect, we can't do much good in the world. Haven't you ever noticed that when someone is going through a rough patch where they are caught up in grief or are in shock over a devastating loss, they aren't capable of expressing much love at that time? They are feeling so off-center that their amount of self-love has dwindled to the point where there is no excess to flow out to others.

If you want to speed up your attraction of prosperity, understand that wealth is a neutral energy. It goes where it is attracted. It does not have a filter to refuse to go because it will be used for evil. It goes where it is made welcome, whether to build war machines or to build schools.

For every aspect of your life where you want to improve results, realize you are capable of having and giving and being and doing absolutely everything you would enjoy.

Affirm: "The divine plan for my life is now speeded up!" Florence Scovel Shinn

***

20

TRUST YOURSELF

If you have a hard time trusting others, or if you have a history of being mistreated, abused or conned by an untrustworthy person...stop and take a look within because your life is trying to point out a potential area of growth.

In fact, trust could very well be the exact value that you need to change in order to take quantum leaps in your life once your issues around it are resolved.

Often a stumbling block such as lack of trust in yourself will show up in many ways. You may procrastinate on important projects, not trusting yourself to complete them correctly and therefore putting off starting them until the last minute.

You may display jealousy in a relationship to the point of suspecting the other person of wrongdoing no matter how innocent they may be in actuality.

Other ways a lack of trust in yourself show up can be at times when you hedge your bets, can't make a decision about what to wear, or what to order in a restaurant, or what car to buy.

If you look "out there" for advice, constantly asking others to help you make even basic decisions, then you have abdicated your self-trust to others, and along with trust you give up your ability to make decisions and to be the master of your fate.

It's easy to get angry.

It's easy to throw tantrums.
It's easy to blame others.

It takes trust in higher principles, and it takes self-discipline to be a man or woman of integrity.

Games of the ego always include ways for the tyrant to attempt control over the other person. This is the basis for all types of abuse: emotional, verbal, physical. It is an indication that the tyrant – no matter how well they hide behind a façade of grins and joviality – is seeking to make sense of his world by dominating everyone in his sphere.

What are some ways you can build your level of trust in yourself and others? Start with something small. Commit to making quick decisions. This doesn't mean racing out to the mall on a shopping spree and allowing impulse buying to take over. It means trusting your first thought. It means opening to the intuition that is available to you. If someone offers you a job and your instant thought is "I'd hate working here!" don't override that thought. It's your true reaction. Decline the job. If you must take it for immediate financial needs, continue job-hunting and get out of that place as quickly as you can.

When someone asks you how you feel about a particular topic, if you've learned the habit of people-pleasing or being on guard, you may pretend you haven't made up your mind, or put them off with some other vague reply.

The truth is, we always know our reaction in an instant. If you're in a bad relationship, you don't have to think about whether you do or do not want to be out of it. You KNOW deep inside that you want out.

But on the heels of that pure clean knowledge, come all the layered responses that stem from lack of trust in yourself to know what is best for you and to take action to achieve it. *I know I should end the relationship, but he'd get so mad...where would I go...my friends would be shocked...my family would be angry...at least I'm in a relationship so I should be glad about that...what can I do anyway...might as well stay.*

When we learn to trust ourselves, we make decisions much more quickly and easily. We learn to align with our core values instead of undermining and sabotaging ourselves.

***

21

UPLIFT YOUR VIBRATION

Vibration is another word for "feeling." When you say someone gives off a bad vibe, you mean they are negative. Good vibrations are positive. If you say you feel upset, it means you are vibrating at a lower than optimal level.

Everything is energy. Everything vibrates. The chair you sit on is a mass of molecules in motion. The clothes you wear are vibrating. All of energy is an ocean of motion, and we are part of it.

This book is about using the power of the law of opposites and the law of attraction to be a new kind of "resistance fighter" who doesn't use guns or sabotage to defeat the tyrants, but instead uses the much more powerful laws of the mind to be victorious and to thrive.

Go beyond karmic debt, beyond fear. Access the power of grace to release all the mistakes you've made up until now and understand those lessons have brought you to this very point in time and the opportunity of opening to great possibilities.

Move out of the Old Worldview and into the kingdom of the One Mind.

We cast the words of our thoughts before us and they create expectations in our minds, and then we experience what we expect to see.

That means relationships and situations and health and a level of prosperity that are on the same wavelength as our thoughts.

If you are worried about Trump's actions, you will be on the Fear Frequency, which matches situations such as car accidents, missing your flight, a sudden health problem, an unexpected bill, and so on. A person diagnosed with cancer might have built up a strong fear inside about getting cancer—or it can arise in reaction to ongoing fears about issues seemingly unrelated to health.

Cancer isn't contagious—the cancer epidemic is an epidemic of allowing yourself to be on the wrong vibration for a long time, long enough to create dis-ease in your physical body, but the dis-ease in your mind, in your thoughts, was there long before the problem showed up in your health. For children, they respond to the vibration of people around them.

We can readily see the relationship between negative thoughts and poor health, and in contrast, when we turn our thoughts toward goodness and optimism, our health can improve.

At this time in our history, it's as if we humans are still using training wheels with the laws of the mind. Even though the law of attraction is told in the stories and parables of the Old and New Testaments and in sacred scriptures and texts from other religions and philosophies, we seem to have grasped the idea and passed it on year after year that those stories were about special people who could do things we cannot.

YOU are special. Yes, you are.

Take a moment to reflect on the incredible miracle that you are, and understand it is not being stuck up or spoiled to agree that you are a wonderful human being, capable of greatness.

You have everything you need right inside your own mind to imagine better things for yourself and your family, and to receive the how-to steps via your intuition and the opportunities that arise when we get in harmony with the mental laws.

What we do with wealth and how we attract it is more important than the dollar amount. To be part of the movement to help the world grow and expand and bring more of good things to more people, it's necessary to have a vision that involves helping others, not merely using them and discarding them.

Helping others includes entertaining, uplifting by being great at playing sports whether it's your local bowling league or the NFL, showing others how to cook, play an instrument, use a computer, write a song or a book. There are countless ways we can be of service in the world even in what we might call a small way in our own little corner of the world.

A song by Rodgers and Hammerstein for the play Cinderella includes an ode to the power of the imagination:

In my own little corner in my own little chair
I can be whatever I want to be.
On the wings of my fancy I can fly anywhere
And the world will open its arms to me.

Picture what you want, imagine it clearly. Your vibration will automatically soar higher when your dream is something that enlivens you. Keep your thoughts up on that Joy Channel, and when you feel yourself dipping down into discouragement or frustration or fear, get happy again.

Affirm: Every day, I strive to live and serve at my highest potential, helping others while I help myself.

***

22

VANQUISH VICTIMHOOD

Here's another area we learned from our race history: how to be a victim in a thousand ways.

Consider the life stories of Mahatma Gandhi, Martin Luther King, Jr., Nelson Mandela, and Mother (now Saint) Teresa. These 20th century world leaders taught us the value of non-violence as the underpinnings of a great change to help many millions of people find freedom from the double yoke of poverty and injustice.

Our victim stories are as varied as we are, and would make great entertainment if they weren't so devastatingly sad. How is that we humans have gone through so many thousands of years of living all around this globe, thumbing our noses at our own power to co-create abundance and loving relationships with the Source from which we all came, and that we are all part of.

Here are some statements that I think are pretty common—see how easy it is to recognize the victim mentality once you know what to look for:

No matter how hard I try, I'll never get ahead.

I've got the worst luck of anyone I know—nothing ever goes my way.

I don't know why I even bother, it's never going to work out.

I've got some kind of crazy hex or curse on me that means I'll never find love.

All of these statements, and many thousands of a similar nature, are affirmations.

We say the phrases again and again, and drill down deep into our subconscious mind until the thought becomes a belief.

Once a belief takes root in the inner recesses of our powerful mind, the law of attraction begins gathering all the elements needed to bring that belief to life.

If you tell yourself again and again, "I'm clumsy and stupid," you will materialize the results of that. It is true, even though it might seem unfair. We get what we ask for and believe we are worthy of receiving.

The clue to changing our results is to amplify our worthiness, and to deliberately do much better in the asking department.

When we make the decision to no longer be victims, we shed an old skin that is dried up and worn out anyway. In our new, more empowered state, we can align with the power of the law of attraction and magnetize joy, creativity and love into our lives, and through us and our actions, into the world at large.

***

23

WAKE UP TO YOUR EVERYDAY POWER

Do you walk around feeling powerless and helpless more often than not? It's a common state of mind, but an unfortunate one because it undermines your true power to create a beautiful life for yourself and your family.

What if you could be Cinderella or Cinderfella for a day? What would you wish for? What would you ask your fairy godmother to grant with that magic wand of hers?

Think about the things on your dream list, and understand that if they are on your list not just as a passing fancy, but as something that makes you feel more alive just dreaming about it, then you have the full capability of manifesting them.

I define a passing fancy or idle wish as being the type of idle wish a teenager might have of being a rock star or celebrity because it would be so cool and you'd get all the clothes you want and travel everywhere. But it's not a serious dream, it's shrugged off and either vanishes from lack of attention or is outgrown.

The difference between that idle wish you don't really believe in, and your dream that you really want is that with focused thoughts, you can bring your dream into reality.

The lesson material has been in front of us for countless centuries in ancient texts which tell us that we become what we think about, and that what we need to do is ask while believing, and then we will receive.

And yet we have not understood the broader application of these principles. With the advent of quantum physics, we've been gaining a better understanding, although certainly not a complete understanding, of how we affect energy with our thoughts and our observations of life going on all around us.

By becoming more awake and aware of our ability to change our results by controlling our thoughts, we access the power to create.

It turns out that demonstrating appreciation is the quickest way to activate this energy of creation. Say "thank you" again and again throughout the day. Doing so puts you in vibrational harmony with the universe and all its abundance.

When we enter and remain in a state of gratitude, we are saying thank you for all that we already have in our lives, and we are also being grateful for all that is to come.

When I was growing up, we always said grace before dinner. At the time I didn't realize I was being taught the universal law of gratitude. While saying the words by rote – *Bless us, oh Lord, and these thy gifts which we are about to receive from thy bounty through Christ our Lord*– my head was bowed and I was looking at dinner on the plate in front of me. And at the end of grace, we always said *Amen.*

However, instead of grasping and learning about the power of being grateful in advance for what I wanted, I simply made the connection that I was thanking God for something that was already there: my dinner.

I didn't see the incredible ramifications of the phrases in that short prayer of thanksgiving:

1. "Bless us" –shower upon me all that I desire and require to create a fulfilling life.

2. "Gifts" – my life is a gift, and so is everything in it.

3. "About to receive" – I must open up to receptivity and not block my good by inadvertently pushing it away in doubt.

4. "Bounty" – there is unlimited abundance in this universe, it expands with each request of mine for more.

5. "Christ" – the Christ consciousness is a metaphysical awareness that we become what we think about and we create our own reality by the power of our emotion-filled thoughts.

6. "Amen" – and so it is. It is done.

When we wake up to our relationship with the One Mind, we become more and more aware of our role here on Earth. We are here to help the universe continue to expand, to blossom, to create more and more new experiences and things that never were before.

When we understand this is an abundance universe that has bottomless wealth available for us, we can let go of the old ideas that there is only a small amount of money on earth and we'd better hurry and grab our share before someone tries to steal it.

When we are constantly grateful in advance for what we desire, we put ourselves in a vibrational state of pure joy that attracts all we want and even more from the benevolence and goodness of the Spirit.

Thank you, thank you, thank you.

Say "thank you" often, say it even when you feel you have nothing to be grateful for. Demonstrate your appreciation for life, and miracles will come to you in unexpected ways.

***

24

X-RAY YOUR THINKING

While we don't know what our next thought will be – we <u>do</u> have control over the habitual direction we allow our thoughts to take.

Update your "Mind App" now – just as we need to update the software programs on our computers and personal devices now and then, we need to learn to do a better job of updating our thinking habits.

When a computer program isn't working right, we don't blame the computer or phone and throw it out a window.

We look for troubleshooting with the software or for the recent update that we just installed. Many times, it will happily turn out that others have reported the same bug(s) and a free update or patch is available to fix the issue.

Other times, it turns out there's a bigger incompatibility going on and we need to upgrade at a cost to the newest software from that company, or from their competitors in the marketplace.

But in all this updating and learning new features, we overlook the fact that our own minds are far superior to any computer that will ever be invented, and yet we take it for granted that it's just "there" and doesn't need any maintenance.

Our own minds get overlooked—because we never learned that we have any control over our thoughts.

It's as if we walk through life under this burden of habitual thinking that's been passed down generation after generation. Even people who are considered the philosophers or intellectuals of their age will be seen to have a minimal or off balanced view about use of thoughts, because we'll see they may have been successful in one area but very unhappy in another area of their life, health or wellbeing.

Seven billion people are walking around on this planet with countless Mind Apps in operation all the time.

These Apps are so bug-ridden that we'd scream in horror if we opened a kitchen cupboard and encountered such an infestation of pests.

What if we could peer under each other's heads and see what was going on?

Actually, we can get a look, by simply noticing the person's outer results. Some are obvious and in fact have become clichés such as the wallflower who has self-esteem issues and must have a Belief App running that says, "*I am painfully shy, nobody likes me, I never know what to say to anybody, I wish I could go home.*"

A person who seems to trip over his own feet may have a Mind App programmed to say, "I am clumsy, I never look where I'm going, I don't have enough sense to come in out of the rain."

Now, how about doing a diagnostic checkup by X-raying your own thinking habits?

Start getting curious about your relationships and social life, your job, your health, your finances and every aspect of your life, and imagine that you can look right through those outer circumstances and see the bare bones of your belief system.

If you don't like what you see, realize that your work lies within, in becoming more congruent with the beliefs and Mind App that you want to update. If your realize you aren't getting anywhere in your job, for example, notice that your lack of confidence is holding you back, and begin installing new software that supports your self-respect.

25

YIELD TO A HIGHER FREQUENCY

When we take drivers education, we learn to yield to traffic that has the right-of-way.

When we start a job, we learn to yield to what our boss wants or risk getting fired or demoted.

That yielding is deeply ingrained in us from early childhood when our parents tell us it is time to go to bed, and even if we protest, they end up winning. We learn, to some degree at least, that it's generally easier to go along with what those in power are telling us to do.

Then along comes Trump. I doubt if even his supporters would call him a man who is interested in spiritual and personal development. We can see from his words and deeds that he operates at a low vibrational frequency.

If we yield to that low frequency, then we come into alignment with the congestion of fear and anger and depression.

A healthier reaction is to observe the other person's behavior, do all you can to prevent devastation, but remain emotionally higher and uplifted.

Imagine being a woman in an evening gown, having to walk down a muddy street. You'd lift up your skirt to avoid being contaminated by the filth.

The higher road is to understand everyone has the right to their own opinion and to the life they are leading. We don't know fully what motivates a person, although we can often guess pretty close to the truth by watching how they act and how they treat others.

Instead of getting caught up in finding fault, however, a better use of our energy is to get fully involved in projects and ideas that bring us alive and are for the greater good of all concerned. Go up higher in your vibration, up to the Joy Channel. Turn away from what you don't want and pour your mental energy into what you do want to create.

It's amazing how much freer we can feel when we stop pushing against something undesired. We have far more power and we are for what we want instead of when we are again something or someone.

Look at yourself in the mirror. Think of something you want. Say "YES!" out loud. The word YES holds incredible energy in it. Find more things to say yes to in your life.

***

26

ZAP YOUR STRESS

Here is a lesson from a program I created a few years back called "Zap Your Stress"—I produced it when I saw that so many people were totally zonked by the housing market downturn and financial crash of 2008. Even though I experienced the shock of a financial hit, I knew that I could help others make the best of the bad situation by moving out of the negativity of focusing on the problem and into the kind of thinking that would create solutions and recovery.

Years ago, a minister named Frederick W. Robertson said, "No one can be great, or good, or happy except through the inward efforts of themselves."

Robertson was born nearly 200 years ago in England. You may not be familiar with his name, but during his relatively brief lifetime – he only lived 37 years – he had a famous ministry at Holy Trinity Church in Brighton, England. His sermons attracted throngs of people in all classes of society and with all shades of religious belief. He had a great insight into the principles of how to lead a spiritual life, and that's what intrigues me about him.

In a recently published book about Robertson's life, his biographer, Christina Beardsley, said that thousands of people found in his sermons "a living source of impulse, a practical direction of thought, a key to many of the problems of theology, and above all a path to spiritual freedom."

Do you feel enslaved by your anxiety and stress?

Are you ready to leap onto a path of freedom?

You may have heard the saying "happiness is an inside job" – but it's easy to repeat platitudes and proverbs, and not know how to put them into practical use in your life. When you are overwhelmed with too much going on all at once, and one crisis after another comes at you from every direction, the big challenge is usually just getting through the day without cracking up.

Who has time for a lot of serious thinking and introspection? Your mind is probably flooded with nonstop worries.

Stop focusing on all the bad stuff going on in your life – you may have studied the Law of Attraction, and if so you already know that the secret to attracting the great things you want in life is to stop paying so much attention to everything that's going wrong.

When you feel frustrated, irritated and discouraged, it's usually because you are resisting reality. Something in your life or in the behavior of people around you isn't going the way you want, but instead of accepting it, you keep slamming your head against it, determined to make things go your way.

The result? Lots of tension and stress.

By learning to pay attention to our emotions, we gain insight into our thought patterns. From there, we can examine what our beliefs are. That's an important part of being able to release stress, because when our results are being driven by hidden beliefs, then we have no control over the outcome in our everyday world.

Once we recognize the disempowering beliefs, we change them by steadily affirming what we do want to believe about ourselves. A simple method is to use a tool created by Benjamin Franklin called the "T-Square"—no, it's not the t-shaped ruler you would find at an office supply store, although that is what it resembles.

Take a plain piece of paper, then draw a line across the page about an inch from the top of the paper. Draw a vertical line down from the horizontal bar to the bottom of the page, making a large "T" on your paper.

On the cross bar, write the issue you're having the most trouble with. Or you might want to just write "MY LIFE TODAY" and use the page to list all the issues that have you feeling stressed.

On the left-hand column of the page, make a bullet list with a brief description of each problem you are trying to handle. Then in the right-hand area, write the polar opposite of each problem next to it.

Realize that the items on the left side of the page are actually affirmations that you are inadvertently repeating day after day by putting your attention on problems.

Affirm instead the beautiful outcome you desire on the right-hand side of the page, and understand that while you may need a transition time for getting yourself out of a financial problem, for example, it can also happen very quickly, as with a phone call out of the blue where someone offers to purchase a car you thought you'd never be able to sell.

Expect miracles in your life, and they will come.

PART FOUR

31-DAY COUNTDOWN TO INAUGURATION 2017

I wrote these articles in support of everyone who has been stressed out and in a total panic over what will come next with a man like Trump in the White House. I hope you enjoy them.

#31 Are You Properly Armed?

Inauguration Countdown Day 31—Are You Properly Armed?

For the next month, until Inauguration Day on January 20, 2017, I will be blogging about how we can "combat" the extreme hate-based agenda of Donald Trump. We will do so in a non-violent way, getting deeper into using the Law of Attraction and other principles of mind power that most of us never learned to access. If you properly arm yourself with faith that love always trumps hate, then you don't have to be afraid of what will happen in the next four years with Trump at the helm. Guess what? He didn't buy the White House and he doesn't get to plaster his name over it...not unless we all fall down in fear and allow him to trample across our great nation.

We have opportunities for growth that will arise from what appears to be the muck of the Electoral College results.

Now is the time to come together. United, We the People, the majority voters in the 2016 election, can make a big difference. We can, in fact, neutralize the radical plans Trump has for destruction and devastation to so many of the progressive issues important to all compassionate and loving people, no matter what "party" affiliation you may have.

My book "America's New Breed of Freedom Fighters" is available now for pre-order on Amazon. It will be released on 1/20/2017. Among other topics and inspiration for change, the book includes information about Trump's Narcissistic Personality Disorder. You may have noticed how easily he is enraged when he feels thwarted, and when he doesn't like what someone else is saying. That's a big clue to his narcissism, but we don't have to lie down and be his doormats.

We the Peaceful have more power than we think. Power to envision the desired outcome in order to stop his agenda in its tracks before he gets started on his path of destroying hard-won advances in civil rights, voter rights, minimum wage, health care for women and children, education, environmental issues and animal rights, and so much more.

If we allow ourselves to dread his taking office, and focus on the anger and fear, then we actually pour more power into his agenda--in essence, we become inadvertent collaborators! Let's not do that. Join with me now and become one of America's new breed of freedom fighters. Together, this new resistance has potential to create wonderful transformation and change in our country.

#30 Don't Be a Wuss

Inauguration Countdown Day 30—Don't Be a Wuss

When I got the idea on 11/9/16 for my new book "America's New Breed of Freedom Fighters," I quailed. As much as I knew I was qualified to write it, and that I could and should write it, I also wanted to push the idea away and hope that someone else was next on the getting-ideas-from-the-cloud database in the universe that all authors and creative people tap into.

But I rallied at once, because I knew that I had a powerful message to share and I wanted to get it out there in a book for all to read. I knew that I needed to have enough courage to step up and help people not only relieve their stress and grief over the election results, but to come together in peace and pick up where we left off with our progressive agenda of creating liberty and justice for all people, not just a self-anointed minority.

Then, on 12/20/16 when I reflected on the fact that the Inauguration ceremony was exactly one month away, I got the idea for this 31-Day Blog Countdown to Trump's Inauguration. My vision for it was that it would be 31 positive and inspiring posts, all about using the law of attraction and tapping into our incredible power to create a better reality for America and the rest of the world, no matter what destruction Trump and his cronies have planned.

Okay, to be honest, when I got the blog countdown idea, my stomach fell. Seriously, I felt gut-punched by the idea. Not only is a blog-a-day a big commitment in itself, I'm still writing the book! Inside, I knew that was just an excuse, because I'm a writer. It's what I do. A deadline or big task doesn't really scare me. The truth beneath my moment of fear was a scared little voice saying, "No way am I going to make myself a total target for radical right agitators and all their hatred!"

You see, I have a lifelong habit of being a people-pleaser in every situation, and at worst a decades-long history of being a total doormat in toxic relationships with men.

214

Deliberately stepping up and saying, "Here I am, this is what I stand for, this is what I believe—and now, go ahead and leave a comment below" filled me with momentary dread.

Again, I kind of hoped someone else would grab the blog countdown idea and run with it.

But, yet again, I realized that if the idea came to me it meant that Source (Divine Mind, Spirit, God) was confident I could handle any push-back. My father was a Colonel in the U.S. Army, and I wasn't raised to back down to the enemy.

Besides that, with my knowledge of the laws of the mind, I understand we never get ideas without the tools to make them come into fruition.

So, here's my advice to you, the same thing I said to myself in the mirror a few minutes ago: "Don't be a wuss. Speak up for what you believe in. Get involved in the issues that are important to you. Let your voice be heard. Make your life count."

If we all cower in the face of Trump's brand of terrorism, then his hate-based agenda will truly win. Let's not let that happen. Together we can prove that love always trumps hate.

#29 The Panic Button

Inauguration Countdown Day 29—The Panic Button

Do you recall the 2008 financial crisis? Of course, you do. Many people panicked over the sudden loss in value of their homes and investments. In response to that situation, realizing that I could help alleviate anxiety, I wrote my first personal development book, called *Forget Your Troubles: Enjoy Your Life Today,* a five-step stress management system that became a bestseller.

215

Now, here comes Donald Trump's shocking win of the Electoral College votes. So many people began panicking as the polls began predicting his win that people seriously talked about leaving the country, unwilling to stay and watch him in action with that deadly 100-day plan of his to create mayhem and a lot of false promises of trickle-down wealth.

It may seem impossible not to panic, and yet when we allow those fearful emotions to gain hold and grow strong roots, we actually abdicate control of our lives to Trump and his pals. I still find it hard to believe that people I know voted for him—that's a head-scratching moment for many progressives to find out someone you thought was on the same page actually voted for a man who has spewed hate at every opportunity. But that topic is for another blog.

Right now, I want to address the sense of panic you may be feeling. I know of some people who are experiencing such distress that they feel life will never be the same. Again, that is handing over our thoughts to Trump on a silver platter and allowing him to pull our strings as if we are nothing but puppets reacting to everything he does and says. That's a dream come true for a narcissist! Everybody watching and reacting to every little bitty thing you do? Most of us wouldn't care for that, but narcissists thrive on that attention as it feels like adulation and envy to them.

I invite you to think about what you really want life to be like, for yourself and your fellow citizens. Put aside your fears of what Trump may or may not do next. Cut the wires to the panic button so it doesn't have the ability to shock you with another charge of fear every time you think of Trump and his stated policies.

He's made it clear he has no interest in the greater good of America and the world at large. That means it is up to the rest of us to step in and continue to work for progress.

Are you in? Okay, then put aside the panic, breathe mindfully, and realize this is an incredible opportunity for all of us to "fight" for the freedom and justice we desire. More to come in the rest of this blog countdown to Inauguration 2017, and in my new book which will be released that day: *America's New Breed of Freedom Fighters: With Liberty and Justice for All*

#28 What Do You Really Want?

Inauguration Countdown Day 28—What Do You Really Want?

Decide what you really want and understand you have the POWER to create it. Let's join together and build progressive change in America!

The topic of this blog is "What do you really want?" –and I know the immediate tendency is to say or think: I want this to not have happened, I want Hillary to have been elected, I want to turn back the clock and get a different result.

It's natural for us to go through a transitional time of accepting a disaster that we cannot totally change. When people survive a natural disaster such as wildfire, hurricane, tornado, or flood, they have probably also experienced the devastation of financial and property loss, as well as changes in the physical and emotional wellbeing of family and friends. We don't expect them to pop up the next morning and say, "Oh well, I'll just carry on—chin up and muddle through!"

We know they need to get past the shock, and come up with a plan of action for recovery.

We are faced with a similar choice post-election: do we cave in, huddle together and grow in bitterness as we watch for what Mr. Trump will do next? … OR, do we realize that we're not beaten unless we give up? We're not his victims. We're not hostages to his anger and hate-based ideas unless we come into agreement with those low-frequency emotions and begin hating him and the voters responsible for his election.

Hatred means we'll always be the losers—it brings us down to his level. We're better than that. We don't look at the world and see what we can grab for ourselves and our cronies. We look at the world and say: *How can I help? How can I lend a hand? How can I be of service?*

We are free citizens of the United States of America and we have more rights than most countries endow their populace with. We have free speech, we have free enterprise, we have capitalism which of course is not perfect and has its flaws, but gives us opportunities to make our own way in life and produce an income for ourselves.

So…what do you really want? More peace and love in the world? Me, too. Let's get started by continuing with our progressive ideals and re-commit ourselves to our agenda to secure liberty and justice for all, even in the face of Trump's threats to destroy all we hold dear.

#27 Grownup Wish List

Inauguration Countdown Day 27—Grownup Wish List

When I was growing up, there was one year in particular when I had an extremely important wish on my Santa list: *Please let my little brother live. Please bring him home to us from the hospital.* I was nine years old and he had been diagnosed with a brain tumor two years earlier.

Despite my fervent wish and prayers for his recovery – for a <u>miracle</u> -- a few weeks before Christmas, my four-year-old brother died of cancer. And I felt it meant that God did not listen to me because I don't matter, that what I do makes no difference at all, that it is useless to pray.

Today, I know there are many millions of us – the majority of American voters, in fact – who have similar feelings of shocked abandonment. How on earth could a benevolent universe allow a hateful man like Donald Trump to win the U.S. Presidency? How could this be? And yet, if we stay focused on the "why, why, why" questions, we'll stay stuck in grief.

In fact, there are many reasons why we can see this situation as an amazing opportunity for great good. Think about the times when you experience the most growth in your own life. Is it when everything is humming along smoothly? Or, in contrast, is it the times when you felt stunned by an accident, a job loss, financial downturn, relationship problems, a health diagnosis that rocked your world? Those are the times when we reach deep within and we overcome seeming disaster by finding a stronger and higher level of love.

And, as a nation, we come together in disasters and create an even better outcome for more people, having been prodded to notice things that were under the surface all along and can now be healed.

This is part of the transformation of the world that we came here to participate in. Yes, we knew we would be challenged, but we are capable of creating great good if we don't let the fear-demons gain the upper hand.

We progressives, liberals and independents have a crucial choice in front of us: do we really believe in our ideals? Do we really want to uphold the U.S. Constitution and the Declaration of Independence which preceded it? Do we really care about creating a better world, not just for a privileged few, but for all in the world who desire "life, liberty and the pursuit of happiness"?

Here's what we can do with our wish for liberty and justice for all— we can imagine our wish fulfilled, hold that beautiful image strong in our hearts, and work with the laws of the mind to create the reality we desire. Together, we can triumph over the seeming disaster of the 2016 election. Together, we can and will make a difference—a positive difference.

In his book *Feeling Is the Secret*, Neville Goddard explains the process for us to use: "To impress the subconscious with the desirable state you must assume the feeling that would be yours had you already realized your wish. In defining your objective you must be concerned only with the objective itself. The manner of expression or the difficulties involved are not to be considered by you. To think feelingly on any state impresses it on the subconscious. Therefore, if you dwell on difficulties, barriers or delay, the subconscious, by its very non-selective nature, accepts the feeling of difficulties and obstacles as your request and proceeds to produce them in your outer world."

Did you notice this sentence: "To think feelingly on any state impresses it on the subconscious"? That's how Trump got elected—too many of us allowed our emotions to be manipulated by Trump's fear and hate-based rantings and promises to create havoc.

#26 Can We Get a Do-Over?

Inauguration Countdown Day 26—Can We Get a Do-Over?

I imagine the desire to get a second chance is something we share with our ancestors going so far back on the family tree that we'd quickly lose track of how many great-great-great-grandfathers that would be.

Election 2016 is certainly no exception to that yearning for a do-over, at least for the majority of voters in the USA, and our progressive and sensible friends around the globe who are appalled that a man with Trump's core values is actually going to be the leader of the free world.

220

Our love for do-overs are seen in our movies, TV shows, and the Monday morning quarterbacking that goes on after a weekend game where every play is analyzed to see what could and should have been done differently.

In *Groundhog* Day, we see Phil (Bill Murray) being given a magical chance to repeat one day in his life hundreds of times until he gets it right and begins thinking and acting from a desire to be of service to others rather than from his prior self-absorption. In *Freaky Friday*, we get to be the fly on the wall and watch a mother and daughter pair grow to appreciate the other's point of view and, again, lead from the heart instead of from self-interest. The TV series *Quantum Leap* tapped into our desire to change history, to fix things that went wrong, to take advantage of the hindsight we enjoy as we look back.

And yet, as we know all too well, we cannot magically travel back to 11/8/2016 and change even one vote.

In all areas of our personal and business lives, we are given countless opportunities (which we may or may not accept and take action on) to make amends, to repair what damage we can in the present. No matter how much we might regret an incident or outcome, however, we can't turn back the clock and actually behave differently in the past in order to get different results in the now. We can't un-do a phone call that led to disaster. We can't turn a different way to avoid that accident. We can't unring the bell.

However, when we get into the mindset of transformation, we can find hundreds of ways to create an improved situation and this is true even about Trump's election.

Take a moment to think about some of the thoughts that coursed through your mind when you realized or got the word that Trump had gotten enough electoral votes to secure the win. Did you feel regret that you hadn't gotten more involved in Hillary's campaign? Did you wish you had gone out to vote instead of staying home because you figured Trump couldn't possibly win? Were your thoughts in a whirl, filled with dread over what a man like Trump in power could mean to our nation, and wishing you share with your friends why you would vote for Hillary, or in some other way helped undecided voters see the facts behind the issues, and not just Trump's dramatic sound-bites, hate-filled Tweets, and rants?

Instead of beating ourselves up for something we can't change, it is time to come together and create the change we desire, to take those actions in-the-moment that support the issues most important to us.

As Gandhi famously did <u>not</u> say, "Be the change you want to see in the world."

It turns out that quote we commonly attribute to Gandhi is actually a paraphrasing of this longer quotation: "We but mirror the world. All the tendencies present in the outer world are to be found in the world of our body. If we could change ourselves, the tendencies in the world would also change. As a man changes his own nature, so does the attitude of the world change towards him. This is the divine mystery supreme. A wonderful thing it is and the source of our happiness. We need not wait to see what others do." – Mahatma Gandhi

Let's not play the "wait and see" game with Trump. He's made it clear he won't play by any rules but his own. If we give up now, he'll truly win, but the world will be a worse place because of it.

#25 Freedom Fighting Is Not for Sissies

Inauguration Countdown Day 25—Freedom Fighting Is Not for Sissies

I noticed a comment on my LinkedIn profile from a guy who was posting in response to my Blog Countdown. Apparently, he saw the update about Day 30, and just had to let me know his opinion: "Ugh, at first I thought this was positive, but it's another anti-Trump attack. Very tiring, can't wait for it to end."

I assume he means he wants my countdown to end. The rest of us are probably thinking we'd like Trump's presidency to end before it gets started.

Meanwhile, however, I had just received a private note from a man who said he was really looking forward to reading my new book "America's New Breed of Freedom Fighters," and closed with "We need all the help we can get."

If I was on a rant about Trump, I would have leapt at the chance to tell that LinkedIn guy a thing or two about how positive in nature my blog posts always are (there are over 500 at my central site evelynbrooks.com and I've been blogging on stress management and the law of attraction since 2009). However, since the whole point of the blog countdown and my new book is to help people understand the laws of the mind better and lift up to a higher level of awareness about all we can achieve together, I simply ignored the LinkedIn comment, and read the private note out loud to myself again.

It can be tempting to try to reach out to someone who is a Trump supporter and coax or cajole or convince them of the error of their ways, but that's really a waste of energy. None of us enjoy having someone try to force their opposing opinion on us, and I don't want to be guilty of doing that to anyone, no matter who they voted for, or if they, like 40% of registered voters, didn't vote at all.

I say that "Freedom fighting is not for sissies" not only because of the slings and arrows we may get from Trump supporters, but also because being a modern-day resistance fighter is going to require us to dig deep into what kind of people we want to be, and to commit to ourselves and each other that we won't let insults or mudslinging stop us.

These are brave words for a recovered people-pleaser, but if I can do this when I have shrunk away from conflict my entire life, then so can you. I'm willing to be the standard-bearer, but I can't do this alone. I hope you'll join me and together we can, with the power of a beautiful vision for our country, create the kind of world we want to live in and pass along to future generations. Life, liberty, and the pursuit of happiness? Oh yeah, all that and more.

#24 Are You Worried?

Inauguration Countdown Day 24—Are You Worried?

Starting when we are very small children, we learn from the people around us how to worry about what is coming next. Sometimes the lessons are subtle warnings as part of everyday conversation that is fear-based in nature and reflects the human history of struggle and very little awareness of our mental powers. Much of it is more overt, such as the bad things that happen to good people and shock us so deeply that we gain the worry habit as a result. It's as if we've got this mass belief passed on from one generation to the next that if only we worry sufficiently we can ward off what we fear the most.

In the 2015 film "Bridge of Spies," Russian spy Colonel Abel (Mark Rylance) is repeatedly asked by his lawyer Jim Donovan (Tom Hanks) the same type of question to find out if the calm-faced Abel is actually terrified inside. Each time Donovan asks a variation of "Are you worried?" Abel replies mildly, "Would it help?"

The answer is: No. Worry never helps. It never has and it never will. It is a complete misuse of our incredible thought power and the laws of the mind.

We are just beginning as a race to understand more about our minds—movies like "What the Bleep Do We Know?" open the door onto more questions than they answer, because there is so much to explore and so little we know at this point. One thing most people in personal development seem to agree on is that we become what we think about.

You can tell from Trump's behavior that he has thought angry thoughts for a really really long time.

here's a lesson from the Old Testament that you may have learned as a child. I know I did, but it never seemed to apply to my own life because I didn't understand it was a metaphor to teach us how to be careful how we use our thought power. It's the story of "Job" – remember him? Terrible things kept happening to him. His life situation went from bad to worse, until he finally cried out (or so the tale goes): "Lo! What I have feared has befallen me!"

That "lo!" statement is comparable to today's "ah-ha" moments where we gain sudden insight into something we've been doing mindlessly all along and realize we need to change what we're doing. When we look at the power in understanding that we draw into our lives what we think about, then we can step back from the habit of worrying all the time and see just how damaging it is. You see, when we fear something, we become in harmony with it.

We draw it to us just as a magnet draws pins and paper clips and metal filings. Not on purpose of course, but by the sheer weight of our misunderstanding about how our world and our universe came into being and how we co-create with the Source energy we are all a part of.

In fact, I'll go ahead and stick my neck out on this because it is something I firmly believe: Fear is what elected Donald Trump. His supporters aligned emotionally with his angry shouting and belligerent accusations—they became fearful of the alternatives he raved about as if they were true. AND, the Democrats who feared he would win added energy to his campaign! That is the truth of the law of attraction in action: whoever has the most energy, negative or positive, will come out winner.

Trump's demand for a Muslim registry is so reminiscent of Hitler's "final solution" for what was called the "Jewish problem" that it really startles me when a Jewish friend tells me that he voted for Trump. I know all the razzle-dazzle of Trump's being a reality TV show host had people fooled, and he drummed up a tremendous amount of fear that is still sweeping the world.

Because I've studied the laws of the mind for a long time, even though for many years I struggled to release my old habits of thought that continued bringing me unwanted results, I decided to speak up and explain how I see things. Yes, it's a bit nerve-wracking when I see a negative or hostile comment, but I can't let that make me back down, because that's how fear wins. Giving up means fear wins. Giving in to Trump's agenda of racism, elitism and tax breaks for the wealthy, along with raping the environment and so many other plans that he proudly announces means fear wins.

I think most voters reacted with emotion and total unawareness of the power of the law of attraction to create our results based on the thoughts we think about with the most passion.

That's why I'm writing this blog series countdown, and why I'm writing my new book *America's New Breed of Freedom Fighters* – I want to help as many people as possible—Democrats, Independents, Republicans, voters, non-voters, Americans and our international friends – to wake up to their innate power to create a better world.

It's up to us whether we continue to cower in fear of what Trump will do in the presidency. But if we do, then we will end up having to join in Job's lament: "Lo! What I have feared has befallen me!"

#23 Find Your Relief

Inauguration Countdown Day 23—Find Your Relief

I was thinking about what a relief it would have been if only the Electoral College had done what the majority of voters wished for, and honored the popular vote, thus giving the win to Hillary Clinton instead of Donald Trump. We use the word "relief" rather loosely in America, for many different things. There's the sense of relief when something bad doesn't happen after all. There's the relief we gain by taking an aspirin for a headache. The feeling of great relief when a long and arduous task has been completed. We also provide relief to people who have experienced a disaster or extreme privation for some reason in their life, by giving them food, shelter, clothing, and sometimes welfare funds to tide them over until they are gainfully employed.

The way I'm looking at "relief" right now, however, is not as something imposed upon us from the outside, or something that is meant to erase an unwanted event, but rather as a stance of empowerment that we can call forth, each of us individually.

Abraham-Hicks points out that "relief is the cure that all medicine is looking for." It's what we seek at the end of a tiresome day at work, and because we haven't learned we have the ability to create our own relief, we look for the quick fix of food, alcohol, distractions, and so on.

As I see it, we progressives, Democrats and Hillary supporters can either drive ourselves crazy over the next four years, feeling anxious and stressed out… OR we can take action now towards creating relief within our own lives and for the country as a whole.

First, imagine something minor that you have felt relief over in the recent past. Perhaps you nearly knocked over a full cup of coffee or tea on your desk filled with important papers. But you caught it just in time, and steadied the cup. Perhaps a few drops splattered here or there, but no real damage was done. Whew! That nervous jittery feeling that popped up in the instant is now released, perhaps with a big sighing exhalation and even a little laugh, or a joke at your own expense.

Now, think about that happy glow of knowing disaster was averted. It felt really good, right? Keep recalling it, until you feel that glow all over, that sense of relief, of joy, of everything being good in your world for those few moments.

Capture that feeling, bottle it up in your imagination, and uncap it as needed to bring a sense of relief into your day whenever you feel anxiety try to take over. If we allow Trump's agenda to terrify us, then we are victims of terrorism. If we allow his rants to scare us, then we are his mental collaborators and feed his type of energy with our fear, thus making the "Dark Force" stronger. And, if we grumble to each other and hunker down to wait him out, we become slaves chained to a feudal lord.

I believe the key to relief is to understand we have the power to create the change we desire, and we can do this no matter what Trump plans. But we have to join together, we have to be bigger than all that hatred. Never forget: love trumps hate. Always.

#22 Stand Guard

Inauguration Countdown Day 22—Stand Guard

Ralph Waldo Emerson was a popular lecturer, author, essayist and founder of the Transcendentalist movement in the mid-19th century. Transcendentalism focused on seeking to understand the philosophy and metaphysical teachings of Jesus Christ so that one could go beyond the mere material realm that we live in and access the far greater power of the world of the mind.

Emerson's advice to "Stand guard at the portal of your mind" is needed now more than ever. It is vital for the health of our country, and for ourselves and our families, that we learn to dismiss the angry rants and destruction of liberty that permeate Mr. Trump's agenda.

When we stand guard at the doorway to our thoughts, it means that we are not passive victims. We stop being "reactive" and begin being responsive instead. We take charge of our thoughts, and focus on the results we want, without letting someone else's agenda terrify us and distract us from our beneficial goals.

When we dismiss the negative in our lives, we actually attract less and less of it. However, when we focus on it, however inadvertently, and fear what will happen next, then we become energetic participants in the problem.

I invite you to continue to be part of the solution in America. Progressives and Democrats traditionally are service-oriented. We look to see what good we can bring to our fellow citizens, and also our international friends who share this journey of expansion with us at this important time of transition in the human race to a higher level of awareness, truly the "Age of Aquarius." We are growing out of our long dark history of greed, struggle, and control by force, and into an awakening wherein each individual is cherished and nurtured, and contributes to the good of the whole.

You came here on purpose at this time in the world, to be part of the change. Perhaps you are part of the stirring up and agitation of fear, perhaps you aligned your energies with Mr. Trump's platform. And in doing so, you've given the rest of us the impetus to grow and move forward even more rapidly than before.

When life is easygoing, we lay back in our hammocks with a fan in one hand and a lemonade in the other, observing how pleasant the garden is. When an infestation arrives in that garden, we move into action and do all we can to protect what is already flourishing, and also to nourish even more growth.

Let's keep growing together. I invite you to affirm: I live and serve at my highest potential each day. I stand guard at the portal of my mind, and I do not allow in thoughts of destruction and resentment. I allow only good into my life. We are all connected.

#21 Emotional Freedom

Inauguration Countdown Day 21—Emotional Freedom

Have you ever felt like you were being held hostage by a highly charged situation not of your own making? It might have been an extended family argument that went ballistic, an issue at the office where people were taking sides and the atmosphere went beyond unpleasant into toxicity. Or, perhaps, you are feeling torn emotionally by the results of the recent U.S. presidential election and its aftermath filled with Mr. Trump's threats ("promises," to his devotees) to destroy freedoms that are integral to healthy American lifestyles, and even to immediately ("on Day One") begin building a massively expensive wall at our southern border. (Hey, anyone remember the Berlin Wall erected by Communists in 1961, and then in 1989, President Reagan's famous words, "Mr. Gorbachev, open this gate! Mr. Gorbachev, tear down this wall!"?)

It's not much fun feeling like a hapless ping pong ball being batted around by what someone else is threatening. However, it is crucial to not allow anyone, including (or especially) Mr. Trump, to dictate your emotional state of mind.

When we gain a fuller understanding that we do indeed create our own daily experience in this world, we can more readily see that if we allow ourselves to feel yanked around like a puppet on its strings, and be terrified one minute, in tears the next, and then angry the following hour, then that person manipulating the strings is the one in charge of your life as completely as if you were enslaved.

Stand up for your own freedom. Join this new movement to be a new breed of Freedom Fighter in America—and our international friends are welcome, too. There's no cost to participate. All it requires is a desire to feel better, to help make the world a better place instead of a worse one, and the willingness to experiment with a few simple methods of deliberately using the law of attraction to improve your results instead of accepting what comes you way by seeming happenstance.

Mr. Spock (*Star Trek*) had the right idea about emotional discipline, although of course his practice was carried to the extreme to be a more exotic and unfathomable alien from the (fictional) planet Vulcan. But we can learn from Spock, that we don't have to leap every time someone says "frog." We don't have to let our hot buttons get pushed again and again.

Let's deliberately turn our attention away from the rants and threats, and towards the good that we want to create for ourselves and our fellow citizens.

The election results may have you feeling like you are stumbling around in the dark, afraid you'll never find the door out. It feels disorienting. It feels like you aren't in charge of your own life anymore. It feels scary that a man who talks the way he does could actually get elected. (Aside: how on earth do rational parents explain to their children that a man with so much hatred for women, for people of color, for people of a different religion than his preference, actually got elected to the highest office in our country?)

When you take a look at the progression of what you observe and what you feel, and what you do next, you can detect the cycle: thought produces an image, the image immediately produces an emotion, and the emotion leads us into action. From the action, we then step into re-action to our results and to what others are doing and saying, and the cycle continues, endlessly.

By the way, action can mean a physical or mental activity or direction of thought; it doesn't have to mean you get up and go do something. Most of our actions take place in our minds. When we gain more control over our mental activities, then we can create order out of chaos. And when we are thus more calm and in charge of our thoughts, there is no stopping us from creating tremendous growth both in our individual lives and for humanity as a whole.

Let's start appreciating our opportunities to produce great expansion and greater freedom for all in the coming four years. Out of great disaster, we can produce great growth.

Now, breathe. As we breathe slowly, deeply, mindfully, it becomes a type of meditation that invites calmness and discipline into our thought processes. It becomes easier to dismiss the threats and focus instead on the action we can take to create more liberty and more justice and more freedom for all. Breathe in: allow Spirit to flow into you and refresh, revitalize and remind you of exactly who you are and why you are here.

#20 Anticipate Miracles

Inauguration Countdown Day 20—Anticipate Miracles

Happy New Year! Last night, I enjoyed the New York Philharmonic's New Year's Eve concert at Lincoln Center, conducted by Alan Gilbert. At the end of the concert, before leading the audience in "Auld Lang Syne," he said, "The opposite of war isn't peace--it's creativity."

Let's join together with our amazing creative thought power and bring about the positive change we desire in our country, and in the world.

As one of my favorite inspirational authors, Florence Scovel Shinn, says in her book *Your Word Is Your Wand* (1928), "God makes a way where there is no way." The full meaning of that seemingly odd statement is that we are not supposed to worry about all the "How can we do anything about this?" questions that leap to mind when we think about a racist taking office in less than three weeks as president of our great country.

When we look to Source (God, Universal Mind) to work with us, we can accomplish anything we set our minds to. By tapping into the true power of our creative thoughts, we create miracles. A miracle, by the way, is the genuine outcome of using our minds the way there were intended, to create desired results—it's the logical result of thinking deliberately about what we want, holding the feeling of already having it in our lives, and allowing it to manifest fully in the physical world we inhabit. But since we've all been trained to believe in things like good luck, bad luck, happenstance, and wishing on stars, it can really seem like a "miracle" when we get what we want instead of a pale imitation of it, if even that much.

Learning to use the universal laws gives us so much power in our lives. It's like being shown how to drive a car for the first time. At first, there's so much to learn and remember, and we grip the wheel in panic, muttering under our breath, "Seat belt! Check the rear-view mirror! Turn on the engine! Release the emergency brake! Put it in gear! No, no—wait! Put your foot on the brake first!" And then, as if by magic, after practicing and practicing, and getting things wrong sometimes and doing better the next time…we're driving like we were born to it. The same process works for using the law of attraction in a far more powerful and effective way than we ever have before.

Go ahead and let your wishes jump-start your engine—but don't count on wish power to make results happen. We can't "hope" that the next four years turn out okay. We have to get creative, and make sure they turn out better than just all right – that they turn out miraculously well because we anticipated great things and we brought them to pass in support of liberty and justice for all.

#19 Stop Badmouthing Trump

Inauguration Countdown Day 19—Stop Badmouthing Trump

The more we send out thoughts of hate and worry about what Trump will do on Day One of his presidency, the more we come into collusion with his agenda. I'm not asking you to say something good about him. Start with not saying something bad. It might feel strange. You may have to catch yourself mid-sentence and change the subject.

Here are some of the things we Democrats and Progressives and Republican Moderates should stop doing immediately:

- – Hating Trump
- – Wishing he'll fail
- – Hoping he gets kicked out of office
- – Hoping he is scorned by our allies and world leaders (other than those like Putin who are thrilled Trump got elected)

- Worrying about the umpteen billion-dollar wall Trump demands must be erected between the United States and Mexico (which, by the way, as any elementary school kid could tell him, used to own our southwestern states including California.)

Resisting Trump by speaking and thinking ill of him is actually the wrong way of going about things. It's contrary to the way our thought power works. In fact, resistance is worse than "futile" as a hostile alien might intone to a hapless Earther—resistance plays into our opponents' hands by strengthening the energy around their agenda.

The natural laws of the mind show us that it can't be otherwise. We can't continue to think unhappy thoughts and create happier results. It doesn't work that way, even though we've stumbled along as a race for many thousands of years doing just that.

Wishful thinking doesn't work either, not unless we amplify it with a higher level of expectation.

In response to our pushing-away thought commands (e.g. "I want Trump to go away!") the Universe can only give us more Trump, and even worse – a bigger and stronger Trump.

The law of attraction draws together all harmonious elements to create the matching result. It's like the children's game of matching colored squares. If millions of us are thinking negative, low sour-green frequency thoughts about Trump and his cronies, we actually align our energy with his because that's where his platform is: on a low energy sour-green vibration of hate and discord.

You may be inwardly protesting that you have stepped up your positive affirmations and meditations since the election results were announced. And that's wonderful. But take a look as well at how you feel about Donald Trump. Do you walk around with a dull ache inside, with anxiety in the pit of your stomach, and fear in the back of your mind? That fear emotion is what the Universal Mind is "reading" and responding to.

It's as if we operate with a stereo system in our mind. On the full volume track, we've got our beautifully crafted positive affirmations, and we repeat them, we listen to them on recordings, we watch positive videos, we write them in our journals and on sticky notes for the bathroom mirror. Example: "I am so happy and grateful now that all is well and only good comes to me."

But—let's look at that other stereo track, which is actually our subconscious beliefs. Imagine it's on a very low volume, so you don't notice it consciously, especially when you're going about your busy day. It's the voice of your inner beliefs, and it might go something like this: "I am so upset that @#${&*^ man got elected! What are we going to do! I'm terrified what is going to happen next!"

That inner voice of anxiety and dread is the one driving your results—and when we all chime in together on that vibration of anxiety, we inadvertently create a big manifestation that's all about stuff we don't want and would never deliberately conjure up.

The key is to change our beliefs, to get a sense of inner calm that good can come out of this, that together we are strong and will create the progressive change we desire, that we have hope for the future because we know a bully can't defeat us unless we let him.

Tip: if you haven't done so already, sign up for my Serenity Gift Collection which includes two meditation audios and the full chapter on removing negative labels from my bestselling stress management book *Forget Your Troubles: Enjoy Your Life Today*. Go here to claim your gifts: http://evelynbrooks.com

Once we get into the rhythm of speaking for what we want (instead of decrying what we don't want and badmouthing the president-elect), we begin to see a shift in our results.

It starts first with feeling a bit better. Not as anxiety-ridden. Not as sleep-deprived. Not as stressed-out. We start feeling that, okay, this isn't the choice we prefer, this isn't the candidate we voted for, he's not even the one who got the most votes, but we still live in a democracy, we still have access to our Congressional representatives and senators to make our voice heard, and we can keep moving forward.

If we buckle under to fear, then Trump truly wins.

#18 Dissolve the Wall Before Trump Builds It

Inauguration Countdown Day 18—Dissolve the Wall Before Trump Builds It

What happened when you first heard about the massive wall Trump plans to build at our southern border? We think in images, so I feel confident you didn't see the letters "W-A-L-L" in your mind's eye. Instead, you no doubt pictured a snaking wall between the United States and Mexico. That picture popped into your mind instantaneously, didn't it?

Our images are powerful. The longer we think about that wall and add details to it in our horrified imagination, the stronger and more realistic the picture gets. Have you ever used a Polaroid instant camera? Remember watching as the picture developed into full color right before your eyes? That's just a small metaphor for how our imagination power works.

If you are appalled at the idea of breaking the economy by building a huge wall across many miles, dividing our citizens ever more firmly into opposing camps, and becoming a police state, then we have to start taking action now.

I'll leave it up to you to support the activist and political sites by signing petitions and helping to share messages from the Democratic Party and other progressive groups.

What I want you to do is to promise you'll stop picturing that damned wall.

Okay, what happened? Did the image magically go away? Of course not. Probably it got even clearer because I told you not to picture it. This is like the old joke: *Hey, don't think about an elephant in your living room!*

The special trick to using the law of attraction is to turn our attention <u>away from</u> the result or experience that we do not want to create. Since most of us never learned to do this growing up, we have very well-established thinking habits, and it can feel like quite a challenge to not automatically join in the worrying and anxiety about all of Trump's plans.

After all, he's got so many of them, and not a single one is beneficial for our country. His agenda is to systematically attack our freedoms and change the landscape of our land into one reminiscent of a fascist regime.

Here's the way to change the picture of what he plans into a beautiful picture of progress and freedom for all. Each time you think about the wall, distract yourself with something else. Don't try to force the image away, simply think about flowers, or puppies, or what you are going to have for dinner. If friends and family and coworkers begin fretting about the wall, don't participate in the conversation. Depending on who you are with, share the idea of turning your focus away from the wall and onto things that are positive and make you feel uplifted instead of frightened.

We can truly turn injustice into justice when we join together in creating positive images. Our thinking power means that we create the experiences and results we share. That means we're either helping to build the wall by being upset and terrified about it...

Or we are dissolving it before Trump can even hire the architects, by virtue of turning our energy AWAY from the mental pictures of walls.

James Allen: "We think in secret and it comes to pass. Environment is but our looking glass." Memorize that quote. Read his book "As a Man Thinketh." Actually, you can pick up a copy of it as a gift from me when you go to the readers page link that is inside my new book "America's New Breed of Freedom Fighters."

Draw on your bottomless reserve of courage and remind yourself that being a Freedom Fighter means we don't back down to bullies no matter how outrageous their antics become. The election itself was a barrier to his plan to build the wall, but once he got in, fear crossed the barrier, and now we have a number of hurdles in front of us.

Trump attracts bullies and people who are fearful and angry. Some of his supporters are no doubt good people who were deluded into voting for him. After all, Hitler was elected in 1932, and many thousands of people adored him and thought he'd bring Germany to "greatness."

Trump whipped people into a frenzy of fear with all of his rants and ravings. He's deadly serious about rolling back freedom, liberty and justice so that only he and his cronies come out on top.

Mr. Trump is an extreme narcissist. Narcissists hate being laughed at. Start laughing at Trump's plan to build a wall at our Mexican border.

239

Each time the image of a wall comes to mind, turn your attention to a peaceful border where sensible immigration laws prevail.

#17 Not My President

Inauguration Countdown Day 17— Not My President

While strolling Fifth Avenue in New York City to view the holiday window displays at famous department stores such as Bergdorf Goodman, Saks Fifth Avenue, and Lord & Taylor, I couldn't help noticing all the police and police barriers around 57th Street...the location of the "Trump Tower" where Donald Trump lives.

On the opposite side of the street, a man shivered on the sidewalk in the freezing cold of the dark evening, holding up a large hand-made sign that read: "NOT MY PRESIDENT." And I thought to myself, *Yeah, I understand where you're coming from, but... actually he IS going to be your President, and mine, too.*

This is a democracy. We elect our leaders, and we elect a President every four years. There has never been a year where the election was called off or postponed due to bad weather or a conflict with the NFL schedule. The election is held in an even year, and the polls are always open on the second Tuesday of November, without fail. On the heels of the election, but not so immediate that it's too swift a change--giving the incumbents time to wrap things up and move out, and the city of Washington, D.C. to prepare for the ceremony, the president-elect is sworn in on January 20th, no matter what day of the week that falls on. It's a 3-step process that is predictable: registered voters make their choice, someone wins, and then that person gets inaugurated for a four-year term.

Demonstrating and holding up signs that say "Not my president" is no doubt a way of stating your opinion, but it doesn't affect the reality of Trump's upcoming move into the White House.

240

Trump is our president now. Even though he is not the People's Choice, he was not the winner of the popular vote, the Electoral College declared him the winner, and we must make the best of a bad situation.

Whenever a really scary situation confronts us, we have three basic choices:

1. Scream and yell and rant. Refuse to accept it. Stay angry and worried and stressed-out. Decide we'll all have to muddle through somehow for the next four years and hope things magically work out.

2. Turn away. In this case, move out of the country and relinquish your citizenship so you can truly say "Not my president" and try not to wince every time you see Trump on international news.

3. Do something about it.

With my new book, "America's New Breed of Freedom Fighters," I invite you to step up and be part of a new type of Resistance. You probably know about the freedom fighters in World War Two who were fought long and hard under desperate conditions, to help Jews escape Hitler, to speak out for freedom, to risk their lives while gaining intelligence to help the Allies, and to spread the word that they weren't going to give up their dream of freedom for themselves and their countrymen.

We are under attack, from within our country.

Let's not give up. Let's not let Trump and his cronies stomp all over America with their jackboots. If you voted for Trump or you don't understand what the big fuss is all about and think Democrats are just being "sore losers," I urge you to look deeper into what is going on and what kind of man Mr. Trump is.

Trump is transparent about being an extremist with a hate agenda, but for dyed-in-the-wool Republicans, they probably never saw those "sound bites" on the TV channels they watch or learned about his actions in the newspapers and radio stations that censored such information. Maybe they even believe he finally turned over his tax returns (he didn't--narcissists don't have to follow the rules because they believe in their inherent superiority to the rest of us) and that he's being hounded for no reason.

Lest you think I'm an alarmist, take a look at what's going on already with Trump's selections of white supremacists and right-wing extremists to be key players in his inner circle, as well as the smoke-and-mirrors efforts of Republicans to push through secret agendas while the nation is distracted by the holidays.

Enough about what we don't want. You know what's going on. We've got a challenge ahead of us. Together, we can picture progress and growth in America and for the rest of the world, too, and with the powerful energy of the law of attraction, we can manifest those positive mental pictures into reality. Start now, start today.

Affirm: "My goodwill is a strong Tower around me. I now change all enemies into friends. All inharmony into harmony. All injustice into justice." -- Florence Scovel Shinn

#16 The Shock Heard Round the World

Inauguration Countdown Day 16—The Shock Heard Round the World

Students of American History will, of course, understand the intended reference in the title of this article to "The shot heard round the world" which marked the beginning of the American Revolution in 1775 to gain freedom from the tyranny of King George III of England.

The phrase comes from the opening lines of Ralph Waldo Emerson's "Concord Hymn" written in 1837:

> By the rude bridge that arched the flood,
> Their flag to April's breeze unfurled,
> Here once the embattled farmers stood,
> And fired the shot heard round the world.

Of course, the "shock" I refer to is Donald Trump's win of the 2016 Presidential Election. This shock was truly felt and heard all around the globe as countless millions of people reeled in stunned dismay over the potential outcome of an avowed misogynist and racist in the White House.

In any disaster, we feel overwhelmed and unable to grasp the full scope of the issue because our expectation for good has been turned totally upside down. It takes some time for our heartbeat to return to normal, and longer for our sense of outrage to settle down.

However, it is vital for progress that we not stay in a state of shock any longer. It is time to keep moving forward, to proceed with the issues that are dear to the hearts of people who want this world to grow and evolve, not to return to dark ages and dark times.

Be a voice for progress. Throughout history, ordinary people have heard the call to action and in spite of the logical reasons to excuse themselves from doing things that were scary or uncomfortable or meant sticking their necks out, they found enough gumption to step up and fight back for what they wanted for themselves, their families, and their country.

We can do this too. We can fight back, with the power of positivity.

I am calling on all Democrats, Progressives and Moderates, and our friends around the world, to join in the new revolution and be Freedom Fighters to push forward with justice, education, environmental protection, clean energy, fair wages, and so many more issues that are vital to the wellbeing of our nation and of the entire globe.

"The Universe is all good; however, in difficult situations we are often not able to see the bigger picture. Even situations we call 'bad' actually have good underneath them. Look at any situation with new eyes and look for the good. If you look for it, you will most assuredly begin to find it, and then you will have burst the illusion of difficulty and allowed all the good to come forth." – Rhonda Byrne

It all comes down to saying yes to what we want to experience—and to stop saying no to what we don't want. That "no" power we learned as two-year-olds was an important part of personality development of the individual, and we use yes/no throughout each day in even minor decisions about what to wear or eat, whether to go to that store or the one a block further but with better produce. The type of yes/no judgments that help us navigate the complexity of daily life are not the same process as powering up a big fat "NO, I DON'T WANT THAT!" which actually energizes the very thing, person, or situation we are trying to push away. This is why "resistance is futile" is not just a line spoken by alien monsters in a sci fi movie.

Resistance truly makes a hate agenda grow stronger and more empowered. We learned that lesson with Hitler and apparently, we must learn it again.

We must learn to direct our thoughts and the incredible power of our emotions towards what we want to build together: liberty and justice for all.

#15 Epiphany

Inauguration Countdown Day 15—Epiphany

244

Today is Epiphany, the Christian holiday commemorating the visit to the baby Jesus by the Magi. These were three Kings or Wise Men who traveled from other lands, following the Christmas star to Bethlehem to bear witness to the birth of the new spiritual King. It is the "12th day of Christmas" known by the popular song and not always remembered for what January 6 means in the Christian religion. The word "epiphany" is Greek in origin and literally means that Jesus was "revealed" to the world in this story of a long-ago tradition.

What has been revealed to us in the election of Donald Trump? Do you believe he is worthy of the gifts that were given to the baby Jesus to show his importance? The gold symbolized his royal rank as the new King bringing love into the world, frankincense is an essential oil that is still much valued for its healing properties but in church language the gift of frankincense related to his divine birth, and myrrh represented his human mortality (myrrh was a holy incense burned in temples, and was also used to embalm the bodies of Pharaohs).

When we have an "epiphany" in modern times, we tend to think of it as a really big ah-ha moment. It's as if we were in a darkened room and someone opens a door to the sunlight. An epiphany can feel deeply spiritual, such as gaining knowledge about your life purpose after struggling to figure it out. With the experience of an epiphany, we step out of our ordinary existence and, with the benefit of this new insight, we take a giant leap into a fullness of meaning that is far greater than we have experienced before. And in this new understanding of who we are and what we are capable of achieving, we look around and we see where we can be of service by living at a higher level of potential than ever before.

I believe that the 65,844,610 Americans who voted against Trump had an epiphany when he won. As a group, we realized that we haven't come as far as we thought in bringing people on board with a healthier approach to citizen rights than just the right-wing white Christian desire for homogenized life in the so-called good ol' days of the 1950s. I grew up in the fifties in segregated Texas, a skinny blonde Catholic girl whose grade school butted up against the beginning of the "colored section" of town. I know that going backwards is never going to help this country. Mr. Trump has declared his intentions of creating mayhem and destruction, and is already gathering around him cabinet nominees who have Putin's approval, and white supremacist's blue ribbon as well.

What can we do? Are we simply going to have to wait it out and pray that nothing too awful happens, and that however bad it is, we'll manage to regroup eventually and regain what we've lost during his tenure? If we take that attitude, well, in my opinion, we're defeated right now, because we become inadvertent collaborators.

Let us pray for deliverance from Trump's extremism, and remember that in our prayers and hopes for the next four years, we have the advantage of being people of diversity who can speak up for a new "epiphany" or "revelation" and that will be to reveal more and more progressive action in the coming four years, and not less. We will reveal our determination to protect the progress we've made to date and continue moving forward in all the issues of importance to Democrats, Progressive, Independents and others who want the country and the world to keep expanding in love, joy and creativity.

I'm counting on all the people in the personal development and spiritual communities to step up and help lead the way for progress.

In his metaphysical books, Dr. Joseph Murphy often reminds us to be careful of our thoughts and to be sure that we are always thinking about what is true and of good report. This means we can't fill our minds with thoughts of what Trump is up to. Avoid being a news junkie and following all his rants and threats. Keep your focus on the desired outcome, and allow the powerful law of attraction to make manifest the good pictures in your mind of liberty and justice for all.

"Be sure that you think on
whatsoever things are true,
whatsoever things are honest,
whatsoever things are just,
whatsoever things are pure,
whatsoever things are lovely,
whatsoever things are of good report;
if there be any virtue,
and if there be any praise,
think on these things."

Philippians 4:8

We can't back down. There have always been times in history when it would be easier to just run inside and bar the door and hope that the fighting going on outside passes you by. There is too much at stake to be passive and let Trump and his cronies trample on our liberties.

#14 Law of Attraction in Action

Inauguration Countdown Day 14—Law of Attraction in Action

How did Trump win? This question has already been discussed in many circles, and no doubt will continue to be rehashed in the coming years and by future historians long past this century's end. I would like to offer a different perspective about this. Donald Trump won the 2016 election because the law of attraction was working in his favor.

Seriously.

The same thing happened with George W. Bush. Twice. That is one of the reasons behind my new book *America's New Breed of*

Freedom Fighters and the sole reason for this 31-day blog countdown to the inauguration. I want to do everything I possibly can to ensure that Trump is a one-term-only president.

Very seriously.

We can ill afford him for four years, but re-election in 2020 is a possibility if we don't take strong steps now to offset that eventuality.

I'm not talking about campaign issues and getting the voters out. All of that is of huge importance. But where we need to shift our awareness is in being much more in congruence with what we want (not AGAINST a candidate and his agenda, but FOR what we do want), and then deliberately use the laws of the mind to bring it forth into manifestation.

In other words, we progressives need to master the law of attraction, and there's no time to waste. We think in pictures, and we react with our emotions, and the picture of Trump in office got stronger and stronger and more awful and terrifying and… we who wanted Hillary to win inadvertently poured our powerful manifestation energy into Trump's campaign as surely as if we gave him our money and lifeblood.

> *"The inner movie that you have seen*
> *with your mind's eye*
> *shall be made manifest openly."*

Dr. Joseph Murphy

The accountants have finished the final tally of votes and we now see that 65,844,610 Americans voted against Trump – a better way would be to say we voted FOR Hillary. However, we are so well trained as a society to think in terms of "battle" and "war" and "defeat" that many people are now repeating the summation as being votes against Trump.

We're all living with unique paradigms that run our lives. The part of our mindset that deals with everyday preferences of ketchup over mustard, sweet pickles versus sour, driving a silver car or a white one, wearing lace-up sneakers or the kind with Velcro fasteners—all those are minor and hardly earth-shaking in nature.

But the assumptions that underlie our beliefs in politics created the result we are faced with today: a misogynist and racist entering the White House on January 20, 2017.

I don't believe all Republicans are "evil" and that they must have agreed with all of Trump's platform. I imagine that many of the people who voted for Trump were simply operating under the hypnotic influence of their decision to be Republican, probably because all their relatives and neighbors have been Republican since way back in the day when it meant a smaller government.

Today's Republican platform is hardly recognizable from that of years gone by. When we have our mind pre-set to vote a certain platform, we reject ideas and information that try to penetrate the barrier.

This is an important skill in many ways, so that we can filter out extraneous information. But in the 2016 election, it meant that all the information flooding the airways and Tweet-ways about Donald Trumps' corruption did not even enter the air space of the "red states." If they got wind of something that caused a frown of concern, they no doubt instantly dismissed it: *This does not compute, it is not in congruence with what I want to believe, so it is not real.*

While some Trump supporters chanted and screamed "Build the wall," other supporters might not have even heard about the plan, or if they did would say, "Well I guess that's a good idea, we need safe borders," and never consider the cost and who would pay for it, let alone the ramifications of walling America off from one of our allies and important part of our culture. Others might have reassured themselves that it would never happen and there are always some extremists when people get hot under the collar in election campaigns.

Many millions of Republican voters really liked Trump's promise to make America great again, whatever that means. To progressives, his plans mean making America a hell-hole. To rural white Christians it turns out to mean a magical fairyland where there aren't black people in power and anybody who doesn't go to your church can be run out of town by the local cops.

When we look at this election and try to understand how people could rationally choose a man with Trump's lack of experience and his hair-trigger temper and his extreme narcissism, it seems like we've entered "The Twilight Zone" because it is illogical. That's the thing about humans: we run by our emotions, and our emotions are driven by the hidden beliefs deep in our subconscious. If you hate women and think life was better when they were barefoot, pregnant and in the kitchen, would you even consider the qualifications of Hillary Clinton? Of course not; it would not compute with the program running your life.

Where we went wrong is in sliding into reactive mode. Without being aware of how dangerous it was, Hillary's team began sending out emails with frightening subject lines about Trump outspending, about being scared, about needing to donate more money fast, about "we could lose this" – all of those statements are affirmations. They are requests to the universal law of attraction to bring back to us the matching experiences. So we got more scared, his spending skyrocketed, and we did lose it.

We are in a very important transitional time in human history, and you and I are here to help, so that this will be the last time a man like Trump ever gets elected in a free country. Last. Time. Ever.

But to do this, we need to start honing our skills in using the law of attraction in our own lives. When we learn to access the power of our thoughts, we truly think into the desired results instead of getting a haphazard mish-mash of sorta good and not so great.

My book is crammed and jammed with information on working with the law of attraction so that we can indeed neutralize Trump's agenda of hate, and instead manifest progress with liberty and justice for all.

#13 Hot Stress Relief

Inauguration Countdown Day 13— Hot Stress Relief

Stress kills. If we could bottle up all the stress that erupted on 11/9/16 with the announcement about Trump's electoral vote win, we'd need such massive vats to hold it that we'd be in manufacturing for years to come.

Consider this hypothetical question: Is it possible our nation (and the world) might be safer because Trump won?

When a narcissist is thwarted, all hell breaks loose. If that narcissist operates in a controlled arena such as his job at a factory, he might do some act of sabotage or vandalism or blow off steam in a pub brawl, then go home and abuse his wife and children. But when that narcissist occupies a high level in the public eye, we can only shudder to imagine his reaction and its repercussions. It might be like an atomic bomb test in the ocean, only not so far from civilization. If you think Trump's behavior during the campaign and in the post-election days leading up to the Inauguration has been scary, what if he was in such a rage at losing that he called for a convention for the "red states" to secede from the Union?

I'm not saying we should feel grateful Trump was elected. Just sayin'… it could've been even worse than what we are facing now.

251

Where does all that stress go? It doesn't vanish. It seeps into every one of your 63 trillion cells. Other estimates of the number of cells in our body are higher, but maybe they make allowance for height and weight. In any case, that's way more cells than we can count or keep track of. When someone is stressed out, it has a ripple effect and spreads out to family, friends, the workplace and more. You know what it's like being filled with anxiety, and you know what it's like to feel relief.

So, let's look at how we can invite relief to come on in and relax all that tension before there's a massive epidemic of high blood pressure and other ills related to chronic stress.

In my stress management book, *Forget Your Troubles: Enjoy Your Life Today*, I explain all the ways being in a state of chronic stress is damaging to health. But more to the point for this article, I give in-depth examples of how to create serenity in your life and let go of all that panic.

In fact, there's a whole chapter on anxiety attacks called "Breathe, Dammit! - quick ways to stop a panic attack or meltdown."

Here's an excerpt:

Method #1 to stop a panic attack - deep breathing

Sometimes, simply noticing that your breath is too fast and shallow is enough to help you take a deep breath and slowly exhale, then relax and breathe normally. This will head off an anxiety attack by giving your brain the proper level of oxygen and nutrients.

At other times, you'll need to mindfully breathe in and out, slowly and deeply. If you are breathing in a shallow fashion when you are tensed up, you'll feed an anxiety attack. It's a vicious cycle. But you are in charge, and that's the good news. Isn't it great to know there's an easy, painless solution and it doesn't cost anything extra?

Here's how to use breathing and affirmative phrasing as a crucial part of your life-changing, panic-reducing regimen:

1. Count slowly and silently as you inhale, and then exhale. Be sure to do the counting and phrasing in your head, instead of wasting oxygen on speaking out loud.

2. As you breathe, add empowering silent phrases: inhale on the silent phrase "I am"... exhale on the word "relaxed," and repeat for at least several minutes... until you feel calmer.

3. After you've mastered the "I am... relaxed" phrasing, add simple variations to your routine with affirmative phrases that involve a key emotion. For example, you could benefit from saying to yourself: "I am... serene," "I am... confident," "I am... happy," "I am... stress-free."

[end of book excerpt]

Related to thinking about Trump and the kind of ideas he comes up with to terrorize an entire population with pictures of what he'll do next, I'm reminded of the popularity of horror films.

I feel that one of the reasons horror movies are so popular is that it is actually such a release of tension to get wound up to the point of sheer terror — and then get to the end of the film, heave a massive sigh of relief, calm your racing heart, and go out for a pizza. In comparison with what happened to the characters in the story, your own life's ups and downs suddenly appear much more manageable.

The key to scaring ourselves silly in order to feel a sense of relief that things aren't so bad after all, is to not linger on the frightening images long enough to build up worry that maybe they could happen or would happen. Drop that image, move on to something fun and pleasant.

I don't advocate horror movies and books that have a really strong level of thrill that you absorb all that fear, but since people do watch and read these stories by the millions, I wanted to take a moment to acknowledge that, and offer a warning: keep track of how you are feeling, and if you're not bouncing back to cheerfulness after these kinds of thrillers, stop watching and reading them.

I used to read a lot of espionage thrillers and action adventure stories but then I realized a few years ago that I was so full of tension while reading, I was undoing the calmness I had so carefully cultivated during meditation. I still enjoy a good mystery, but I choose the cozier variety rather than the more violent ones that can be very disturbing as they stimulate thoughts of anger, fear, and helplessness.

Always remember that we think in pictures and we create what we are emotionally imagining. Be careful with your mind power and don't bring disaster into your life inadvertently by thinking scary thoughts, whether those thoughts are about imagining someone in your family getting into an accident, or worries about the Trump presidency.

Learning to control our thoughts opens up access to truly manifesting what we desire instead of being the hapless victims of an angry narcissist.

#12 Narcissism Unmasked

Inauguration Countdown Day 12—Narcissism Unmasked

It's ironic that so many millions of Americans voted for a man who has made it clear he doesn't care about anyone but himself. Do they really believe he will make their lives better? I grew up in a family where one parent was a Democrat and the other was a Republican, but I can tell you that neither would have ever considered voting for an extreme narcissist like Trump.

I believe it is important to understand the mental processes of narcissism, because this personality "type" evokes either adulation or revulsion, and sometimes both in the same person. I know, because I spent many years of my life tied up in knots trying to please the whims and demands of narcissistic men in my relationships.

You may share the assumption I once had, long ago, before daily experience shattered my illusion, that a narcissist is simply a guy who is a bit vain, kind of conceited, what you might call a clothes horse. He loves to dress up, and be admired. He thrives on being the center of attention. In a child, we call it being a show-off, but by the time a full-blown narcissist is swaggering around the business world, he's got his act down pat. He knows how to push buttons, and senses when he needs to back off, smooth things over with flattery or claim that he was only kidding (Hey, can't you take a joke?).

At its heart, the behavior of a narcissist means controlling and manipulating others to get his way all the time. And when he feels thwarted, to erupt in rage and thus ease his inner turmoil.

A few traits common to the classic narcissist are: erratic behavior, shrewd, unreliable, predatory, disdainful, cunning, bigoted, offensive, and a formidable foe.

You can find many narcissists in the bloodied pages of history, stomping their way across nations and demanding fealty and gold.

However, in order to get what he wants, the most adept narcissists learn they have to play by our rules at least part of the time. This means showering people with compliments, particularly in public or in front of others whose esteem he is cultivating.

An example would be at a dinner party where the narcissist wants to impress his guests with the façade of a happy marriage. He'll glowingly praise his wife—then, after the guests have gone and are safely out of earshot, he'll lambast her for embarrassing him, being cold to the guests or not serving the food the way he told her to, or any number of invented reasons for blowing up at her. Why? It is his habitual, practiced way of releasing the tension which was building up inside all evening as he fretted that the guests might judge him unfavorably and thus withhold their esteem of him.

In order to get the love and friendships he craves, the narcissist is fully capable of being Mr. Dream Man, Mr. Nice Guy, Mr. Fantastic Boss…at least while it is necessary to do so. Then, once you've taken the bait, it does indeed turn out to be a bait-and-switch swindle.

The term bait-and-switch popularly describes an offer too good to be true, where the advertisement promises a fabulous item for sale, but when you get there, the skilled salesperson switches the offer and pushes you to buy a higher priced item, claiming they are sold out of the advertised merchandise.

In the narcissist's game, bait-and-switch is a bit different. He lures you in with friendliness, with being such a great guy you can hardly believe your luck in meeting him. Perhaps the relationship is for business instead of a romantic relationship. That's okay, the narcissist readily adapts like a chameleon when he scents admiration in the air.

Praise and attention are catnip to the narcissist: he can't get enough, and panics when adoration is in short supply. In those moments, you can count on the narcissist to agree to trips you want to take, to authorize that new piece of office equipment, or even give you a raise.

The "switch" comes about when the narcissist has tested you enough by jabs of sarcasm which you overlooked or readily forgave. After all, if you are basically an amiable person who wants everyone to get along, it didn't seem bad enough to speak up and say "Please don't talk to me that way." You didn't want to make a big deal over his being out of sorts, you didn't want to rock the boat, you know he's under a lot of stress so it's easier to go along with his denial and reminder yourself it's no big deal to excuse his behavior.

You pass his frequent tests when you avoid confronting him or setting limits. When you go along with his program, and begin your part of the game which is to carefully watch him and try to head off his anger before he erupts in a full-blown rage.

Now he feels a great sense of joy inside: he can count on you to stay! He doesn't have to be nice unless others are around, or unless he wants something. It takes a lot of energy for the narcissist to be generous with genuine affection, so he doesn't bother unless he sees the advantage to be gained.

So, here's the switch: that sting of cruelty, the pain of physical, emotional and verbal abuse, the bruises from being someone's verbal punching bag.

And yet, millions of people manage to cope with a narcissist in their life and keep on hoping for change, or taking any little sign of niceness that he has seen the error of his ways and is on the way toward treating you better. That "honeymoon" phase in the narcissist's cycle is when he is feeling a release of his tension and is more relaxed. But the tension quickly builds because the narcissist takes everything (literally <u>everything</u>) personally, and so the cycle continues, endlessly. He has no motivation for personal growth or development, because he is the center of his world and it is running smoothly.

Inconsistencies of thought are rampant in the minds of a narcissist. He likes to believe the image of himself as a nice guy, someone admired and even loved by many. When he rages, it feels good to get rid of that inner tension, and yet since that kind of behavior is not consistent with Mr. Nice Guy, he has to simply pretend it didn't happen.

When you get adept at watching a narcissist's behavior and noticing the signs of building tension, you can learn to back away and spare yourself the explosion fallout as much as possible, and you can also figure out when to approach to have a more rational conversation with him. When would that be? I'm sure you can guess that it is when he is playing his favorite role, that of benevolent and beloved king.

#11 Fifty Shades of Dread

Inauguration Countdown Day 11—Fifty Shades of Dread

Imagine you've just been handed an assignment to write down fifty things you dread about Donald Trump's presidency. At first you might be taken aback. Fifty? That's a lot of different things. But once you started the list, your fingers would be flying over the keyboard or pad of paper, as your mind brought to the forefront of your memory words he has spoken, bigoted threats he has made, derogatory and misogynist comments, remarks about bombing other countries, deporting people whose skin color and religion he doesn't like, and the list goes on.

It would be bad enough if Trump "merely" had a nasty temper, but his agenda truly is horrific the more you read and learn about it. I'll leave it up to you how much you want to be informed. I feel we must strike a healthy balance between learning what Trump and his administration intend to do--particularly those things they try to sneak in and get approval for by hiding it within other more benign issues—and overloading ourselves with fear and stress by being news junkies.

Worry never accomplishes anything good, and dread just keeps us in a helpless state (right where he wants us).

There are sites that provide email updates along with petitions to sign and share, and fact-checkable summaries of what a given issue is and the qualifications of the people involved.

For example, CredoAction.com (a network of 4 million activists) makes it very easy to find out the background of people Trump puts forth for approval. It's eye-opening to read their CVs and see the kind of people they are and what their business history and prior association with Trump has been.

How people treat their employees is very revealing of how they intend to treat the rest of the country.

Not surprisingly, Trump's nominees have something in common: they are more interested in feathering their own nests and enjoying power over other people than in creating progress and improving the quality of life for everyone in America.

The law of attraction tells us that what we focus on will increase. So I'd like you to take that "Fifty shades of dread" list and delete or tear it up. Otherwise, the more we pay attention to the things we dread and want to run from, the more powerful they become, and the more prevalent in our experience.

A sense of dread can be an important manifestation tool because it brings our attention to an issue or situation we would like to change. And then, once we have our focus, we can release the energy from the "dread state" and use it to empower ourselves for progressive action.

I think you'll enjoy the following true story about a woman who confronted a situation she had been in dread of for years, due to a superstition no doubt taught to her by a well-meaning or unaware parent when she was a small girl.

From *The Game of Life* by Florence Scovel Shinn:

"I have a friend who said nothing could induce her to walk under a ladder. I said, 'If you are afraid, you are giving in to a belief in two powers, Good and Evil, instead of one. As God is absolute, there can be no opposing power, unless man makes the false of evil for himself. To show you believe in only One Power, God, and that there is no power or reality in evil, walk under the next ladder you see.'

"Soon after, she went to her bank. She wished to open her box in the safe-deposit vault, and there stood a ladder on her pathway. It was impossible to reach the box without passing under the ladder. She quailed with fear and turned back. She could not face the lion on her pathway. However, when she reached the street, my words rang in her ears and she decided to return and walk under it. It was a big moment in her life, for ladders had held her in bondage for years. She retraced her steps to the vault, and the ladder was no longer there! This so often happens! If one is willing to do a thing he is afraid to do, he does not have to.

"It is the law of nonresistance, which is so little understood.

"Someone has said that courage contains genius and magic. Face a situation fearlessly, and there is no situation to face; it falls away of its own weight.

"The explanation is that fear attracted the ladder on the woman's pathway, and fearlessness removed it."

By the way, *The Game of Life* ebook is one of the gifts I'm making available for readers of *America's New Breed of Freedom Fighters*.

[That gift link is evelynbrooks.com/readers-freedom-fighters]

We can all learn from the story about the ladder, and it is a helpful image to keep in mind when you realize you are feeling in dread of a situation ahead of you. Assuming the situation that scares you or evokes fear is something that will empower you in the confronting of

260

it, think of ways you can walk up to a "ladder" and then walk boldly under it—to find freedom on the other side.

Affirm: I will walk up to that situation and do the thing that terrifies me.

#10 Deliver Us from Evil

Inauguration Countdown Day 10—Deliver Us from Evil

Have you ever walked into a room and sensed evil? Have you picked up on the fact a friend is upset even though they tell you earnestly that they are perfectly fine and nothing is the matter? Have you had a bad feeling about something, gone ahead anyway, and regretted not following your initial hunch?

Our early training has drilled us in the habits of logic, but our intuition persists in picking up vibrational clues about the world around us and the people we interact with or come in to contact with through our amazing communication system of broadcasts and telephones and internet videos and social media.

We sense when someone is lying. But then what? If you've been taught to disregard your own inner dialogue, you dismiss that feeling and believe the words the person is saying instead.

In thinking about Mr. Trump, I keep coming back to the command to God, "deliver us from evil" that is in The Lord's Prayer beloved by many millions of people. It is sometimes called the perfect prayer, and metaphysically speaking that is true, regardless of what your religion or lack of religious beliefs.

The prayer is a series of demands and praise, in the perfect balance. It establishes our relationship with the Law (Lord) of the Universe, and invokes the blessings we desire to lead a happier and healthier life.

When we say "deliver us from evil"—there's an implication that we are being sent elsewhere, away from it. Right? Think about ordering a delivery from your favorite restaurant. You mull over what to get, place the order, and sooner or later it arrives. You got a delivery from… and it was delivered to…

In asking to be delivered from evil, where are we asking to be delivered to? I think it is a matter of looking at opposites and realizing if we want to move away from evil or sin, which is the lack of love, then we must logically intend to move towards more love.

Evil and sin are both the absence of love. There is no such entity as the devil or evil, no matter what we've been taught by churches and temples with a goal of frightening us into behaving.

If there really was a force of nature called evil, then there could be no love, because the two would cancel each other out.

Toxic behavior is rampant in our culture, promoted by rudeness on popular TV shows, biting sarcasm that gets applause and a laugh track, and the growing prevalence in social media to say whatever one feels like saying in the moment and then tap "send" or "post" without filtering for common courtesy. It's as if someone shouted "no holds barred" and the melee began. People who don't have a photo on their profile seem to really go wild, but maybe that's just my perception that they feel the safety of anonymity means they can lambast anyone and everyone.

Our words truly are boomerangs—when someone transmits messages of hate, then acts of hate come hurling right back to land at their own feet. Anything that is on the same vibrational frequency as hate will return as a "reply to sender." That means poor health, sudden problems at work, unexpected car or house repairs, a financial gut clench, a relationship disaster seemingly out of the blue. But it is never out of the blue, it is always something we have attracted into our experience by virtue of our emotional thoughts and hidden beliefs.

Trump's supporters, primarily in the "Red States" seem to be operating under mass hypnosis, believing in his promises to make America "great again"—meaning, get rid of anyone who is not a white Christian.

They want to bring back the homogenized white milk days, and disallow any chocolate.

They want to bring back the so-called good old days when people of color were barred from restaurants, restrooms and public transportation (other than seating in the back) and many other rights granted to whites. There is ample information online about the days of segregation that you can read about if desired.

I was a child in segregated Texas way back when, and somehow I managed to grow up and out of that mindset and supported Civil Rights when all that came along while I was still young. My mother enjoyed records from Broadway musicals, and I learned all the words to many different songs. One that I feel applies in a deep sense to what our country is going through right now is this one, from the musical *South Pacific* by Rodgers and Hammerstein.

"You've Got to Be Taught"

You've got to be taught
To hate and fear
You've got to be taught
From year to year
It's got to be drummed
In your dear little ear
You've got to be carefully taught
You've got to be taught

To be afraid
Of people whose eyes
Are oddly made
And people whose skin
Is a different shade

Whatever we have been taught, we can make a decision to change our belief to something of a higher nature. But first we must become aware of what those beliefs are! When we have hidden beliefs, we walk around on auto-pilot, not questioning our opinion of others.

One thing that Trump's election is good for is that it has brought greater awareness to the issues of human rights in our own country. Progressive thinkers—meaning all people who want to grow and enjoy life, regardless of political party—are speaking up and demanding to be heard.

People who probably thought everything was going along fine in our country, maybe not perfect, but better than elsewhere, got a rude awakening and are now responding to demonstrate what they want.

I think what we consider "evil" are people who have no principles, no moral compass, and yet who brag and scream that they are the ones who have been saved and the rest of us are damned for all eternity. From my perspective, it's sad to see that we cannot free them from their narrow perceptions and lack of awareness, because they don't see they are trapped in a small way of thinking. People who lead small lives often are not interested in growing: it's too scary to break out of their generational rut and risk offending family and friends.

But the rest of us, the progressives, the people who are eager to create more joy and love in the world, we can sing out and say: *Deliver us from evil—let us turn our attention and vibrational force of love toward expansion and a better life for all Americans.*

#9 Magnetize Gratitude

Inauguration Countdown Day 9—Magnetize Gratitude

We have much to be thankful for. Turn your thoughts away from thinking about Donald Trump and all his ranting and raving, and the bigots and racists he's nominating for positions of great power in our country. Do what you can to make your voice heard to your people in Congress, sign petitions, let your opinion be known.

But…don't get so focused on pushing against Trump and his cronies that you stir up a resonance within yourself that is so fear-based you are putting yourself at risk for dis-ease and all the curses of the world that come in response to deeply negative thinking. You don't want to be on Trump's wavelength for more than a couple of seconds! Less, if possible.

Focus on all the things you intend to do to help our country progress, with liberty and justice for all.

The feeling to evoke in ourselves is one of appreciation for all the good that we already have. Look around your life and notice how much you have to be grateful for, starting with the basic material things like food, clothing and shelter, and going on to your relationships, your ability to learn and grow and make choices about your lifestyle that many people in the world don't have access to.

Think about things that make you feel happy no matter what, such as a garden in bloom, a cup of tea on a chilly day, playing with your pet, children or grandchildren, reading a good book. That welling up of gratitude for the small gifts of life is the feeling of appreciation. When we nurture appreciation, the universe sends us – all of us— more experiences to be grateful for. Gratitude in advance of the results we want actually brings us those results faster.

Dr. Joseph Murphy recounts the story of one of his clients, a young engineer who was upset about the religious beliefs he'd been raised with. Murphy explained to him that "irritation causes oysters to give birth to pearls."

You may have had a similar experience at least once in your life, and more likely a dozen or more times, when a person or situation was so annoying or troublesome that you ended up using your feelings to propel you into action to change things. Perhaps you got fed up with your boss, and ended up striking out on a new career that brings much more satisfaction than you could ever have achieved at the safe old job.

Murphy reports that the engineer began studying the world's religions and discovered the inner meaning of parables and fables, going on to find success by applying the techniques he learned. Dr. Murphy sums up the anecdote by pointing out to us, "If you are supremely happy along religious, political and social lines, you don't seek truth. It is because certain things went wrong that you sought a greater answer and a way out. Then your subjective self-opened a new door for you, and a new light or spiritual awareness was born. When you look back upon the irritation or the problem, you should be grateful and thankful for the challenge, and praise and bless the experience."

Donald Trump's irritation factor is off the charts. But let's think about all those "pearls" we can create in spite of Trump, spurred on by that very irritation so that we bring forth wondrous things in the world that are as precious as pearls.

Instead of viewing Trump through the lens of fear and anger, let's look at him in a more detached way—remove all that emotion he manipulated and stirred up in the hearts of countless millions—and see him as a catalyst.

Merriam-Webster dictionary defines catalyst in this way:

266

1. a substance that enables a chemical reaction to proceed at a usually faster rate or under different conditions (as at a lower temperature) than otherwise possible;

2. an agent that provokes or speeds significant change or action

In chemistry, a catalyst is a substance that sparks an energy change, but by itself is nothing.

That's Trump to a "T"—nothing.

It's what we do with this catalyst (Trump's election) that is going to count.

Let's not waste this opportunity to create huge, wonderful change across our country, and by the ripple effect, around the world.

When we magnetize gratitude to ourselves, it means we find something good everywhere we look, and when necessary we "turn the other cheek" so we are looking in the opposite direction from a sight that was bringing up feelings of fear and uneasiness.

Every good thought you think, every good word you speak, every good emotion you feel, and every act of kindness you perform, is lifting the frequency of your being to new heights. And as you begin to raise your frequency, a new life and a new world will reveal themselves to you. You will emit positive forces of energy across planet Earth that will reach every single living thing on it.

You will lift yourself, and as you lift yourself, you lift the entire world.

When you magnetize gratitude to yourself, it's like creating a magic carpet that rolls out in front of you every day, bringing joyful experiences, happy relationships, prosperity, and great health.

#8 Profiles in Courage

Inauguration Countdown Day 8—Profiles in Courage

When I was growing up and there was any situation that felt overwhelming, my mother's advice was always to "rise above it." I value that advice more now than I did in my younger years when I didn't really understand what she meant or what the process entailed.

Looking back, I realize I thought she meant I was supposed to pretend nothing bad was happening, that I was to be cool and unruffled. I got really good at insisting I was "fine" when I was anything but that. Growing up, I learned to be passive, compliant, easy-going, but also an easy target for abusers seeking their next pliable victim. I was someone you could count on to never show anger, to always offer words of peace. I was the harmonizer, the peace-keeper, the one who smoothed things over in one relationship after another in my effort to avoid conflict, which I viewed as very scary indeed.

But about twenty years ago, I realized nothing was going to change on the outside of my life if I didn't do something about the inside. As I steadily changed my thought habits, my actions changed too, and I moved beyond my auto-pilot behavior of being a doormat in toxic relationships with narcissistic men. I have a different point of view now, and with it comes the gift of being able to cast a kind glance over my past behavior and love that girl who hurt so much inside she didn't know how to speak up for herself.

I spent too many years of my life in thrall to angry men, and now that I no longer feel I have to do that to get along in life, I'm speaking up at this time of Donald Trump's election to the position of President of the United States. And I'm saying: we won't back down to bullies. Won't. Back. Down. To. Bullies.

Yes, it takes strength of your convictions to speak up, to step out of the familiar comfort zone of our daily lives where all of us are so busy with work, families, projects, that never-ending To Do list that dominates our schedules. But if we don't speak up now, if we don't act in favor of creating change, then we miss out on an incredible opportunity for personal growth as well as all the good we can bring to others through our service.

What would you like to do about Mr. Trump and the destruction he has envisioned for our health care, environment, education, labor, the minimum wage, equal pay for equal work, women's rights, human rights, foreign policy, immigration, and other issues near and dear to the hearts of progressives?

Go ahead and think for a moment about what you would like to do. Perhaps it is to start a blog, or host a Blog Talk Radio program where you interview people involved in the issues you care about the most. Maybe you feel inspired to volunteer with different groups whose funds are at risk from budget cuts, such as programs supporting the elderly or homebound.

When we allow ourselves to daydream and just think about what we'd like to do to help, ideas will bubble up inside you in response to your interest and your request for inspiration. When you find yourself drawn toward an idea, you'll feel a sense of joy and light-heartedness. Don't let yourself immediately leap into "How would I do that!" limiting questions that kill our dreams.

When you feel happy about a new idea, it means it's got your name on it, no matter how many others might be doing something similar. You'll bring your own personality and experience to any idea you have. And don't worry that it is too big and you aren't capable of doing it. You wouldn't feel exhilarated by the idea if it wasn't something you can carry out.

As Ralph Waldo Emerson pointed out, "Once you make a decision, the Universe conspires to make it happen." That was his observation as he delved into studying the metaphysical teachings of Jesus Christ, wanting to understand the mental techniques that were hidden in the parables and stories of the New Testament.

When I thought of writing this countdown blog, and the book whose launch it was leading up to, I knew it would be a lot of work in a condensed period of time—but I felt such joy in the ideas I couldn't possibly say no. As I opened myself to allow inspiration free rein, the ideas just kept coming. I let them flow through me and on out into the world, to help others relieve their stress over the election results, and to begin planning what our next steps can and should be.

Now, what about the amount of courage you think you'll need for that great idea you just had? A whole lot more than you've got right now? Guess what—you don't need courage at all. Courage is a label we put on other people's activities after the fact, as a way of praising what they have accomplished and recognizing that it took bravery to go against the odds or speak up despite scary opposition.

In 1955, when John F. Kennedy as a junior senator from Massachusetts, he wrote a book that became an instant classic, called "Profiles in Courage." If you haven't read it, I urge you to do so, as it makes great inspirational reading especially in this challenging time of Trump's election to POTUS.

A few years later, when he was President, Kennedy dealt diplomatically with the Cuban Missile Crisis, and averted nuclear war with Russia. In a speech after the crisis, President Kennedy said: "Let us not be blind to our differences—but let us also direct attention to our common interests and to the means by which those differences can be resolved. And if we cannot end our differences, at least we can help make the world safe for diversity. For, in the final analysis, our most common link is that we all inhabit this small planet. We all breathe the same air. We all cherish our children's future. And we are all mortal."

Those words are clearly applicable to the state of our emotionally divided country today. President Obama has given an indelible message to Democrats and Progressives: "Stand with me. Let's finish what we started."

We have created a lot of good in this country. Of course, it's not perfect, it's evolving. Let's prevent Trump from going the other direction to the white bread, white pasteurized milk fantasy land his supporters angrily demand.

Below is the official transcript from the White House of President Obama's farewell speech to the nation on January 10, 2017. I feel it is the perfect call to action for all of us to allow courage to flow in our veins and keep on working together despite the challenges we face after Trump's election.

President Obama's Farewell Address

THE PRESIDENT: Hello, Chicago! (Applause.) It's good to be home! (Applause.) Thank you, everybody. Thank you. (Applause.) Thank you so much. Thank you. (Applause.) All right, everybody sit down. (Applause.) We're on live TV here. I've got to move. (Applause.) You can tell that I'm a lame duck because nobody is following instructions. (Laughter.) Everybody have a seat. (Applause.)

My fellow Americans — (applause) — Michelle and I have been so touched by all the well wishes that we've received over the past few weeks. But tonight, it's my turn to say thanks. (Applause.)

Whether we have seen eye-to-eye or rarely agreed at all, my conversations with you, the American people, in living rooms and in schools, at farms, on factory floors, at diners and on distant military outposts — those conversations are what have kept me honest, and kept me inspired, and kept me going. And every day, I have learned from you. You made me a better President, and you made me a better man. (Applause.)

So, I first came to Chicago when I was in my early 20s. And I was still trying to figure out who I was, still searching for a purpose in my life. And it was a neighborhood not far from here where I began working with church groups in the shadows of closed steel mills. It was on these streets where I witnessed the power of faith, and the quiet dignity of working people in the face of struggle and loss.

AUDIENCE: Four more years! Four more years! Four more years!

THE PRESIDENT: I can't do that.

AUDIENCE: Four more years! Four more years! Four more years!

THE PRESIDENT: This [Chicago] is where I learned that change only happens when ordinary people get involved and they get engaged, and they come together to demand it.

After eight years as your President, I still believe that. And it's not just my belief. It's the beating heart of our American idea — our bold experiment in self-government. It's the conviction that we are all created equal, endowed by our Creator with certain unalienable rights, among them life, liberty, and the pursuit of happiness. It's the insistence that these rights, while self-evident, have never been self-executing; that We, the People, through the instrument of our democracy, can form a more perfect union.

What a radical idea. A great gift that our Founders gave to us: The freedom to chase our individual dreams through our sweat and toil and imagination, and the imperative to strive together, as well, to achieve a common good, a greater good.

272

For 240 years, our nation's call to citizenship has given work and purpose to each new generation. It's what led patriots to choose republic over tyranny, pioneers to trek west, slaves to brave that makeshift railroad to freedom. It's what pulled immigrants and refugees across oceans and the Rio Grande. (Applause.) It's what pushed women to reach for the ballot. It's what powered workers to organize. It's why GIs gave their lives at Omaha Beach and Iwo Jima, Iraq and Afghanistan. And why men and women from Selma to Stonewall were prepared to give theirs, as well. (Applause.)

So that's what we mean when we say America is exceptional — not that our nation has been flawless from the start, but that we have shown the capacity to change and make life better for those who follow. Yes, our progress has been uneven. The work of democracy has always been hard. It's always been contentious. Sometimes it's been bloody. For every two steps forward, it often feels we take one step back. But the long sweep of America has been defined by forward motion, a constant widening of our founding creed to embrace all and not just some. (Applause.)

If I had told you eight years ago that America would reverse a great recession, reboot our auto industry, and unleash the longest stretch of job creation in our history — (applause) — if I had told you that we would open up a new chapter with the Cuban people, shut down Iran's nuclear weapons program without firing a shot, take out the mastermind of 9/11 — (applause) — if I had told you that we would win marriage equality, and secure the right to health insurance for another 20 million of our fellow citizens — (applause) — if I had told you all that, you might have said our sights were set a little too high. But that's what we did. (Applause.) That's what you did.

You were the change. You answered people's hopes, and because of you, by almost every measure, America is a better, stronger place than it was when we started. (Applause.)

273

In 10 days, the world will witness a hallmark of our democracy.

AUDIENCE: Nooo —

THE PRESIDENT: No, no, no, no, no — the peaceful transfer of power from one freely elected President to the next. (Applause.) I committed to President-elect Trump that my administration would ensure the smoothest possible transition, just as President Bush did for me. (Applause.) Because it's up to all of us to make sure our government can help us meet the many challenges we still face.

We have what we need to do so. We have everything we need to meet those challenges. After all, we remain the wealthiest, most powerful, and most respected nation on Earth. Our youth, our drive, our diversity and openness, our boundless capacity for risk and reinvention means that the future should be ours. But that potential will only be realized if our democracy works. Only if our politics better reflects the decency of our people. (Applause.) Only if all of us, regardless of party affiliation or particular interests, help restore the sense of common purpose that we so badly need right now.

That's what I want to focus on tonight: The state of our democracy. Understand, democracy does not require uniformity. Our founders argued. They quarreled. Eventually they compromised. They expected us to do the same. But they knew that democracy does require a basic sense of solidarity — the idea that for all our outward differences, we're all in this together; that we rise or fall as one. (Applause.)

There have been moments throughout our history that threatens that solidarity. And the beginning of this century has been one of those times. A shrinking world, growing inequality; demographic change and the specter of terrorism — these forces haven't just tested our security and our prosperity, but are testing our democracy, as well. And how we meet these challenges to our democracy will determine

274

our ability to educate our kids, and create good jobs, and protect our homeland. In other words, it will determine our future.

To begin with, our democracy won't work without a sense that everyone has economic opportunity. And the good news is that today the economy is growing again. Wages, incomes, home values, and retirement accounts are all rising again. Poverty is falling again. (Applause.)

The wealthy are paying a fairer share of taxes even as the stock market shatters records. The unemployment rate is near a 10-year low. The uninsured rate has never, ever been lower. (Applause.) Health care costs are rising at the slowest rate in 50 years. And I've said and I mean it — if anyone can put together a plan that is demonstrably better than the improvements we've made to our health care system and that covers as many people at less cost, I will publicly support it. (Applause.)

Because that, after all, is why we serve. Not to score points or take credit, but to make people's lives better. (Applause.)

But for all the real progress that we've made, we know it's not enough. Our economy doesn't work as well or grow as fast when a few prosper at the expense of a growing middle class and ladders for folks who want to get into the middle class. (Applause.) That's the economic argument. But stark inequality is also corrosive to our democratic ideal. While the top one percent has amassed a bigger share of wealth and income, too many families, in inner cities and in rural counties, have been left behind — the laid-off factory worker; the waitress or health care worker who's just barely getting by and struggling to pay the bills — convinced that the game is fixed against them, that their government only serves the interests of the powerful — that's a recipe for more cynicism and polarization in our politics.

But there are no quick fixes to this long-term trend. I agree, our trade should be fair and not just free. But the next wave of economic dislocations won't come from overseas. It will come from the relentless pace of automation that makes a lot of good, middle-class jobs obsolete.

And so we're going to have to forge a new social compact to guarantee all our kids the education they need — (applause) — to give workers the power to unionize for better wages; to update the social safety net to reflect the way we live now, and make more reforms to the tax code so corporations and individuals who reap the most from this new economy don't avoid their obligations to the country that's made their very success possible. (Applause.)

We can argue about how to best achieve these goals. But we can't be complacent about the goals themselves. For if we don't create opportunity for all people, the disaffection and division that has stalled our progress will only sharpen in years to come.

There's a second threat to our democracy — and this one is as old as our nation itself. After my election, there was talk of a post-racial America. And such a vision, however well-intended, was never realistic. Race remains a potent and often divisive force in our society. Now, I've lived long enough to know that race relations are better than they were 10, or 20, or 30 years ago, no matter what some folks say. (Applause.) You can see it not just in statistics, you see it in the attitudes of young Americans across the political spectrum.

But we're not where we need to be. And all of us have more work to do. (Applause.) If every economic issue is framed as a struggle between a hardworking white middle class and an undeserving minority, then workers of all shades are going to be left fighting for scraps while the wealthy withdraw further into their private enclaves. (Applause.) If we're unwilling to invest in the children of immigrants, just because they don't look like us, we will diminish the prospects of our own children — because those brown kids will represent a larger and larger share of America's workforce. (Applause.) And we have shown that our economy doesn't have to be a zero-sum game. Last year, incomes rose for all races, all age groups, for men and for women.

So, if we're going to be serious about race going forward, we need to uphold laws against discrimination — in hiring, and in housing, and in education, and in the criminal justice system. (Applause.) That is what our Constitution and our highest ideals require. (Applause.)

But laws alone won't be enough. Hearts must change. It won't change overnight. Social attitudes oftentimes take generations to change. But if our democracy is to work in this increasingly diverse nation, then each one of us need to try to heed the advice of a great character in American fiction — Atticus Finch — (applause) — who said "You never really understand a person until you consider things from his point of view...until you climb into his skin and walk around in it."

For blacks and other minority groups, it means tying our own very real struggles for justice to the challenges that a lot of people in this country face — not only the refugee, or the immigrant, or the rural poor, or the transgender American, but also the middle-aged white guy who, from the outside, may seem like he's got advantages, but has seen his world upended by economic and cultural and technological change. We have to pay attention, and listen. (Applause.)

For white Americans, it means acknowledging that the effects of slavery and Jim Crow didn't suddenly vanish in the '60s — (applause) — that when minority groups voice discontent, they're not just engaging in reverse racism or practicing political correctness. When they wage peaceful protest, they're not demanding special treatment but the equal treatment that our Founders promised. (Applause.)

For native-born Americans, it means reminding ourselves that the stereotypes about immigrants today were said, almost word for word, about the Irish, and Italians, and Poles — who it was said we're going to destroy the fundamental character of America. And as it turned out, America wasn't weakened by the presence of these newcomers; these newcomers embraced this nation's creed, and this nation was strengthened. (Applause.)

So regardless of the station that we occupy, we all have to try harder. We all have to start with the premise that each of our fellow citizens loves this country just as much as we do; that they value hard work and family just like we do; that their children are just as curious and hopeful and worthy of love as our own. (Applause.)

And that's not easy to do. For too many of us, it's become safer to retreat into our own bubbles, whether in our neighborhoods or on college campuses, or places of worship, or especially our social media feeds, surrounded by people who look like us and share the same political outlook and never challenge our assumptions. The rise of naked partisanship, and increasing economic and regional stratification, the splintering of our media into a channel for every taste — all this makes this great sorting seem natural, even inevitable. And increasingly, we become so secure in our bubbles that we start accepting only information, whether it's true or not, that fits our opinions, instead of basing our opinions on the evidence that is out there. (Applause.)

And this trend represents a third threat to our democracy. But politics is a battle of ideas. That's how our democracy was designed. In the course of a healthy debate, we prioritize different goals, and the different means of reaching them. But without some common baseline of facts, without a willingness to admit new information, and concede that your opponent might be making a fair point, and that science and reason matter — (applause) — then we're going to keep talking past each other, and we'll make common ground and compromise impossible. (Applause.)

And isn't that part of what so often makes politics dispiriting? How can elected officials rage about deficits when we propose to spend money on preschool for kids, but not when we're cutting taxes for corporations? (Applause.) How do we excuse ethical lapses in our own party, but pounce when the other party does the same thing? It's not just dishonest, this selective sorting of the facts; it's self-defeating. Because, as my mother used to tell me, reality has a way of catching up with you. (Applause.)

Take the challenge of climate change. In just eight years, we've halved our dependence on foreign oil; we've doubled our renewable energy; we've led the world to an agreement that has the promise to save this planet. (Applause.) But without bolder action, our children won't have time to debate the existence of climate change. They'll be busy dealing with its effects: more environmental disasters, more economic disruptions, waves of climate refugees seeking sanctuary.

Now, we can and should argue about the best approach to solve the problem. But to simply deny the problem not only betrays future generations, it betrays the essential spirit of this country — the essential spirit of innovation and practical problem-solving that guided our Founders. (Applause.)

It is that spirit, born of the Enlightenment, that made us an economic powerhouse — the spirit that took flight at Kitty Hawk and Cape Canaveral; the spirit that cures disease and put a computer in every pocket.

It's that spirit — a faith in reason, and enterprise, and the primacy of right over might — that allowed us to resist the lure of fascism and tyranny during the Great Depression; that allowed us to build a post-World War II order with other democracies, an order based not just on military power or national affiliations but built on principles — the rule of law, human rights, freedom of religion, and speech, and assembly, and an independent press. (Applause.)

That order is now being challenged — first by violent fanatics who claim to speak for Islam; more recently by autocrats in foreign capitals who see free markets and open democracies and and civil society itself as a threat to their power. The peril each poses to our democracy is more far-reaching than a car bomb or a missile. It represents the fear of change; the fear of people who look or speak or pray differently; a contempt for the rule of law that holds leaders accountable; an intolerance of dissent and free thought; a belief that the sword or the gun or the bomb or the propaganda machine is the ultimate arbiter of what's true and what's right.

Because of the extraordinary courage of our men and women in uniform, because of our intelligence officers, and law enforcement, and diplomats who support our troops — (applause) — no foreign terrorist organization has successfully planned and executed an attack on our homeland these past eight years. (Applause.) And although Boston and Orlando and San Bernardino and Fort Hood remind us of how dangerous radicalization can be, our law enforcement agencies are more effective and vigilant than ever. We have taken out tens of thousands of terrorists — including bin Laden. (Applause.) The global coalition we're leading against ISIL has taken out their leaders, and taken away about half their territory. ISIL will be destroyed, and no one who threatens America will ever be safe. (Applause.)

And to all who serve or have served, it has been the honor of my lifetime to be your Commander-in-Chief. And we all owe you a deep debt of gratitude. (Applause.)

But protecting our way of life, that's not just the job of our military. Democracy can buckle when we give in to fear. So, just as we, as citizens, must remain vigilant against external aggression, we must guard against a weakening of the values that make us who we are. (Applause.)

And that's why, for the past eight years, I've worked to put the fight against terrorism on a firmer legal footing. That's why we've ended torture, worked to close Gitmo, reformed our laws governing surveillance to protect privacy and civil liberties. (Applause.) That's why I reject discrimination against Muslim Americans, who are just as patriotic as we are. (Applause.)

That's why we cannot withdraw from big global fights — to expand democracy, and human rights, and women's rights, and LGBT rights. No matter how imperfect our efforts, no matter how expedient ignoring such values may seem, that's part of defending America. For the fight against extremism and intolerance and sectarianism and chauvinism are of a piece with the fight against authoritarianism and nationalist aggression. If the scope of freedom and respect for the rule of law shrinks around the world, the likelihood of war within and between nations increases, and our own freedoms will eventually be threatened.

So, let's be vigilant, but not afraid. (Applause.) ISIL will try to kill innocent people. But they cannot defeat America unless we betray our Constitution and our principles in the fight. (Applause.) Rivals like Russia or China cannot match our influence around the world — unless we give up what we stand for — (applause) — and turn ourselves into just another big country that bullies smaller neighbors.

Which brings me to my final point: Our democracy is threatened whenever we take it for granted. (Applause.) All of us, regardless of party, should be throwing ourselves into the task of rebuilding our democratic institutions. (Applause.) When voting rates in America are some of the lowest among advanced democracies, we should be making it easier, not harder, to vote. (Applause.) When trust in our institutions is low, we should reduce the corrosive influence of money in our politics, and insist on the principles of transparency and ethics in public service. (Applause.) When Congress is dysfunctional, we should draw our congressional districts to encourage politicians to cater to common sense and not rigid extremes. (Applause.)

But remember, none of this happens on its own. All of this depends on our participation; on each of us accepting the responsibility of citizenship, regardless of which way the pendulum of power happens to be swinging.

Our Constitution is a remarkable, beautiful gift. But it's really just a piece of parchment. It has no power on its own. We, the people, give it power. (Applause.) We, the people, give it meaning. With our participation, and with the choices that we make, and the alliances that we forge. (Applause.) Whether or not we stand up for our freedoms. Whether or not we respect and enforce the rule of law. That's up to us. America is no fragile thing. But the gains of our long journey to freedom are not assured.

In his own farewell address, George Washington wrote that self-government is the underpinning of our safety, prosperity, and liberty, but "from different causes and from different quarters much pains will be taken...to weaken in your minds the conviction of this truth." And so, we have to preserve this truth with "jealous anxiety;" that we should reject "the first dawning of every attempt to alienate any portion of our country from the rest or to enfeeble the sacred ties" that make us one. (Applause.)

America, we weaken those ties when we allow our political dialogue to become so corrosive that people of good character aren't even willing to enter into public service; so coarse with rancor that Americans with whom we disagree are seen not just as misguided but as malevolent. We weaken those ties when we define some of us as more American than others; when we write off the whole system as inevitably corrupt, and when we sit back and blame the leaders we elect without examining our own role in electing them. (Applause.)

It falls to each of us to be those anxious, jealous guardians of our democracy; to embrace the joyous task we've been given to continually try to improve this great nation of ours. Because for all our outward differences, we, in fact, all share the same proud title, the most important office in a democracy: Citizen. (Applause.) Citizen.

So, you see, that's what our democracy demands. It needs you. Not just when there's an election, not just when your own narrow interest is at stake, but over the full span of a lifetime. If you're tired of arguing with strangers on the Internet, try talking with one of them in real life. (Applause.) If something needs fixing, then lace up your shoes and do some organizing. (Applause.) If you're disappointed by your elected officials, grab a clipboard, get some signatures, and run for office yourself. (Applause.) Show up. Dive in. Stay at it.

Sometimes you'll win. Sometimes you'll lose. Presuming a reservoir of goodness in other people, that can be a risk, and there will be times when the process will disappoint you. But for those of us fortunate enough to have been a part of this work, and to see it up close, let me tell you, it can energize and inspire. And more often than not, your faith in America — and in Americans — will be confirmed. (Applause.)

Mine sure has been. Over the course of these eight years, I've seen the hopeful faces of young graduates and our newest military officers. I have mourned with grieving families searching for answers, and found grace in a Charleston church. I've seen our scientists help a paralyzed man regain his sense of touch. I've seen wounded warriors who at points were given up for dead walk again. I've seen our doctors and volunteers rebuild after earthquakes and stop pandemics in their tracks. I've seen the youngest of children remind us through their actions and through their generosity of our obligations to care for refugees, or work for peace, and, above all, to look out for each other. (Applause.)

So that faith that I placed all those years ago, not far from here, in the power of ordinary Americans to bring about change — that faith has been rewarded in ways I could not have possibly imagined. And I hope your faith has, too. Some of you here tonight or watching at home, you were there with us in 2004, in 2008, 2012 — (applause) — maybe you still can't believe we pulled this whole thing off. Let me tell you, you're not the only ones. (Laughter.)

Michelle — (applause) — Michelle LaVaughn Robinson, girl of the South Side — (applause) — for the past 25 years, you have not only been my wife and mother of my children, you have been my best friend. (Applause.) You took on a role you didn't ask for and you made it your own, with grace and with grit and with style and good humor. (Applause.) You made the White House a place that belongs to everybody. (Applause.) And the new generation sets its sights higher because it has you as a role model. (Applause.) So, you have made me proud. And you have made the country proud. (Applause.)

Malia and Sasha, under the strangest of circumstances, you have become two amazing young women. You are smart and you are beautiful, but more importantly, you are kind and you are thoughtful and you are full of passion. (Applause.) You wore the burden of years in the spotlight so easily. Of all that I've done in my life, I am most proud to be your dad. (Applause.)

To Joe Biden — (applause) — the scrappy kid from Scranton who became Delaware's favorite son — you were the first decision I made as a nominee, and it was the best. (Applause.) Not just because you have been a great Vice President, but because in the bargain, I gained a brother. And we love you and Jill like family, and your friendship has been one of the great joys of our lives. (Applause.)

To my remarkable staff: For eight years — and for some of you, a whole lot more — I have drawn from your energy, and every day I tried to reflect back what you displayed — heart, and character, and idealism. I've watched you grow up, get married, have kids, start incredible new journeys of your own. Even when times got tough and frustrating, you never let Washington get the better of you. You guarded against cynicism. And the only thing that makes me prouder than all the good that we've done is the thought of all the amazing things that you're going to achieve from here. (Applause.)

And to all of you out there — every organizer who moved to an unfamiliar town, every kind family who welcomed them in, every volunteer who knocked on doors, every young person who cast a ballot for the first time, every American who lived and breathed the hard work of change — you are the best supporters and organizers anybody could ever hope for, and I will be forever grateful. (Applause.) Because you did change the world. (Applause.) You did.

And that's why I leave this stage tonight even more optimistic about this country than when we started. Because I know our work has not only helped so many Americans, it has inspired so many Americans — especially so many young people out there — to believe that you can make a difference — (applause) — to hitch your wagon to something bigger than yourselves.

Let me tell you, this generation coming up — unselfish, altruistic, creative, patriotic — I've seen you in every corner of the country. You believe in a fair, and just, and inclusive America. (Applause.) You know that constant change has been America's hallmark; that it's not something to fear but something to embrace. You are willing to carry this hard work of democracy forward. You'll soon outnumber all of us, and I believe as a result the future is in good hands. (Applause.)

285

My fellow Americans, it has been the honor of my life to serve you. (Applause.) I won't stop. In fact, I will be right there with you, as a citizen, for all my remaining days. But for now, whether you are young or whether you're young at heart, I do have one final ask of you as your President — the same thing I asked when you took a chance on me eight years ago. I'm asking you to believe. Not in my ability to bring about change — but in yours.

I am asking you to hold fast to that faith written into our founding documents; that idea whispered by slaves and abolitionists; that spirit sung by immigrants and homesteaders and those who marched for justice; that creed reaffirmed by those who planted flags from foreign battlefields to the surface of the moon; a creed at the core of every American whose story is not yet written: Yes, we can. (Applause.)

Yes, we did. Yes, we can. (Applause.)

Thank you. God bless you. May God continue to bless the United States of America. (Applause.)

Thank you, Mr. President, for your years of service and inspiration. My response to his farewell speech: Together, we can continue to make a beautiful difference in our country, even with Mr. Trump in the White House.

#7 What You Can Do

Inauguration Countdown Day 7—What You Can Do

On January 20, 1961, the first Catholic President of the United States took office. In his Inaugural Address, John F. Kennedy shared his vision for our country and the world we share with billions of other people. His speech included these memorable words:

"And so, my fellow Americans: ask not what your country can do for you — ask what you can do for your country.

"My fellow citizens of the world: ask not what America will do for you, but what together we can do for the freedom of man.

"Finally, whether you are citizens of America or citizens of the world, ask of us the same high standards of strength and sacrifice which we ask of you. With a good conscience our only sure reward, with history the final judge of our deeds, let us go forth to lead the land we love, asking His blessing and His help, but knowing that here on earth God's work must truly be our own."

It's easy to read inspirational messages such as the excerpt above, but not always so easy to follow the advice given. What exactly <u>can</u> we do for our country? If you are one of the 65,844,610 Americans who voted for progress and Hillary Clinton's platform, you may be feeling too sucker-punched to do anything more than sign petitions to hold Donald Trump accountable for his actions and his extreme right-wing nominees, and demand the release of his income tax returns (Mr. Trump said, "I don't pay income tax—I don't have to!").

But there is always something we can do, and when we individually do good things on a regular basis, then steadily we uplift the collective vibration of our nation to the frequency level where good things can continue to be attracted into our experiences.

In one of Agatha Christie's mysteries, *Murder at the Vicarage*, her famous sleuth Miss Marple says, "For sheer primitive rage, commend me to a thoroughgoing humanitarian when you get him well roused."

Let's harness the power of our rage and make a commitment that we won't back down to the Trump administration. Together, we can be well-roused directly into righteous action.

"The horror of the Hitler Experience was not that he perpetrated it on the human race, but that the human race allowed him to. The astonishment is not only that a Hitler came along, but also that so many others went along." — Neale Donald Walsch

It is never too late to begin creating change, and moving towards a better way of living. When we create progress for ourselves, we can't help but create it for others at the same time, because we are all connected.

It is the misuse of power that produces tyrants and bullies—they don't know how to share and they don't want to learn. They strut through life, heedless of how many others they trample and destroy, but they will not escape scot-free. Perhaps it appears they will not get any "payback" but the soul memory will always be there and they will have to reconcile the damage they cause against the potential they had for creating greater goodness instead.

We choose our lives. We create them with our everyday actions, those small decisions and the larger ones as well. Primarily, we build up our life resume in the way we act under stress.

We've seen how Mr. Trump handles stress. He has a hair-trigger temper, and is volatile. But that doesn't mean we have to react to everything he does, because in our reactions we become puppets, leaping at his command. A narcissist thrives on that kind of control, where by a mere glower, he can make others scurry into action.

He cracks the whip, and we're supposed to stampede toward the slaughterhouse? I don't think so. Don't play into his hands by becoming fearful of what he'll do next, or anxious about what is to come. Even though worry seems like a sign of caring, actually it is a misuse of our incredible powers of creation. Your attention to him increases his power.

If you were in a train wreck, once you were stabilized physically and had helped others in need, you would probably do your best to salvage what you could of your luggage and belongings. And then you would rebuild your life from that disaster. You wouldn't feel that the accident had to define you from that point forward. It's unlikely you would look at the disaster and decide you might as well make it total, so why bother to salvage anything. You wouldn't pick up a sledgehammer and destroy what was still standing or useable, or toss your suitcase over the nearest bridge.

And yet with a shock like the 2016 election results, it can feel so devastating that it seems life will never be the same, just as if we were indeed in a virtual train wreck, and one where instead of ending, the destruction is going to continue at the hands of the very person elected to supposedly guide the country toward prosperity and security as our Commander-in-Chief.

In writing my book *America's New Breed of Freedom Fighters*, my intention is to create a safe and empowering landing space for everyone who feels hurled out of their normal orbit by the election of a hate-based extremist to the highest office in our country.

About 13,000 years ago, hunters from northeastern Asia crossed the Bering Land Bridge (which no longer exists, having melted) and entered what was later called "North America." From that time forward, this land we call the United States has been a magnet for explorers, adventurers, prospectors, those seeking freedom of religion and personal expression, and many others seeking opportunities to build better lives for their families and friends.

In my own family, we have two precious letters written in 1862 by an ancestor who was the wagon train secretary on the way to Utah, having come from England to Kansas, and then across the Great Plains. The letters were to his parents back in England, and described the same sort of thing we would write home in such a situation: a wagon wheel broke and they were delayed in the fixing of it, a little girl fell in a stream and was drowned, they were looking forward to reaching their destination.

Today, we are so used to our instant communication that it can be difficult to think of waiting months if not years to hear from our loved ones who have set off for far off lands. But what about the far off lands of our imaginations? Can we travel there while taking a walk in the park or relaxing beneath a favorite shade tree? And when we imagine what we want, can we bring back those ideas and by picturing them strongly and steadily, make them materialize for the growth of our country? Yes, yes, yes. Yes, we can.

We are faced with a challenge: if Trump gets his way, walls will be built, people will be deported according to their skin color and religion, and the back of the middle class will be broken by financial burdens while the super-wealthy celebrate their tax breaks. That's just a short list. I don't want to depress you by listing the whole array of devastation he has planned for the environment and just about everything else you could think of. This man is such an extreme narcissist that all he sees is a bigger opportunity to inflate himself with power.

Ask yourself what you can do to help this country survive the next four years—not only to survive Trump's administration but to thrive in spite of him and his cronies.

Allow the question "What can I do?" to settle itself quietly in your heart. Walk around with the question, get curious about the feelings you have when you think about getting more involved in your community and in issues of importance to you. You'll recognize the answers, because you'll feel warm in the region of your heart, and you'll know that, perhaps for the first time in your life, you've discovered the purpose you came for.

For years I have been coaxing my readers and clients to get their emotions up on the Joy Channel, to tune in to that feeling of joy even before it arrives so that you are in harmony with everything you want. All the good things are of a higher finer vibration—loving relationships, fulfilling work and hobbies, vibrant health, financial abundance, and a wealth of creativity. By being grateful and happy in advance, the law of attraction brings us those happy experiences.

Keep your focus on positive change, and when you do, the ideas for what you can do next will begin flowing…and will continue to come into your life on the wings of love and hope.

#6 Reprogram Your Paradigm

Inauguration Countdown Day 6—Reprogram Your Paradigm

A paradigm or mindset is a collection of thousands of beliefs we hold hidden in the deep recesses of our minds.

It's akin to the idea of a complex software program that is installed in our minds in early childhood and continually updates itself with new data and evidence that makes each pattern within the program either stronger or weaker.

For instance, you may have learned at age three from watching a sibling that it is funny to stir all your food together on your dinner plate before eating. For a while, you did it too, until the game wore off or you realized you didn't like your food mushed together. That's a simple example of changing one's mind.

You may also have grown up in a family where there was a lot of sarcasm and belittling, where your ideas and dreams were mocked or discounted, and without knowing you were doing so, you formed a belief that you're not worthy of joy or love or happiness. But as your life progressed, you got so tired of feeling that way about yourself and you looked around and realized there was information available to help you change your self-image. And you decided to take the task seriously, and steadily move toward your goals. Now, each time you slide back into thinking thoughts of discouragement, you catch yourself and replace that with a feeling of "Yes, I can" gumption.

In my opinion, we greatly need an overhaul of our collective paradigm about the power of our thinking.

While walking through Central Park during the writing of this book, I heard two men on the path behind me talking about Meryl Streep's speech at the Golden Globes ceremony the previous evening. Golden Globes are awards bestowed by members of the Hollywood Foreign Press Association. During her acceptance of the Cecil B. DeMille Lifetime Achievement Award, Streep asked the press to hold Mr. Trump accountable now and in the future, citing his well-documented mocking of a disabled news reporter.

Here is part of Meryl Streep's speech:

"They gave me three seconds to say this, so: An actor's only job is to enter the lives of people who are different from us, and let you feel what that feels like. And there were many, many, many powerful performances this year that did exactly that. Breathtaking, compassionate work.

But there was one performance this year that stunned me. It sank its hooks in my heart. Not because it was good; there was nothing good about it. But it was effective and it did its job. It made its intended audience laugh, and show their teeth. It was that moment when the person asking to sit in the most respected seat in our country imitated a disabled reporter. Someone he outranked in privilege, power and the capacity to fight back. It kind of broke my heart when I saw it, and I still can't get it out of my head, because it wasn't in a movie. It was real life. And this instinct to humiliate, when it's modeled by someone in the public platform, by someone powerful, it filters down into everybody's life, because it kind of gives permission for other people to do the same thing. Disrespect invites disrespect, violence incites violence. And when the powerful use their position to bully others we all lose. O.K., go on with it. [She was being prompted to speed up.]

"O.K., this brings me to the press. We need the principled press to hold power to account, to call him [Trump] on the carpet for every outrage. That's why our founders enshrined the press and its freedoms in the Constitution."

Now, let's go back to the two men talking behind me in Central Park. What drew my attention to their conversation is that I heard one of them say, "Okay, so he played a dirty game and he won but now he's the president and Meryl Streep had no business mocking him."

In other words, now that Trump has won, we are supposed to accept whatever he does because he is the president, and if you hold up his behavior to the light, you are the one doing the mocking?

The words that man spoke reveal his paradigm: he believes that being president gives Trump a free pass to do and say what he wants, and it is unreasonable to hold him accountable.

What can we do about such thinking? We can't force people to change. Change has to come from within each of us in order to be real change and not just a surface compliance with what someone more powerful than you has decreed.

No one can think our thoughts for us.
No one can feel our feelings for us.
No one can create the pictures in our minds for us.
No one can take our actions for us.

But we can be pushed and goaded—and if we haven't learned to disconnect those buttons and are hot-wired to react, then that other person does indeed call the shots.

Want to be a free agent instead of a puppet on a string? Learn more about using the law of attraction in your life. Understanding is the key to lasting, beneficial change in our lives.

For change to be effective, each individual must want to experience better results in life than what they now realize is their limiting set of beliefs about their abilities and self-worth, and they must be willing to try new things and open up to new ideas.

When someone tries to force change on any of us, no matter how well-meaning, we always resist. Think about all the times your parents scolded you to stop being messy or to change a certain habit they labeled as bad—didn't you dig in your heels and become more determined than ever to hold onto the behavior or belief that was seemingly under attack?

Let's not waste energy on trying to change other people's minds and opinions. We've got more than enough work to do in mastering the laws of the universe so that we can attract the greater good we progressives desire for our country, even with a misogynist and racist in the White House.

Charles Haanel (1866-1949) was a New Thought teacher whose books remain popular today with those studying personal development. Below are eight lessons that Haanel offered as part of his "Master Key System" to help us better comprehend the universe we live in and the mental power we all are born with.

1. That much gathers more is true on every plane of existence and that loss leads to greater loss is equally true.

2. Mind is creative, and conditions, environment and all experiences in life are the result of our habitual or predominant mental attitude.

3. The attitude of mind necessarily depends upon what we think. Therefore, the secret of all power, all achievement and all possession depends upon our method of thinking.

4. This is true because we must "be" before we can "do," and we can "do" only to the extent which we "are," and what we "are" depends upon what we "think."

5. We cannot express powers that we do not possess. The only way by which we may secure possession of power is to become conscious of power, and we can never become conscious of power until we learn that all power is from within.

6. There is a world within a world of thought and feeling and power; of light and life and beauty and, although invisible, its forces are mighty.

7. The world within is governed by mind. When we discover this world we shall find the solution for every problem, the cause for every effect; and since the world within is subject to our control, all laws of power and possession are also within our control.

8. The world without is a reflection of the world within. What appears without is what has been found within. In the world within may be found infinite Wisdom, infinite Power, and infinite Supply of all that is necessary, waiting for unfoldment, development and expression. If we recognize these potentialities in the world within they will take form in the world without.

Once we learn that there are specific rules that control the results we live with each day, then we gain access to the power of creating more joy, freedom, justice and prosperity for all.

#5 I Have a Dream

Inauguration Countdown Day 5—I Have a Dream

We the Peaceful have the opportunity to stretch and grow, to become bigger than we were before, to expand beyond the point in history where we are now, instead of retreating to lick our wounds.

When we access the power of the universe, when we plug into progressive ideals, then our motivation to improve life works with that power the same as plugging a lamp into a socket. We come alive! We light up! We feel joyful and energized.

Let's imagine future historians are looking back on the aftermath of Election 2016. What will they report? Will they say there were strong ongoing protests to Trump's agenda and his nominees for the cabinet, and the progressives held him accountable?

Will they say that we never gave up? That we kept moving forward with our dream for all that this great country can be? Will they praise the progressives for refusing to be rattled by the threats of an extremist?

Years ago, in the early days of the Civil Rights movement to gain freedom for people of color in our country, Martin Luther King, Jr., whose birth we celebrate today, commemorated by a national holiday in his honor, delivered a speech on August 28, 1963 in Washington, D.C. as part of a nonviolent march on the capital. The initial title of his speech was "Normalcy, Never Again" but due to his repetitive use of the phrase "I have a dream" that became the name of this, his most famous speech. Dr. King was assassinated less than five years later.

These words are excerpted from Dr. King's "I Have a Dream" speech:

"In the process of gaining our rightful place we must not be guilty of wrongful deeds. Let us not seek to satisfy our thirst for freedom by drinking from the cup of bitterness and hatred. We must forever conduct our struggle on the high plane of dignity and discipline. We must not allow our creative protest to degenerate into physical violence. Again, and again we must rise to the majestic heights of meeting physical force with soul force."

If we worry that it's going to be too hard to fight Trump and neutralize his extremist agenda, or that it's hopeless anyway, so we might as well hunker down and wait out his term, then we are becoming part of the problem in our nation instead of standard-bearers in the realm of solutions.

When we abandon disempowering thoughts, then we create space in our hearts and minds to harness the energy of the universe and use it to manifest the results we want.

Affirm: "I do not resist this situation. I put it in the hands of Infinite Love and Wisdom. Let the Divine idea now come to pass." Florence Scovel Shinn

I believe in the cardinal virtues of a true statesman:

> ➢ Self-control
> ➢ Capacity for listening to others and considering new ideas
> ➢ Ability to compromise
> ➢ At ease with himself
> ➢ Deeply spiritual and aware of a power greater than himself
> ➢ Desire to be of service to others

- ➢ Healthy ego, acts like the parent on an airplane, taking care of his own oxygen need first in order to be of use to his children
- ➢ Compassionate and kind
- ➢ Self-discipline
- ➢ Soft-spoken and well-mannered
- ➢ Even-tempered
- ➢ Interested in other people's point of view

At every time in history when oppression reigned there have always been freedom fighters and resistance movements. The weight of fear and the inertia of despair caused prolonging of tyranny, but eventually we as a race always move upward into a higher level of awareness and freedom. The bondage of fear keeps us entrapped. Instead of titling my next screenplay "Nightmare on Pennsylvania Avenue" I'd rather write that dreams do come true when we work together and focus on progress.

Here is the dream I have for our country:

I dream of a nation where our leaders and citizens work together to create greater good for all.

I dream that we the people enjoy and expand our material wealth and enjoy a healthy and vibrant social structure that allows all individuals to prosper and to express their natural gifts.

I dream of a time when everyone lives in peace and harmony, having abandoned the old ideas that we must compete against each other in order to survive and struggle to afford the bare necessities. I dream that all schoolchildren learn how to use the laws of the mind and have ready access to all the support they need from their local communities and states, and at the federal level too, in order to fulfill their destinies and create more love and expansion in our great nation.

Peace in our time? Yes, it is possible. If we want it enough, we can create peace. However, it won't come by decree from outside of us. It starts within, in our own hearts. Releasing your emotional reaction to Trump's election is the first place to start. Replace it with a sense of calmness and surety that all is working out, and together we will indeed triumph.

"This one simple change—seeking and finding peace within—could, were it undertaken by everyone, end all wars, eliminate conflict, prevent injustice, and bring the world to everlasting peace. There is no other formula necessary, or possible. World peace is a personal thing! What is needed is not a change of circumstance, but a change of consciousness." Neale Donald Walsch, from *The Complete Conversations with God*

We fly our nation's flag at half-staff (some say "half-mast") as a sign of mourning, such as on Memorial Day in honor of our war dead, on the day before and the day after a member of Congress dies, and by proclamation from the President as well as from the Governors of individual states. The proclamations include the specific days for the flag to be at half-staff, and when the flag should be returned to full-staff, sometimes from sunrise to sunset on the same day and sometimes to be lowered to half-staff and not be returned to full-staff until a week later.

On Wednesday November 11, 2016, the day after the presidential election, I noticed that the American flag atop Belvedere Castle in New York City's Central Park was flying at half-staff. No doubt it was a "coincidence" and there was an official reason for the signal of grief. But it seemed a providential coincidence indeed.

Over half the voters of America were in deep mourning, shocked and dismayed that our fellow citizens would actually elect a reality TV show host known for his utter disregard for the rights of others to be President of the United States. As a whole, it seems that Trump's party is deep in anger and they want to spread it around as much as possible. I've been attacked (via email and social media) for writing my countdown blog and writing this book. Seriously? You can't tolerate a writer who is offering stress relief to others?

A signal of dire distress: flying the American flag upside down.

Let us do everything we can to be sure we never need to display that signal.

#4 Advance Confidently

Inauguration Countdown Day 4—Advance Confidently

From this point on, the choice is ours: do we move forward, or do we collectively allow fear to mire us in the mud of inaction? It's not enough to be "against" what Trump proposes and has already begun putting into effect. We progressives must be <u>for</u> what we want, and use our thought energy in a much more powerful way than we have up until now.

Decide now what you want. Make a list of the issues and principles that are most important to you. Write about the big dream you have for your life, that "thing" that will bring you satisfaction and a sense of a life well-lived. If you don't have that dream yet, take time to reflect on what you enjoy doing the most. Our hobbies and interests always contain the seed of our greatness. The reason you are drawn to sports, for instance, could be that you have an inner dream of helping others be better athletes by coaching a local team as a volunteer, inventing a new improved fabric for athletic clothes or shoes, or creating a mobile app that allows fans to track their favorite teams.

In my ecourse called "Unstoppable Confidence" I share lessons on how to go deeper into developing healthy self-confidence so that you can achieve both short-term and long-term goals in your life. Here is an excerpt from the course workbook:

Imagine you've reached the end of your life and – as a friendly spirit – you're eavesdropping at your own memorial service. You nod with satisfaction as you hear the recounting of all the good you did during your journey on Earth. There's even some good-natured ribbing over mistakes you made in a well-meaning way while learning and growing. You laugh along with the listeners as the person at the podium recounts a few anecdotes that really bring your life into full flavor.

ASSIGNMENT: Write your own eulogy NOW!

Rationale

This tool is valuable for identifying the major achievements you most desire to accomplish in your lifetime. It points out the holes where you need to pay more attention to what is important to you, and underscores the values that you hold dear.

Instead of rushing through this with a few quick comments about what a nice person you were and how much you'll be missed, take time to do this exercise with care. You will find it helpful to use as a visionary document that can be a "map" to guide your action steps from now on.

And, of course, you can keep revising it as the years pass and you accomplish more and more of your big dreams for expressing yourself fully in the world with all of your gifts to humanity such as kindness and caring.

Earl Nightingale is known as the "Dean of Personal Development" because he was not only a popular radio personality, author and speaker on the topics of human character development, he was the first to create home study courses that were recordings. Prior to that time, you could get written course material mailed to you, but no one had thought of preparing and mailing a vinyl record so that students of the course could feel they were in the room with their teacher, and listen to the lesson again and again, thus retraining their thought habits and inculcating the lesson material. He was co-founder of the world-renowned Nightingale-Conant personal development company. Nightingale defined success this way: "Success is the progressive realization of a worthy ideal or goal."

Notice the two key words: "progressive" and "worthy." So let's put aside any comments that might come to mind about Donald Trump's seeming financial success which he created with the perverted tactics of an old-style robber baron, and instead focus on how we can progressively move forward with plans that are worthy of fruition and bring value for the greater good of all.

Dr. Joseph Murphy reminds us, "Decide now to make your life grander, greater, richer, and nobler than ever before. Within your subconscious depths lie infinite wisdom, infinite power, and infinite supply of all that is necessary, which is waiting for development and expression. Begin now to recognize these potentialities of your deeper mind, and they will take form in the world without."

It is only when we really focus on constructive goals that we can be part of the magic of manifesting true progress in our society. The powers of the mind are neutral and therefore can obviously be used to bring about recession, unemployment, and other ills. So, let's keep our attention on creating more good in the world, both for ourselves and our families and for society as a whole.

Murphy goes on to say, "In order to change external conditions, you must change the cause. Most men try to change conditions and circumstances by working with conditions and circumstances. To remove discord, confusion, lack, and limitation, you must remove the cause, and the cause is the way you are using your conscious mind. In other words, the way you are thinking and picturing in your mind. You are living in a fathomless sea of infinite riches. Your subconscious is very sensitive to your thoughts. Your thoughts form the mold or matrix through which the infinite intelligence, wisdom, vital forces, and energies of your subconscious flow."

Donald Trump and his camp followers manipulated the world with fear and hatred just the way a war general stirs up the populace in favor of aggressive action and restrictions of those who are "different." Trump targets the female majority of this country with threats of punitive restrictions of access to affordable care and reproductive health screenings. He successfully agitated so much fear in the hearts of listeners that people who were against his plans inadvertently poured the energy of fear into his campaign as if their emotions were attached to a funnel empowering him.

That's not science fiction, it is science fact. Our thoughts are all connected. We are not Borgs, however; we all have our independent minds. But when we are accustomed to making choices based on reactive emotions, without understanding the power of our thoughts, we create results collectively that we would never wish for if we knew what we were doing.

Think again about your own life, and the direction you are going. Are you advancing, or are you sliding backwards, or are you at a full stop? Are you following your big dream, or just following the money from paycheck to paycheck?

We are all deserving of prosperity in every area of our lives. Wealth isn't a problem by itself, it's what people do with the money once they have it, and how they get it in the first place.

If you bring the world a better product or something that is of service and makes money, that's terrific! Becoming successful with a worthy ideal will bring you satisfaction and a sense of fulfillment along with the abundance and financial freedom.

Just following the money without consideration for your core values and what you are aligning your soul with, may bring you material goods and all that money can buy, but without that satisfaction of living your dream, that type of financial success will not bring you happiness.

Do you want to remain safely on the sidelines and be a bystander for the next four years? Or do you want to take action on behalf of the issues that are most important to you?

It doesn't mean having to go march on the White House or picket Congress. It doesn't mean donating money, although of course you are welcome to donate to your favorite organizations such as those supporting environmental protection, feeding the hungry, educating the overlooked.

Did you know that our embarrassingly high illiteracy rate hasn't improved in many years? 32 million adult Americans cannot read. The last thing this country needs is making education even harder for people to access. But Trump doesn't care about that—it's a line budget item he intends to sacrifice to make way for other things such as tax cuts for the super-wealthy.

You can continue to tell yourself things like: I feel so tired all the time, I'm really stressed out, this project (family, house, job, economy) is going to be the death of me!

OR

Start a new trend in your life with self-chat that is far more empowering and delightful such as, I really feel energized by this new project, I feel relaxed and happy, I know that everything is working out for me and I'm right where I planned all along.

Begin today. Choose the commands you give to your subconscious mind, which is the driver on the road of your life.

Affirm: Every day in every way, I advance with confidence in my heart, to help create more good in the world.

#3 Be a Freedom Fighter

Inauguration Countdown Day 3—Be a Freedom Fighter

During World War II, "fifth columnists" were people the Nazis could count on to help Hitler's gaping maw gulp down yet another village, city, or country. Fifth columnists lived and worked in those towns, usually having been born and raised there. These collaborators secretly worked with the enemy from within the targeted region. The first "four columns" meant the advancing formation of soldiers in four military columns, grimly marching in lockstep. So, if you were known as a fifth columnist, it meant you were a traitor to your own country, and you aided and abetted the enemy either for monetary gain, power and favors (such as getting more food and fuel than the average villager), and sometimes because you also believed in the values the enemy proposed.

A collaborator can be seen as someone who is more interested in what they can gain than in what they can do to help their fellow citizens in times of great need. They look for the easy way out, the door to riches and power over others, and they turn their backs on social issues that help their country.

Is any of this beginning to feel familiar about what we face today? As they say, history repeats itself, but the only reason it does is because we continue thinking the same outworn thoughts about struggle and lack and limitation, and we have failed until now to systematically access the power of the subconscious mind to create the results we want.

If we align our thinking with Trump's hate agenda and get on that low level vibration with him and his cronies, we inadvertently become fifth columnists, helping to undermine and destroy the very freedoms we wish to defend and protect.

During the American Revolutionary War that resulted in the colonists' breaking away from the rule of King George III of England (and yet eventually becoming Allies and at times BFFs), the colonists who remained loyal to the King were called Tories or Loyalists or Whigs. As a whole, the colonists and American's eastern shore had considered themselves "Englishmen," but a big thorn in their side was the lack of representation in Parliament that all Englishmen (meaning white adult males) expected as a God-given right. Trouble kept brewing and boiled over into a battle cry. Further attempts to create harmonious relationships with the implacable King were abandoned in favor of revolution.

It was totally illegal to align yourself with the freedom fighters of 1775-6. Totally. I mean, like, you could be shot for this, because basically the colonies were owned by Great Britain and the King did not look kindly upon an uprising across the pond. I'll let you discover the details of our fight for independence on your own. I just wanted to be sure to point out that being on General Washington's side was not your immediate ticket to an easy life of sitting by the fire and toasting a scone while sipping tea from a dainty cup.

It was scary, it was dangerous, it required a firm belief in the high stakes of freedom. And meanwhile, back at the ranch, you had to be

306

careful around your neighbors and villagers who remained loyal to the King.

I have been a bookworm all my life. Before the advent of ebooks, you could always find me near a stack of books bristling with notes, and I still enjoy having several books in progress at any given time. To me, books are comfort food and my first refuge.

When I was growing up, we went to the library on a regular basis and I always came home with an armful of mysteries and historical fiction to dive into. One of my favorite book series for middle-grade girls involved a heroine who was a Patriot girl about age ten or twelve, and who had a dangerous mission to perform in total secrecy, such as smuggling a crucial message to General Washington. I adored those adventures! At the time, I didn't even know that I was actually a Daughter of the American Revolution, although not a member. One of my sisters discovered that fact years later when doing a genealogy search about our family history.

Perhaps an angel perched on my shoulder those years ago while I was thrilling to the tale of Patriots, and whispered in my ear: "One day, when you are grown up, you will write a book to help a new kind of freedom fighter in America."

So, let's see exactly what's different about being a freedom fighter today compared to being on in World War II or any other great conflict where the stakes were high. We have it easier now, because from the safety of our homes, we can reach the entire world. We don't have to print pamphlets in a hidden room and risk our lives to distribute them. We just tweet and our message is instantly heard around the world.

Mr. Trump used social media to lambast the globe with hatred and lies and promises of his idea of "greatness."

Now let's turn around that mis-use of a wonderful tool and instead of hammering people over the head with hatred, use the "hammer" of justice to promote progress in all areas of our society not just for a favored few.

How can you become one of America's "new breed" of freedom fighters? Instead of printing a few dozen leaflets in a back room and furtively passing them around, we have the incredible power of instant communication around the world via social media. Let's use technology in a positive way to share messages of hope and liberation, of freedom and justice.

The new resistance fighter doesn't needs weapons, doesn't need to skulk in the shadows. The new activist is someone who sees something going wrong and is willing to help. I think there's confusion surrounding the idea of peaceful action, or of nonviolent demonstrations. It doesn't mean you're weak. It doesn't mean sitting calmly and letting someone be abusive to you. It does, however, mean learning about the laws of the mind and thus understanding how to activate a sense of indifference toward the rants of people like Donald Trump and his cronies. When we are indifferent to a negative force, it will cease to exist. Our attention to it, our desire to push it away, those feelings and actions just make the negative grow stronger.

What exactly is a new kind of resistance fighter? Using the law of attraction to neutralize Trump's plans for America, together we can achieve constructive progress instead of being the victim of expensive plans that favor the wealthy and that promote an agenda of hatred for anyone Trump disfavors.

There are so many things you can do to support progress as you go about your daily life. Although it would be wonderful if you felt called to support your favorite issues and get actively involved in supporting those causes, you don't have to leave your house to help.

Join us in the frequency wavelength of love and expansion that circles our globe. It's invisible, but it's there, and all of us can access it by simply inviting in feelings of peace, light, and calmness.

When thoughts pop up that make you feel agitated or fearful, dismiss them as you would a mosquito or gnat. You don't have to get out a cannon and angrily rant at a gnat, now do you? Of course not.

But when someone like Donald Trump strikes fear into the hearts of so many millions of people around the world, it can feel like only something "big" could possibly combat his agenda of hatred.

Not true. Love trumps hate, and you can start with love in your daily life. By doing so, by adding to the energy of love in the world, you help neutralize the negativity of Trump's proposed agenda. He cannot win, he cannot dominate, he cannot appoint himself emperor unless we stand back and allow it by energetically aligning with the fear that rules his behavior.

When a classic narcissist such as Donald Trump gets in power, it can be terrifying indeed to listen to the rants, to watch the enraged facial expressions, to hear that fury in his voice.

Pause and put aside your anxiety--listen for the two-year-old in Trump. You'll hear him, having a tantrum. And you will find it much easier to look away, and to stop inadvertently empowering him by being afraid and letting him call the shots.

It's odd, but we progressives must essentially act like the loving parent to Donald Trump and set firm limits so he doesn't destroy all of us with his out-of-control demands for walls, for deportation, for eliminating women's affordable access to cancer screening and reproductive health care, and so many other issues he intends to stomp beneath his boots.

Perhaps his voters had already decided they would vote Republican no matter who the candidate was, even if they felt distaste when he revealed his opinion that it's okay to grope women, it's okay to make racist slurs and it's okay to deport people based on their religion. They voted for him anyway, even when he bragged he doesn't have to pay income tax, and even when he refused to make his tax returns public. They had a belief inside that a Republican would be better than a Democrat, and that belief punched the voter ballot.

Some Republicans, of course, voted for Trump because they are racist, they hate women, they don't want anyone of color to have advantages, they want wealth for themselves and find glee in sticking it to the middle class in as many ways as possible. Their mentality is me-first and ignore the rest of the country.

Other Republicans were unable or unwilling to look past the paid ads and sound bites that glorified Trump as some sort of business wizard who would help the economy. They didn't look past the glitter and bombast to the man beneath the self-wrought tinsel crown.

Trump enjoys taking hostages. Our trained beliefs—installed by parents, teachers, society we live in – dictate our behavior. If you're tired of being held hostage by Trump's constricting definition of who you are and what you are capable of achieving, then activating an understanding of the laws of thought will free you.

Pause for a moment when you feel frustrated about Trump's supporters and their inexplicable desire for things to revert to what they consider the "good old days." Think about when you were in high school and played with a small child or sibling. Perhaps you did some babysitting for the neighbors. From your higher perspective about life and relationships and the subjects you were studying at school, you weren't at the same level as the little children. It didn't mean you took a superior stance or tried to shame or scold them for their lack of awareness of geometry while they were struggling to handle multiplication.

In a similar vein, it can be liberating to realize that everyone alive at this time is helping humanity move forward. We are ever evolving upward. We are never going backwards even if it sometimes might seem that way.

The people who cling the hardest to old ways actually give motivation and impetus to those of us who are on the leading edge of change. We are the "tip of the arrow" thinkers as some people put it. We are the ones willing to keep pushing for progress.

And we can't back down. Trump will be in office for 1,461 days. Let's state our intention now that we will use these four years wisely to gain a firmer stronghold in grassroots community efforts for progress, that we will help get out the vote not just for the presidential election in 2020 but for local and state elections, too.

Together we can and will continue to make a positive difference for our country and our allies.

#2 Love Trumps Hate

Inauguration Countdown Day 2—Love Trumps Hate

Power Tip of the Day: Open your heart to love and forgiveness.

Forgiveness can feel like we're being weak, like we're saying "Oh, yeah, no big deal that Trump played a very dirty game and won even though Hillary had the popular vote." It can feel like we're being asked to say it doesn't matter what Trump and his campaign did to manipulate fear throughout the world, and to rile up rural Americans nostalgic for a trip back in time to the nasty days of white supremacy where "faith" meant believing in a vengeful God and it's okay to put the Christian injunction to "Love thy neighbor as thyself" on hold while you hate anyone who looks different from you and doesn't attend the same church.

In an article I read years ago about Dorothy Bridges, the actress and poet who was the wife of Lloyd Bridges and mother of actors Jeff and Beau Bridges, she was quoted as saying that she raised her children to understand if they ever felt a challenge in believing in "God" to simply add another "o" to the word...and believe in "Good."

We can all understand and relate to "good" and we can state an intention to create more of good and less of its opposite, and to hold our elected officials to the same standard.

We can't hold grudges and also profess that we are transmitting love in response to hate.

"When they go low, we go high."-- Michelle Obama, First Lady

The process of forgiveness is actually a simple one. It involves letting go of the thoughts and feelings that you have clutched to yourself with rage, anger, resentment, and wishes for vengeance. Wherever you feel those negative emotions, it's an indication that forgiveness will free you from that slavery to hatred.

Release the anger. Release the desire to get back at the person or organizations who have hurt or upset you. Let go of your grim determination to make someone pay for what they've done.

Stop looking in the rearview mirror of life. Instead, free up that energy to create good, harmony, and growth.

Transmuting fear into love is a powerful process. This goes for all issues where there is strife in our lives, not just this election debacle.

When we open to allowing love to flow and goodwill to flourish, we become aligned with the emotional vibrations of joy, peace, bliss, happiness. And in that alignment, we find our true power to create our desired results.

On the other hand, when we hang onto vengeful thoughts or the angry rehashing of events, we stay chained to emotions that, by virtue of the laws of our universe, can only bring us more things to feel angry and resentful and upset about.

Here's a trick to making forgiveness more palatable: you're taking the high road, you're taking a superior position over the "you" who has until now been less aware of your own thought activities. Congratulate yourself on being willing to grow.

Once you gain the forgiveness habit, I think you'll discover, as I did, that it makes life so much easier and more congenial to let the anger go and focus instead on what you are doing today and how you can be of service to others.

If you feel challenged to forgive and understand friends and family members who voted for Trump, take the important step of making love more important than politics. Calm your breathing, get still within, and ask for help in being a channel for universal love. Remind yourself that in one hundred years, all of us who participated in Election 2016 will be long dead. Don't allow the anger over the election to spoil the rest of your life, don't let it harden into bitterness or hatred. Remember always that love trumps hate, because love is of a higher nature than hate and fear and worry.

Send compassion to people who voted for Trump, and realize they followed their own hidden beliefs that are obviously fear-based in nature. They are a dying breed. As our world evolves, and the mental laws are more freely and readily understood, more and more individuals will transition upward into a greater level of awareness.

People like Donald Trump will never be allowed near positions of power.

We can let go of them now, without sharing in their narrow Old Worldview of struggle and domination, of control and fear.

"When we come to see that Thought is a force —a manifestation of energy —having a magnet-like power of attraction, we will begin to understand the why and wherefore of many things that have heretofore seemed dark to us.... When we think we send out vibrations of a fine ethereal substance, which are as real as the vibrations manifesting light, heat, electricity, magnetism." -- William Walker Atkinson

Here is something else to consider about loving others, in spite of their opinions and behavior. When we try to make the other person or group wrong, the natural reaction on their side is to push back and prove that they are right. That clash can quickly escalate into angry shouts (and Tweets).

The higher road is to understand everyone has the right to their own opinion. We can turn away from what we don't want and pour our mental energy into what we do want to create. It's amazing how much freer we can feel when we stop pushing against something undesired. Even though at first it may seem the only logical recourse that we have, that isn't true. We have far more power when we take inspired action for what we want, than when we angrily push against what we dislike or fear.

From adventures to explorers to people seeking greater freedom and prosperity – America has ever sounded the clarion call as the land of opportunities. Let us take full advantage of the freedoms we have: the right to free speech, the right to vote, the right to get a job and be paid for it, the right to create your own business and set your own prices, the right to live where you desire without discrimination, the right to life, the right to due process of law, the right to the pursuit of happiness.

Many rights and freedoms are at risk due to Trump's election. Get involved now and let's keep moving forward in service to the greater good.

#1 Take the Oath

Inauguration Countdown Day 1—Take the Oath

In America, we vote for our president every four years, and after the election, the power of that office is transferred non-violently to the incoming President-elect, unless the current administration was re-elected (maximum of two terms).

As stipulated in an amendment to the US Constitution, the President and Vice President are sworn in at noon on January 20th in the year following the election.

Various traditions are upheld on the day of the president's inauguration. It is always held in our nation's capital, and takes place outside instead of behind closed doors. Citizens are welcome to witness the ceremony and the informal parade as long as space in the streets permit, and as long as they retain order and self-discipline.

The incoming President, Vice President and their immediate families arrive at the Capitol steps by car, and customarily walk part of the way to wave and interact with the crowds lining the street. On the evening of the swearing-in ceremony, inaugural balls are held throughout the city of Washington, D.C.

The ceremony itself is brief, and consists of both the president and the vice president taking a solemn oath, as directed in our Constitution:

Oath of Office for President of the United States

US Constitution, Article II, Section 1

Before he enters on the execution of his office, he shall take the following oath or affirmation: "I do solemnly swear (or affirm) that I will faithfully execute the office of President of the United States, and will to the best of my ability, preserve, protect, and defend the Constitution of the United States."

The Constitution established the national government and its fundamental laws, while guaranteeing certain basic rights for its citizens, which at that time were the white adult males of the population. The current oath of office was passed by Congress in 1884, changing the wording somewhat, and is the same oath that Members of Congress take.

When we take an oath, it is a special moment.

In times of danger in our society, ordinary citizens can perform an arrest, which, not surprisingly, is called a "citizen's arrest." The practice dates back to medieval times and allows citizens to hold a suspected felon even without the official right to do so.

If you're a fan of classic television comedies you may remember the episode in *The Andy Griffith Show* where Deputy Barney Fife (Don Knotts) tickets Gomer Pyle (Jim Nabors), and in retaliation Gomer Places Barney under citizen's arrest for making an illegal U-turn. "Citizen's arrest! Citizen's arrest!" If you haven't seen it, the clip is on YouTube and is considered one of the funniest episodes of that long-running series set in small town America.

If we can perform a citizen's arrest under extraordinary conditions, then why can't we take a citizen's oath as well? These are indeed extraordinary, perilous times, when Donald Trump's election feels more like we've landed in *The Twilight Zone* than *Mayberry, RFD*.

Are you ready to be one of America's new breed of freedom fighters? Are you ready to put your commitment into words and turn the weakness of wish power into the boundless "yes, we will" power? Do you want to help create progress, liberty and justice for all?

If so, then please place your right hand over your heart and say these words:

"I [your name] do solemnly affirm that I will create more goodness, more love, more joy, more kindness, and more expansion in my own life, and help others do the same."

My new book *America's New Breed of Freedom Fighters* is now available. Thank you for taking this blog journey with me for the past month leading up to the inauguration of Donald Trump as the 45th President of the United States.

God bless America—keep us safe from all harm, foreign and domestic.

PART FIVE
IN GOD WE TRUST

*"The ground I am on is holy ground.
The ground I am on is successful ground."*

Florence Scovel Shinn

Whatever your religious beliefs or lack of them, you can tap into a higher power, whether you call that force God, Nature, Spirit, the Super Conscious Mind, the Christ Consciousness, the universal creative energy, or whatever feels comfortable to you. The word "Good" encompasses the Spirit of God and is readily understood by most people to be beneficial and loving without carrying the taint of religious dogma.

The Pledge of Allegiance

I pledge allegiance to the flag
of the United States of America
and to the republic for which it stands,
one nation, under God, indivisible,
with liberty and justice for all.

E Pluribus Unum

E Pluribus Unum is the motto of the United States of America. Latin for "out of many, one" it signifies the union of the thirteen original colonies into one nation instead of separate ones. The motto is carried by the American eagle on the Great Seal of the United States.

318

Since the motto was first proposed by the U.S. Continental Congress in 1782 for use on the seal, our country has grown and expanded far beyond the original thirteen stars on our nation's red, white and blue flag.

But how is *E Pluribus Unum* of value or interest today, so many years later? Does it have real meaning to anyone, other than being part of our currency and tradition? I think that it does. Progressives focus on finding ways to be of service for the greater good of all citizens, and not just a few. Out of the many, one.

Let's keep progressing, and keep our sight on all the good we desire for ourselves and others. When we magnetize unity of purpose to our goals, the universe indeed conspires to bring about great miracles in unexpected ways.

The key is to not get divided into splintered factions over the issue of Trump's election. We must bravely carry on as Americans, and find more unity in what we have in common with our fellow Americans, no matter who they voted for.

In his Farewell Address, President Obama said, referring to our nation's founders, "they knew that democracy does require a basic sense of solidarity — the idea that for all our outward differences, we're all in this together; that we rise or fall as one."

Relying on God's Assistance

Every child knows that U.S. dollars and coins carry the words "In God we trust"...but what does that mean today, when so many people are asking, "How could a loving God allow Donald Trump to be elected to the highest office in the land?" Many people feel abandoned by God at this time, and worry that only evil and suffering will come out of this situation.

When I was a child, the catechism I memorized in second grade asked me, "Who made us?" and my learned response was "God made us." Over the years, I delved into theology, philosophy, spirituality, New Thought and metaphysics. As I gained a fuller awareness of our eternal nature, and our timeless, unbreakable connection with each other, I came to believe in a benevolent Spirit of which we are all an important part.

I believe that the beauty of our universe is proof of the love and delight our Creator feels for us. And I believe that our power to co-create with Source is our greatest gift, and our least understood one. We inadvertently cast doubt and fear on our path and prevent our greater good from streaming into our lives.

"The Supreme Power of the Universe is the supplier of all things, and the law of attraction is the distribution manager of those things.
You are a central point of creation on Earth, and it is through you and your use of the law that the Universe can bring creation into our physical world. What a beautiful system!"

Rhonda Byrne (*The Secret*)

We call this Supreme Power by many names, including God, Source, Great Spirit, Divine Intelligence, Creative Intelligence, the Super Mind, Nature, and more. Whatever your culture, religion, beliefs or lack of beliefs may be, I feel we are all seeking to name the ineffable, and to corral the integral and limitless energy of our universe by describing it in a way that feels comfortable to us based on what we learned from our families as a child.

Science shows us that we inhabit the quantum field of infinite possibilities, and we are at the very early stage of understanding even a small bit of how things work. It's amazing that we all came here at this time to help bring about more love and expansion through the power of the One Mind.

"You must stop seeing God as separate from you, and you as separate from each other. The only solution is the Ultimate Truth: nothing exists in the universe that is separate from anything else. Everything is intrinsically connected, irrevocably interdependent, interactive, interwoven into the fabric of all of life. All government, all politics, must be based on this truth. All laws must be rooted in it. This is the future hope of your race; the only hope for your planet."

Neale Donald Walsch

"On Holy Ground"

"On Holy Ground" is by songwriter Geron Davis. This is a quote from the lyrics:

When I walked through the doors I sensed His presence
And I knew this was a place where love abounds
For this is a temple, the God we love abides here

Oh, we are standing in His presence on holy ground

The Statue of Liberty Poem

Emma Lazarus (1849-1887) was a Jewish-American poet born in New York City who is most famous for the sonnet she wrote to help raise money for the statue's 89-foot tall pedestal. She wrote the poem in 1883, but did not live to see the bronze plaque with her poem installed on the pedestal in 1903.

The words of her poem are just as important today as they were a hundred years ago.

"The New Colossus"

Not like the brazen giant of Greek fame,
With conquering limbs astride from land to land;
Here at our sea-washed, sunset gates shall stand
A mighty woman with a torch, whose flame
Is the imprisoned lightning, and her name
Mother of Exiles. From her beacon-hand
Glows world-wide welcome; her mild eyes command
The air-bridged harbor that twin cities frame.
"Keep ancient lands, your storied pomp!" cries she
With silent lips. "Give me your tired, your poor,
Your huddled masses yearning to breathe free,
The wretched refuse of your teeming shore.
Send these, the homeless, tempest-tost to me,
I lift my lamp beside the golden door!"

Desiderata by Max Ehrmann

(1872-1945)

Quote from the poem:

Go placidly amid the noise and haste,
and remember what peace there may be in silence.
As far as possible without surrender
be on good terms with all persons.
Speak your truth quietly and clearly;
and listen to others,
even the dull and the ignorant;
they too have their story.

The Optimist's Creed by Christian D. Larson

(1874-1962)

Quote from the poem:

Promise Yourself…

To be so strong that nothing can disturb your peace of mind.

To talk health, happiness, and prosperity to every person you meet.

To make all your friends feel that there is something worthwhile in them.

To look at the sunny side of everything and make your optimism come true.

To think only of the best, to work only for the best and to expect only the best.

John F. Kennedy's Inaugural Address, January 20, 1961

Let us take hope and inspiration from the immortal words of President Kennedy, who defeated Richard Nixon in the presidential election of November 1960:

We observe today not a victory of [the Democratic] party, but a celebration of freedom — symbolizing an end, as well as a beginning — signifying renewal, as well as change. For I have sworn before you and Almighty God the same solemn oath our forebears prescribed nearly a century and three quarters ago.

The world is very different now. For man holds in his mortal hands the power to abolish all forms of human poverty and all forms of human life. And yet the same revolutionary beliefs for which our forebears fought are still at issue around the globe — the belief that the rights of man come not from the generosity of the state, but from the hand of God.

We dare not forget today that we are the heirs of that first revolution. Let the word go forth from this time and place, to friend and foe alike, that the torch has been passed to a new generation of Americans — born in this century, tempered by war, disciplined by a hard and bitter peace, proud of our ancient heritage — and unwilling to witness or permit the slow undoing of those human rights to which this Nation has always been committed, and to which we are committed today at home and around the world.

Let every nation know, whether it wishes us well or ill, that we shall pay any price, bear any burden, meet any hardship, support any friend, oppose any foe, in order to assure the survival and the success of liberty.

This much we pledge — and more.

To those old allies whose cultural and spiritual origins we share, we pledge the loyalty of faithful friends. United, there is little we cannot do in a host of cooperative ventures. Divided, there is little we can do — for we dare not meet a powerful challenge at odds and split asunder.

To those new States whom we welcome to the ranks of the free, we pledge our word that one form of colonial control shall not have passed away merely to be replaced by a far more iron tyranny. We shall not always expect to find them supporting our view. But we shall always hope to find them strongly supporting their own freedom — and to remember that, in the past, those who foolishly sought power by riding the back of the tiger ended up inside.

To those peoples in the huts and villages across the globe struggling to break the bonds of mass misery, we pledge our best efforts to help them help themselves, for whatever period is required — not because the Communists may be doing it, not because we seek their votes, but because it is right. If a free society cannot help the many who are poor, it cannot save the few who are rich.

To our sister republics south of our border, we offer a special pledge — to convert our good words into good deeds — in a new alliance for progress — to assist free men and free governments in casting off the chains of poverty. But this peaceful revolution of hope cannot become the prey of hostile powers. Let all our neighbors know that we shall join with them to oppose aggression or subversion anywhere in the Americas. And let every other power know that this Hemisphere intends to remain the master of its own house.

To that world assembly of sovereign states, the United Nations, our last best hope in an age where the instruments of war have far outpaced the instruments of peace, we renew our pledge of support — to prevent it from becoming merely a forum for invective — to strengthen its shield of the new and the weak — and to enlarge the area in which its writ may run.

Finally, to those nations who would make themselves our adversary, we offer not a pledge but a request: that both sides begin anew the quest for peace, before the dark powers of destruction unleashed by science engulf all humanity in planned or accidental self-destruction.

We dare not tempt them with weakness. For only when our arms are sufficient beyond doubt can we be certain beyond doubt that they will never be employed.

But neither can two great and powerful groups of nations take comfort from our present course — both sides overburdened by the cost of modern weapons, both rightly alarmed by the steady spread of the deadly atom, yet both racing to alter that uncertain balance of terror that stays the hand of mankind's final war.

So, let us begin anew — remembering on both sides that civility is not a sign of weakness, and sincerity is always subject to proof. Let us never negotiate out of fear. But let us never fear to negotiate.

Let both sides explore what problems unite us instead of belaboring those problems which divide us.

Let both sides, for the first time, formulate serious and precise proposals for the inspection and control of arms — and bring the absolute power to destroy other nations under the absolute control of all nations.

Let both sides seek to invoke the wonders of science instead of its terrors.

Together let us explore the stars, conquer the deserts, eradicate disease, tap the ocean depths, and encourage the arts and commerce.

Let both sides unite to heed in all corners of the earth the command of Isaiah — to "undo the heavy burdens – and to let the oppressed go free."

And if a beachhead of cooperation may push back the jungle of suspicion, let both sides join in creating a new endeavor, not a new balance of power, but a new world of law, where the strong are just and the weak secure and the peace preserved.

All this will not be finished in the first 100 days. Nor will it be finished in the first 1,000 days, nor in the life of this Administration, nor even perhaps in our lifetime on this planet. But let us begin.

In your hands, my fellow citizens, more than in mine, will rest the final success or failure of our course. Since this country was founded, each generation of Americans has been summoned to give testimony to its national loyalty. The graves of young Americans who answered the call to service surround the globe.

Now the trumpet summons us again — not as a call to bear arms, though arms we need; not as a call to battle, though embattled we are — but a call to bear the burden of a long twilight struggle, year in and year out, "rejoicing in hope, patient in tribulation" — a struggle against the common enemies of man: tyranny, poverty, disease, and war itself.

Can we forge against these enemies a grand and global alliance, North and South, East and West, that can assure a more fruitful life for all mankind? Will you join in that historic effort?

In the long history of the world, only a few generations have been granted the role of defending freedom in its hour of maximum danger. I do not shrink from this responsibility — I welcome it. I do not believe that any of us would exchange places with any other people or any other generation. The energy, the faith, the devotion which we bring to this endeavor will light our country and all who serve it — and the glow from that fire can truly light the world.

And so, my fellow Americans: ask not what your country can do for you — ask what you can do for your country.

My fellow citizens of the world: ask not what America will do for you, but what together we can do for the freedom of man.

Finally, whether you are citizens of America or citizens of the world, ask of us the same high standards of strength and sacrifice which we ask of you. With a good conscience our only sure reward, with history the final judge of our deeds, let us go forth to lead the land we love, asking His blessing and His help, but knowing that here on earth God's work must truly be our own.

America, the Beautiful

Written by Katharine Lee Bates, music by Samuel A. Ward

Bates was an English professor at Wellesley College in Massachusetts. Her train trip in 1893 to teach a summer session in Colorado inspired her with the words for this poem, which was set to music later. On her trip she saw the World's Columbian Exposition in Chicago, which is referenced in the "alabaster cities" as a promise for an undimmed future.

Over the years there have been attempts, particularly in the Kennedy administration, to make *America, the Beautiful* with its theme of brotherhood, our national anthem, replacing the more war-like theme of *The Star-Spangled Banner*. The uplifting music in *America, the Beautiful* was composed by Samuel A. Ward, a choirmaster in Newark, New Jersey.

There were a few variations of the song before we settled on this version in 1911. It is sometimes referred to as a poem or song for July 4th.

O beautiful for spacious skies,
For amber waves of grain,
For purple mountain majesties
Above the fruited plain!
America! America! God shed His grace on thee,
And crown thy good with brotherhood
From sea to shining sea!

O beautiful for pilgrim feet,
Whose stern impassion'd stress
A thoroughfare for freedom beat
Across the wilderness!
America! America! God mend thine ev'ry flaw,

Confirm thy soul in self-control,
Thy liberty in law!

O beautiful for heroes proved In liberating strife,
Who more than self their country loved,
And mercy more than life!
America! America! May God thy gold refine
Till all success be nobleness,
And ev'ry gain divine!

O Beautiful for patriot dream
That sees beyond the years
Thine alabaster cities gleam,
Undimmed by human tears!
America! America! God shed His grace on thee,
And crown thy good with brotherhood
From sea to shining sea!

The Star-Spangled Banner

Our national anthem. Francis Scott Key was an amateur poet at the time he witnessed the American victory over the British during the Battle of Baltimore in the War of 1812. He was inspired to see that the large American flag was still standing, and wrote a poem called "Defence of Fort McHenry" in 1814.

(And, no, the final line of the anthem is not "Play ball!")

Personally, I believe if the composer, John Stafford Smith, had possessed a crystal ball and could view crowds straining to reach those high notes at the start of a baseball game, well, surely he would have taken pity on us and dropped the music an octave lower.

Below is the complete version of the poem as originally written, followed by our modern-day one-stanza anthem. *The Star-Spangled Banner* became our national anthem in 1931.

Original poem

O say can you see, by the dawn's early light,
What so proudly we hail'd at the twilight's last gleaming,
Whose broad stripes and bright stars through the perilous fight
O'er the ramparts we watch'd were so gallantly streaming?
And the rocket's red glare, the bomb bursting in air,
Gave proof through the night that our flag was still there,
O say does that star-spangled banner yet wave
O'er the land of the free and the home of the brave?

On the shore dimly seen through the mists of the deep
Where the foe's haughty host in dread silence reposes,
What is that which the breeze, o'er the towering steep,
As it fitfully blows, half conceals, half discloses?
Now it catches the gleam of the morning's first beam,
In full glory reflected now shines in the stream,
'Tis the star-spangled banner - O long may it wave
O'er the land of the free and the home of the brave!

And where is that band who so vauntingly swore,
That the havoc of war and the battle's confusion
A home and a Country should leave us no more?
Their blood has wash'd out their foul footstep's pollution.
No refuge could save the hireling and slave
From the terror of flight or the gloom of the grave,
And the star-spangled banner in triumph doth wave
O'er the land of the free and the home of the brave.

O thus be it ever when freemen shall stand
Between their lov'd home and the war's desolation!
Blest with vict'ry and peace may the heav'n rescued land
Praise the power that hath made and preserv'd us a nation!
Then conquer we must, when our cause it is just,
And this be our motto - "In God is our trust,"

And the star-spangled banner in triumph shall wave
O'er the land of the free and the home of the brave.

Modern anthem

Oh, say can you see
By the dawn's early light
What so proudly we hailed
At the twilight's last gleaming?
Whose broad stripes and bright stars
Through the perilous fight
O'er the ramparts we watched
Were so gallantly streaming?
And the rocket's red glare
The bomb bursting in air
Gave proof through the night
That our flag was still there
Oh, say does that star-spangled banner yet wave
O'er the land of the free
And the home of the brave?

PART SIX

CALL TO ACTION

"God makes a way where there is no way."

Florence Scovel Shinn

The Hero's Journey

The hero's journey always begins with a threat from outside the village or the world as we know it. And then, without his asking to be the one to resolve it, our hero is pressed forward, and something happens to make him realize that if he doesn't say "Yes" to this call to action, then no one will. He may not be fully qualified in his mind's eye, but he's the best choice for the job, sometimes the only choice because no one else will step up.

"If you don't do everything you can,
you will always be beaten
and you will deserve it.
If you don't fight on even after
it doesn't seem to be any good,
you are not worth saving."

Patricia Wentworth (from *The Benevent Treasure*)

During his journey, the hero begins to see the bigger picture, and he realizes that he desperately wants to defeat the enemy. He grows and expands, while being of service to his fellows, and by the end he is admired and appreciated for his big heart.

332

Affirm: I attract only <u>good</u> into my life.

We Are Bilbo & Frodo

In the Lord of the Rings trilogy by J.R.R. Tolkien, ordinary gentle "Hobbits" who live in Middle-earth are called on to save the world from an all-pervasive cloud of evil that threatens their very existence.

The hero's journey always involves wishing we didn't have to leave our comfort zone, and to hope someone else will take get rid of the villains on our behalf.

> *"I wish it need not have happened in my time," said Frodo.*
> *"So do I," said Gandalf, "and so do all who live to see*
> *such times. But that is not for them to decide.*
> *All we have to decide is what to do with the time*
> *that is given us."*

J.R.R. Tolkien, The Fellowship of the Ring

We don't need the power of magical rings. We have the ring of truth. There is no need to wait for Gandalf to show the way. We have all we need right now, and total access to the power of the natural laws of our universe.

By using our word as our wand, we can cast out demons and bring forth all the goodness we desire for our countrymen, our environment, the beasts and flora, and for the entire world.

Use Constructive Anger to fuel your desire to help. Sometimes it can feel discouraging, it can seem much easier to quit and let that magically invisible "somebody else" take over. But when we do that, we wedge the door open for Trump to truly win with his agenda.

Emotions such as fear, anger, resentment and hatred are what we call our "baser" emotions because they are much earthier and reactive than the higher-level emotions of love, compassion, kindness and caring for others.

Together We Are Strong

Mind control methods have been used to great effect by Hitler Mussolini and other dictators as well as by lesser known tyrants.

We the Peaceful have the power to neutralize Trump's agenda before he can carry it out. This will require learning to shift our collective thinking away from all that we fear and toward the outcome we do want to achieve: liberty, prosperity, justice and freedom for all citizens, not just the favored insiders and their deluded followers who might get a few crumbs from the feasting table.

The reason our bright ideas for great progress don't always come off the way we planned or intended is that the undercurrent of doubt derails the manifestation.

We SAY: We will overcome! But inside we BELIEVE: Yeah, right, like this is gonna work.

How many times in a day do we sabotage our own dreams and success? Countless times! It's such a habitual way of thinking, inbred for thousands of years.

Throughout history, ordinary people have felt helpless to do anything about injustice, because the ruling few had the weapons, the fire power, the armed troops.

But also, throughout our history, there have always been groups of resistance, who had to meet in secret and carry out their plans in stealth.

Today, with the ability to communicate globally in an instant, we don't have to hide. We can speak up and be heard. We can use the weapons of truth, justice and free speech to combat the perverted power of people like Donald Trump and his supporters.

Are all people who voted for Trump evil and racist? No, but a significant percentage do fall in that category—they align with his agenda of white supremacy.

> *"It is an exciting time to be alive for the consciousness expansion in the human experience. Beings will see the limitless nature of the mind. So, there would be great things changed, advanced upon, but more importantly, what one sees is the innate capabilities of humankind to love. That is the greatest change of all, is it not?"*

THEO

Stop being bitter and angry about Trump's election.

Start seeing the opportunities to neutralize his agenda. It is not too late—but we must work together on this, because our collective power is so much greater than if only a few of us do this.

Bitterness and resentment are not neutral emotions. They lead to more situations to feel bitter and resentful about. This is the law of attraction—send out bitterness, get bitterness-related experiences in return. Just like ordering a take-out delivery.

Our base feelings actually play right into the hands of the enemy— that situation or person you are trying to defeat. What this means to us, once we grasp the concept in its fullness, is that we have much more control over our lives than we ever imagined. Just think about the relationships and situations you would like to change but feel helpless to affect.

You're not helpless! You have the same power that creates worlds and stars and orchids. Tap into that Divine Mind we are all part of, and see your own power.

Access your innate ability to create whatever you imagine and get involved with emotionally. Reverse any limiting statements so that they are positive and inspiring. Clear the static of doubt and fear that is cluttering your vibrational frequency—let your emotions tell you when you are dipping into worry or anxiety, and do what it takes to get your feelings higher up on the scale just as if you were singing Do-Re-Mi and then go higher and higher! Go up to where your dreams reside. To manifest what you want, keep a steady flow of happiness long enough to affect the molecules of change.

When we call on God for help, Light comes to us and uplifts us collectively, and with the law of multiplication, the synergy of *E Pluribus Unum* (out of the many, one) propels us forward and proves the old adage that together we are stronger than all our individual selves added up singly.

*"I dreamed, and behold, I saw a man clothed with rags,
standing in a certain place, with his face from
his own house, a book in his hand, and
a great burden upon his back. I looked, and
saw him open the book, and read therein; and,
as he read, he wept, and trembled; and,
not being able longer to contain, he brake out
with a lamentable cry, saying, 'What shall I do?'"*

John Bunyan (from *The Pilgrim's Progress*, 1678)

Affirm: All is well—great good will come out of this dark night.

ABOUT THE AUTHOR

Evelyn Roberts Brooks is a writer, lightworker, and speaker. She's shared the stage with Bob Proctor ("The Secret"), Gay Hendricks, Peggy McColl, Arielle Ford, Misa Hopkins, Dr. Steve G. Jones, and other experts in personal growth and development.

She's the author of 25 fiction and non-fiction books .

Evelyn is passionate about helping others experience a transformational healing in their lives, reduce stress, heal heartache from loss, divorce, grief and trauma, and lead happier lives.

With an emphasis on helping others gain clarity about the life changes they would like to make and then showing them how to expand in awareness, Evelyn inspires and encourages while making the lessons entertaining and inspiring.

Her goal is to show people how to heal and be happier.

evelynbrooks.com

NOTES

NOTES

www.ingramcontent.com/pod-product-compliance
Lightning Source LLC
Chambersburg PA
CBHW070758280326
41934CB00012B/2968